❖ Confrontation at Winnipeg

David Jay Bercuson

Confrontation at Winnipeg

Labour, Industrial Relations, and the General Strike

MCGILL-QUEEN'S UNIVERSITY PRESS
MONTREAL & KINGSTON • LONDON • BUFFALO

First edition
© McGill-Queen's University Press 1974

Revised edition
© McGill-Queen's University Press 1990
ISBN 0-7735-0794-9

Legal deposit third quarter 1990
Bibliothèque nationale du Québec
Printed in Canada

The first edition of this book was published with the help
of a grant from the Social Science Research Council of
Canada, using funds provided by the Canada Council.

Canadian Cataloguing in Publication Data
Bercuson, David Jay, 1945–
    Confrontation at Winnipeg

    Includes bibliographical references.
    ISBN 0-7735-0794-9

    1. General Strike, Winnipeg, Man., 1919.
    2. Industrial relations—Manitoba—Winnipeg—History.
    I. Title.

    HD5330.W46B4 1990   331.89′29712743   C90-090145-4

❖ *To Alex Shepherd*

❖Contents

❖ Preface

This study is a survey of the history of the labour movement in Winnipeg from the late nineteenth century to 1919 and is intended to explore areas untouched by others. Almost all the works dealing with western labour radicalism or the Winnipeg general strike have concentrated on political causes and ramifications rather than the industrial background. The impression has thus been created that there was little extraordinary in employer-employee relations in the city prior to 1918; in fact, the roots of the general strike may be traced as far back as 1906. In this work I have attempted to fill this large gap and at the same time examine part of society at war and a smaller portion of that society—labour—to see what additional strains were placed on the social fabric by the stresses of a major conflict.

The successful completion of this work depended on the generosity and co-operation of many people and institutions. I am grateful to the staffs of the Public Archives of Manitoba, the Public Archives of Canada, the Government Documents Centre of Sir George Williams University Library, the United Church Archives at Victoria University and the University of Winnipeg, and the McCord Museum of McGill University. The Dominion Bridge Company in Montreal extended permission to examine their minute books for the period under study and furnished important material bearing on the company's history. The Canada Department of Labour Library at Ottawa was invaluable and the staff patient and helpful.

The individuals who came forward to offer their time, material, or helpful suggestions are too numerous to mention. Those generous persons who consented to be interviewed and to whom I will always be grateful were Graham Spry, Les Paulley, F. G. Tipping, Alex Shepherd, Miller McKinnon, R. W. Durward, A. L. Crossin, A. P. Crossin, G. O'Grady, and B. Wallis. Captain Alastair Ketchen and the family of Murray Wilton were helpful, and W. A. Pritchard and A. D. Longman generously shared material and recollections.

Special thanks must be extended to Mrs. R. B. Russell and Mrs. Margaret Sykes for allowing me to study the important papers of R. B. Russell. Kenneth McNaught and Ramsay Cook offered helpful advice and support, and Craig Brown challenged many opinions formed too quickly and helped channel my approach into new directions. Mary Cottrell worked tirelessly preparing lengthy drafts and typing and retyping major portions of the manuscript in incredibly little time. David Millar saved months of tedious work at several points and shared transcripts of his interviews with Col. J. Dunwoody, Col. Macpherson, W. A. Pritchard, and Alex Shepherd.

Finally, I have dedicated this study to one who was witness to and player in so many of the events recorded here and who tracked down information, wrote anecdotes, sat for long interviews, completed a lengthy questionnaire, and spent much time discussing the people and places he had known along the way—Alex Shepherd who died in March 1970.

❖ Preface to the Revised Edition

When this book appeared in 1974, it was the first full-length study of the Winnipeg general strike in more than two decades. It followed D.C. Masters' ground-breaking *The Winnipeg General Strike* which had been published in 1950 as part of a series of books tracing the background to the rise of the Social Credit movement in Alberta. Masters emphasized the political and ideological roots of the strike; I looked more closely at the tensions between workers and employers that had developed after 1900 as by-products of Winnipeg's urban development.

Confrontation at Winnipeg appeared at the dawn of what one prominent historian called the "golden age of Canadian historical writing," a period that witnessed "a remarkable renaissance in working-class studies."[1] It was an era when non-Marxist "labour" historians such as Irving M. Abella, A. Ross McCormack, Robert Babcock, and I began to add a social-history dimension to Canada's then endless horizon of traditional political history.[2]

The reception given this book very much depended on the ideological proclivities of the reviewers. Marxists and followers of the so-called "new" labour history generally dismissed it. Bryan Palmer was typical: "Bercuson breaks no new ground, and essentially reiterates that the strike was merely a struggle for collective bargaining rights gone wrong. This piece of conventional wisdom has had a long life. . . ."[3] Non-Marxists gave it a warmer welcome; Irving Abella called it a "masterful, thorough, engrossing study."[4]

It is somewhat surprising that no new full-length treatment of the strike has appeared since *Confrontation* was first published. Thus even detractors such as Palmer must still admit that it "provides the essential chronology and narrative of the conflict."[5] As such, it warrants republication. The first twelve chapters of the original book have been retained unchanged, but a new chapter has been added summarizing the book's reception, outlining the new work that has been done on the strike since 1974, and repositioning the strike in Canadian history.

David Jay Bercuson
Calgary, 1989.

1. Ramsay Cook, "The Golden Age of Canadian Historical Writing," *Historical Reflections* 4 (1977) as quoted in Bryan Palmer, "Working-Class Canada: Recent Historical Writing," *Queen's Quarterly*, winter 1979–80, p. 598.

2. See I.M. Abella, *Nationalism, Communism and Canadian Labour* (Toronto: University of Toronto Press 1973); A. Ross McCormack, *Reformers, Rebels and Revolutionaries* (Toronto: University of Toronto Press 1977), and Robert Babcock, *Gompers in Canada* (Toronto: University of Toronto Press 1974).

3. Palmer, "Working-Class Canada," p. 595.

4. I.M. Abella, "Confrontation at Winnipeg" in *Newsletter of the Committee on Canadian Labour History* 6, 1975.

5. Bryan D. Palmer, *Working-Class Experience: The Rise and Reconstitution of Canadian Labour, 1800–1980* (Toronto: Butterworth & Co., 1983), p. 174.

1. ❖ The Early Years

Had it not been for the railways, Winnipeg might have remained a small prairie town nestled in the arms of the Red and the Assiniboine rivers. Pierre Gaultier, Sieur de la Vérendrye, established Fort Rouge with the help of his sons on the present site of Winnipeg during his explorations in the fall of 1739. From those first days the settlement was meant to be both a junction and the link of a chain; it lay astride Indian trails from the south to Lake Winnipeg and joined a string of French fur-trading posts stretching from the Great Lakes to the Rocky Mountains. It is perhaps significant that, from the beginning, Winnipeg served as a depot—a transmitter of supplies and information to the scattered points of civilization that lay west over the great plains.

For the first century and a half of its existence, Winnipeg was an isolated outpost serving the needs of fur traders, farmers, freighters, and missionaries. For a brief but important moment two years after Confederation the settlement served as a stage for Louis Riel's first dramatic struggle for the rights of the Métis nation. The most significant event in the early history of Winnipeg, however, was played out to the east on the farm of David Fife in Peterborough County, Ontario. There, in the spring of 1841, a new strain of wheat renowned for its fruitfulness and hardy qualities was discovered which became known as Red Fife. In 1875 a committee of farmers from Manitoba, searching the western United States for a new grain to transplant to the dry plains of their province, returned with this new strain and by

October 1876 were able to ship a little over 857 bushels of seed wheat to Toronto.[1]

This was the first faltering step that began Winnipeg on its long journey as a world grain centre. The demand for wheat in eastern Canada and Europe became the key to unlock the potential of this strategically placed community. Though Winnipeg was known primarily in the 1870s as a frontier town of whiskey, saloons, and wild women, the human resources needed to bring about a metamorphosis from idolatory to industry already existed within the settlement. The trickle of immigration brought talented individuals from eastern Canada and Europe who deeply believed in the potential of their adopted community. A core of business and professional people raised their sights beyond the muddy trails and teeming bars to envision a great trading centre funnelling grain out of the grasslands while pulling in settlers and supplies to populate the plains. The adoption of a civic coat of arms with a locomotive and three sheaves of wheat was prophetic.[2]

The locomotive, however, did not come easily. If the original plans for construction of a transcontinental railway had been adhered to, Winnipeg might not have become the metropolis of the prairies. At first, in the early 1870s, the Canadian Pacific planned to cross the Red River at the head of navigation—a point later named Selkirk. As a result the town enjoyed a short-lived boom and began to consider itself a rival of Winnipeg. In 1880 and 1881, however, Winnipeg was able to come to terms with the railway, and in return for its capture of the Red River crossing, granted the CPR exemption from municipal taxation in perpetuity, rights of way, and land for station and yards.[3]

With rail connection to the east, Winnipeg began to assume vital importance as a transfer point. Grain and rails pushed the city forward slowly in the eighties. By the beginning of the last decade of the nineteenth century Winnipeg's Main Street boasted horse-drawn streetcars and shop windows lit at night by coal-oil hanging lamps. The main axis of the city took shape from old cart trails, Main Street running north and south along the Red River and Portage Avenue branching off west, to Portage La Prairie and "The Saskatchewan," as the flat country beyond the western horizon was called.[4]

The gay nineties ushered in expansion. Laurier's capture of the federal government and his appointment of Clifford Sifton to the Interior Ministry marked the beginning of a new effort by Ottawa to attract immigrants to western Canada. The effect on Winnipeg of this new and successful campaign was revolutionary. In 1891 Winnipeg's population totaled 25,639, of whom 18,000 were either British or Canadian born. By 1901 the population had almost doubled to 42,340. Sifton's efforts to attract potential settlers from central and eastern Europe did not, however, greatly affect the city's demographic profile until the first decade of the twentieth century. By 1911 the tidal wave of immigration washing over Winnipeg had transformed the city. There were now 136,035 people, 22 percent of whom were of non-Anglo-Saxon origin, while thousands of others were recently arrived British immigrants.[5]

Those ten years witnessed the beginnings of significant industrialization outside the railway shops and yards. Winnipeg's industrial plant in 1891 contained 307 firms which employed 2,359 individuals. Total fixed capital amounted to a little over $1.5 million and total working capital amounted to some $1.3 million. Three million dollars' worth of raw materials were used, wages of approximately $1.2 million were paid to employees, and $5.6 million worth of goods was produced.[6]

Ten years later the number of establishments in Winnipeg's non-railway industrial plant had decreased to 103, but total production had increased to over $8.6 million worth of goods. This is an indication, perhaps, of greater industrial maturity and a result of consolidation and the growth of fewer but larger companies. Twenty-five establishments, for example, accounted for over $7.2 million worth of the total output, and the other seventy-eight factories shared the remaining $1.5 million of production. Total wage earners employed in the city was still only 2,741.[7]

By 1911 Winnipeg had become, by prairie standards, a major industrial centre. Its 177 establishments, with total capitalization of over $26 million, produced approximately $32.7 million worth of goods. The industrial plant was fed with $18.4 million worth of raw materials annually. Industry had now diversified to over thirty-five different types of establishments producing everything from agricultural implements to cookies. Two years later industrial output finally topped the $50 million mark, and over 130 new industries were established in the years from 1911 to 1913 alone. In the spring of 1913, *Industrial Canada,* the official journal of the Canadian Manufacturers' Association, observed: "The example of Winnipeg's rise in a little more than a decade to the position of fourth industrial city in the Dominion, has had the effect of limbering the imagination of conservative Canada, and now very often the remark is made that

Manitoba is more like an eastern province than a member of the middle western family."[8] As a result of this expansion the segregation of the rich and not-so-rich, the middle class and the poor became pronounced. This marked the beginning of class division. The social elite, mainly Anglo-Saxon and Protestant, gathered themselves in certain well-defined bastions of affluence: Armstrong's Point, Wellington Crescent, and River Heights. The working population, laced with new immigrants, lived in parts of Fort Rouge, northwest Winnipeg, and the "north end." The latter area was Winnipeg's "across the tracks," situated for the most part north of the sprawling Canadian Pacific yards, which stretched from Weston to Point Douglas, site of the CPR station and the Royal Alexandra Hotel.

The raw manpower needed to construct factories, office buildings, and houses, to stoke the fires of industry, drive the delivery wagons, bake the bread, and maintain the electrical turbines came primarily from eastern Canada, the British Isles, and central Europe. Immigrants arrived in CPR colonist cars, checked in at the Immigration Hall at Point Douglas, then streamed in their thousands into the north end. The majority of the central Europeans were Ukrainians, most of whom were unskilled workers and secured what low-paying manual labour they could find on construction and track-laying gangs. Many of them could afford nothing more than to pack together in rickety crowded shacks or tenements. Streets were often unpaved, basic sanitary facilities rare, and sources of fresh water for drinking and washing few and far between. Some immigrants never experienced the luxury of wooden floors or walls thick enough to keep out the bitter prairie winters. Sometimes several families were forced to share the rent of a flat or a single house, and privacy fell victim to the squalid realities of slum living.

Another type of immigrant was arriving at the same time. Less heralded because of his Anglo-Saxon background and Protestant religion he was, nevertheless, a very different animal from his upper-class countryman. He was the skilled British tradesman leaving the crowded industrial cities of north England and Scotland in search of better opportunities in the promised lands across the Atlantic. By the time he arrived he had usually served his apprenticeship in any of a number of trades and might have achieved journeyman status. These British immigrants brought with them an outlook and sometimes an ideology forged in the factory cities of industrial England. Many believed deeply in the principles of trade unionism and labour political action. Some were socialists, others advocates of industrial unionism or syndicalism, but most shared a desire to put the lessons they had learned to good use; these were the men who soon formed the elite of union leadership in Winnipeg and the west.

The combination of industrialization, immigration, and rapid expansion created complex difficulties within this new society. In the areas populated largely by immigrants from central Europe over-crowding, illiteracy, crime, and seasonal unemployment ruled. Skilled tradesmen were far from immune to these difficulties, and although employed more steadily at better-paying jobs, they found themselves in dark factories, unprotected by safety equipment, forced to compete with child labour, and at the mercy of the job market in matters of wages. Most shop and factory owners automatically assumed that labour was just a commody to be paid for on the basis of market dictates. Under such circumstances it is not surprising that various movements for social reform, political and religious in nature, began to appear in the 1890s and grew steadily as the problems of this industrial city became more complex.

The social gospel movement in Winnipeg contained the seeds of promise for the amelioration of the living conditions of thousands of immigrants and workers. A concise definition of this phenomenon has been given by A. R. Allen: "The social gospel rested on the premise that Christianity was a social religion, concerned when the misunderstandings of the ages was stripped away, with the quality of human relations on this earth. More dramatically it was a call for men to find the meaning of their lives in seeking to realize the kingdom of God in the very fabric of society."[9] Acting on these principles a legion of men and women, lay and clerical, attempted to bring the Kingdom of Heaven to north Winnipeg.

The All Peoples' Mission, supported by various Methodist organizations in the city, was founded by Miss Dolly McGuire in 1898. At first it was simply one of a number of missions and settlement houses established to do traditional religious salvation work and was only a small part of Winnipeg's disjointed charity machinery. In 1907, however, it came under the influence of Rev. James Shaver Woodsworth, who proceeded to fashion it into an instrument for the attainment of social gospel ends.[10] Woodsworth was an original thinker, but he was undoubtedly influenced, along with a host of other reformers, by Rev. Salem Bland, who taught at Winnipeg's Wesley College during this period. Perhaps it is fair to say of these prewar years that Bland was the philosopher of the movement while Woodsworth was the man of practical action.

Rev. Salem Bland was born in Lachute, Quebec, in 1859. He graduated with a bachelor of arts from McGill University, was ordained as a Methodist minister in 1884, and earned his Doctor of Divinity from Queen's University in 1900. He arrived in Winnipeg in 1903 to become Professor of Church History and New Testament Exegesis at Wesley College. Bland was, by religious conviction, a radical, and he used every available opportunity to espouse the cause of heavenly salvation through earthly social improvement. He believed the perfect man would only emerge in a perfect society. Social regeneration, he maintained, could not be left to the workingman alone—the church must play a strong role in the battle for redemption. He urged his followers and co-religionists to throw themselves into the fight against slums, monopolies, and unearned profits until the society based upon competition was destroyed.[11] He did not, however, restrict himself to general denunciations of the system. He called for a living wage for workers, support for trade unions, and sweeping urban reforms to drain and widen streets, plant trees, construct proper sanitary facilities, and lay out parks and playgrounds. He set forth a program to create more and better schools, hospitals and asylums, found art galleries and libraries, and hold free concerts.[12]

Bland ceaselessly attacked the free enterprise system which, to him, was wasteful and destructive and only allowed success at the expense of competitors and workers. Industrialists, he charged, took "meat from children's mouths to pay dividends on watered stock" and forced workers to suffer low wages and an increasing cost of living.[13] Bland preached that God wanted His church to join the fight because the workers, irrevocably involved in the struggle, were one-sided and bitter. The efforts of the church would balance this shortsightedness, and together the forces of reform would be successful in the effort to stop the few great fortunes from gobbling up the riches of Canada's natural resources.[14]

Social reform efforts in Winnipeg were not confined to the activities of religious organizations. The city was host to several political movements aiming at the improvement of social ills and the structural reform of democratic institutions. Winnipeg was relatively young and small compared with the great industrial cities of eastern Canada and the United States, but it was fertile ground for its own brand of mugwump progressivism. Middle-class reformers allied themselves with representatives of religious organizations, suffragettes, and old family pioneers with a sense of *noblesse oblige* to produce a variety of political movements aimed at wiping out the evils produced by rapid industrialization.

Winnipeg's political progressives concerned themselves to varying degrees with four chief causes: direct legislation, the single tax, female suffrage, and temperance. One of the more influential movements was the Manitoba League for the Taxation of Land Values based on Henry George's single tax ideology, which gained support from organized labour, agrarian progressives, and middle-class reformers. Its ideas were espoused by Rev. Bland and its chief spokesman in Winnipeg was F. J. Dixon.

Dixon was a well-groomed Englishman with a resonant voice who became one of the early leaders of the scattered but growing reform groups in the city. He was an insurance salesman by occupation and his passion for social change led him to work tirelessly for the Political Equality League and the Direct Legislation League as well as the League for the Taxation of Land Values. Dixon worked on committees, spoke from numerous platforms and contributed a column to *The Voice;* he built up for himself a reputation for reason, moderation, and clear thinking in the service of his various causes. Over the years he won the respect of farmers, businessmen, and workers, as well as middle-class reformers and was able to gather a faithful following in the city.

The "ironclad" laws of economics, adhered to so closely in the nineteenth century's golden age of laissez faire, dictated that labour was a commodity. Supply and demand determined wages, hours, and working conditions—when men were plentiful they were also inexpensive, when skilled workers were at a premium they could obtain satisfactory conditions. Thus the first workers to organize trade unions were usually skilled individuals who could not be replaced easily by an obstinate employer. In Winnipeg literate and highly trained men who set type formed the first unions in the city in 1872. Other crafts followed in the next decade with the establishment of a moulders' union in 1883, a carpenters' and joiners' union in 1887, and a masons' organization in 1888.[15]

In the midst of the depression of 1884, the Knights of Labor came to Manitoba. A local assembly was established and paved the way for three others, one of which was composed entirely of CPR employees.[16] In the winter of 1884—85 they combined with the existing craft unions to set up a central council, which also issued Manitoba's first workingmen's newspaper, the *Winnipeg Labor Call.*[17]

The influence of the Knights in Manitoba was short-lived, but during their brief life they gave Winnipeg its first taste of trade union power. In 1886 District Assembly 204 was formed from five locals with a total membership of over five hundred workers. This number fluctuated during these uncertain years, but the Knights were still instrumental in securing the province's first piece of trade union legislation, the Manitoba Shops Regulation Act.[18] This short period of activity in the 1880s was a false dawn for labour organization in the province, however; in 1886 the central council ceased to operate, and by the early 1890s the Knights had all but disappeared from Manitoba.

The Canadian Pacific Railway brought the promise of a lucrative future to Winnipeg in the 1880s and substantial riches of trade and immigration in the 1890s. In its path it also brought unions. The organizations which grew across the prairies in the train of the CPR were not the products of a half-formed industrial ideology, they were combinations forged by practical men who repaired locomotives, maintained the right of way, and manned passenger and freight trains. The railway unions, shop craft and running trades, formed the substantive core upon which the Winnipeg labour movement was built. They provided the bulk of the membership with the practical ideology and organizational desire so necessary to sustain the movement in times of adversity and drive it forward in propitious days.

The last decade of the century witnessed the establishment of the first railway shop union, International Association of Machinists (IAM) Local 122 in 1893, the formation of the Winnipeg Trades and Labor Council, and the publication of *The Peoples' Voice* in 1894.[19] The appearance in 1903 of a council of building trade unions marked further efforts of workingmen to unite beyond the bounds of their particular crafts. Their entrance into politics through the auspices of the Winnipeg Labor Party in March 1896[20] demonstrated a sophisticated awareness of the problems labour would face in restricting their efforts to "pure and simple" unionism. By the end of the decade and the end of the century, trade unions were firmly established; they would in future continue to be affected by economic conditions, but were no longer so frail that the merest hint of depression in the wind would blow them over.

Across the nation the trade union movement was growing as well. The Trades and Labor Congress of Canada (TLC) had developed, since its founding in the 1880s, as an all-inclusive national centre. Knights of Labor assemblies were affiliated, as well as purely Canadian unions and locals of United States–based international unions. The pressures to affiliate to the American Federation of Labor (AFL) grew stronger, and in 1899 fraternal delegates were exchanged by the two organizations. The final step in this process was taken in 1902 when the United States unions forced the TLC to expel all unions which directly competed with those in the AFL.

The almost total absence of any attempt by owners or managers to provide adequate minimum wages, decent working conditions, and civilized hours of work was bound to create a self-defence impulse among the working classes. Governments might have used their influence to humanize the industrial system but were usually reluctant to do anything but a bare minimum. Canada's earliest factory legislation had been passed in Ontario by the government of Oliver Mowat in the 1880s, but by the turn of the century the state of such regulation had advanced little.

In Manitoba labour and factory legislation was only slightly more than primitive as late as the outbreak of the First World War. The Shops Regulation Act of 1888 and the Factories Act of 1900 were designed to guard against the worst abuses of extended hours of work and child labour, but both contained large loopholes, were weakened by amendments, and were not stringently enforced. By 1913, for example, children were still allowed to work a maximum of seventy-two hours a week. Adults were also limited to twelve hours a day, six days a week, but only if they worked in establishments employing five or more persons. If they worked in a smaller shop or store they had no protection whatsoever.[21] In promulgating such restricted and primitive legislation and further amending it so that its effectiveness, debatable at best, was undercut, the provincial government created a legacy of mistrust and ill will that stimulated the growth of trades unionism.

Strikes tend to increase the individual workman's awareness of his position in society and heighten his identification with others of his group. Winnipeg experienced several key industrial disputes in the decade between 1901 and 1911 which focused organized labour's attention on its relatively weak position in society and forced it to recognize the long road to be travelled before trade unions would be universally accepted. Employers who would readily accede to demands for higher wages, shorter hours, better working conditions, and, ultimately, union recognition and collective bargaining were rare indeed in the early years of this century.

In 1901 a portion of Winnipeg's working population was involved in a strike by maintenance-of-way employees (trackmen) against the CPR system. The two-month-long dispute centred around demands for a wage increase and, although the strike was focused on a few major industrial centres, the railway's operations were affected across

Canada. The dispute was eventually settled through mediation by a conciliation board made up of representatives of the Railroad Brotherhoods.[22] The Brotherhoods were U.S.-based international unions independent of the AFL whose members were amongst the first railway employees to organize and who carried the primary responsibility for running the trains. The Brotherhood of Locomotive Engineers was formed in 1863, the Order of Railway Conductors in 1868, the Brotherhood of Railroad Trainmen in 1873, and the Brotherhood of Locomotive Firemen in 1883. The four organizations were exclusive and aristocratic craft unions that became more conservative with the passing years and rarely resorted to strikes in their own negotiations with management. Since they were, at the same time, unions, they were often called upon to act as independent arbitrators.

In this particular case, suspicion arose soon after the settlement that the arbitors had not been entirely honest in their dealings with the trackmen. *The Voice* reported rumblings among members of the maintenance-of-way union that the prestige of the Brotherhoods within the labour movement had been used by CPR officials to hoodwink the strikers.[23] This charge was not substantiated, but is important in what it reveals about the labour movement at this point —an appearance of solidarity on the surface but with major factions which could be turned against each other by management or governments.

In May of 1902 a strike on the Canadian Northern Railway, centred in Winnipeg, combined the skilled forces of machinists, boilermakers, and sheet metal workers with unskilled labourers. The unskilled workers were largely represented by a new organization that appeared in Manitoba in the spring and summer of 1902, the United Brotherhood of Railway Employees (UBRE), a radical, western-oriented industrial union affiliated to the American Labor Union. Founded in San Francisco in 1901, the latter was a potential rival of the American Federation of Labor and had been established by a radical coalition of western unions, including the Western Federation of Miners and the UBRE, to spread the gospel of industrial unionism on a nationwide scale.[24]

The UBRE claimed to have a membership of approximately one thousand in Winnipeg by the summer of 1902, combining freight handlers, clerks, switchmen, and brakemen. As the walkout dragged on, support grew among the city's working population, and a large demonstration was held in mid-July to back the beleaguered strikers.

At this point, the Railroad Brotherhoods intervened, sending representatives to Winnipeg to confer with the management of the Canadian Northern. A settlement was reached which only covered the skilled workers, leaving the UBRE without the support of the most important segment of the CN working force. The strike collapsed. Later in the year the Manitoba Executive of the Trades and Labor Congress charged that the Brotherhoods had sacrificed the interests of the unskilled workers at the instigation of management; it considered the episode "the blackest page in the history of trade unionism in Manitoba."[25]

In the early months of 1906 the Winnipeg Electric Railway Company, a holding of William Mackenzie, railway entrepreneur and part owner, with Donald Mann, of the Canadian Northern Railway, locked horns with Street Railwayman's Union Local 99 in a bitter dispute which touched off violent clashes between company police and pro-strike demonstrators in the downtown streets of the city. The company had never actually extended recognition to the union, but simply negotiated and signed agreements with a "committee" of their employees who, not surprisingly, happened also to be union officials. In 1906, however, the Electric Railway decided that Local 99 had become a thorn in its side and decided to use the negotiations to undermine the union's position amongst its employees. For several weeks prior to the initiation of discussions between the two sides union officials were harassed and some were suspended for alleged infractions of company rules. Two days after negotiations began the president and executive secretary of Local 99 were dismissed from the company's employ for "insulting" company officers. The union, for its part, had lived with its unofficial status long enough and was now determined to force management to extend bona fide recognition.[26] The hard-nosed attitudes of the company and Local 99 soon produced a complete impasse in the negotiations and set the stage for an increase in tensions.

On Monday, March 26, officers representing international union headquarters arrived in the city from Detroit to take charge of negotiations. After investigating the dispute they announced they were prepared to sanction a strike of Local 99 should it prove necessary.[27] Two days later reports reached Winnipeg, amid company denials, that approximately one hundred men with experience in streetcar operations had been recruited in Montreal and were being sent to Winnipeg as strikebreakers. The report indicated that representatives of the Electric Railway were hiring all the experienced men they could get, most of them former employees of the Montreal system.[28] The company, meanwhile, claimed publicly that they had actually agreed to most of the union's demands. One thing, however, was clear —the most important issue as far as the men were concerned, one they were willing to strike for, was union recognition, and this the company had not afforded.[29]

In the early hours of Thursday, March 29, the battle was joined; 237 union members voted unanimously to strike at a four-hour meeting which had commenced at midnight on Wednesday. The company announced it had made its last offer and intended to operate car service as usual. The strike thus began immediately, as men streamed out of the meeting hall and set up picket lines. Many apprentices who had been ordered by company officials to work as strikebreakers refused and joined their union colleagues.

Violence broke out the first day of the strike. The company brought in private police recruited in the east by the Thiel Detective Agency, an American concern, to protect equipment being operated by imported strikebreakers. The Thiel men were recklessly running streetcars down tracks attempting to clear crowds from the right of way and attacking people trying to obstruct service. The thousands who blocked streets, jeered the strikebreakers, and threw stones at the cars were, for the most part, rowdies or private citizens sympathetic to the strikers. The *Free Press* observed that public demonstrations against streetcar operations came from "thousands of [the company's] patrons." The majority of the regular customers supported the strike and refused to ride the cars. By mid-afternoon service was virtually halted. In the face of this determined opposition, the company demanded militia protection. Under the terms of the Militia Act passed in 1904 the mayor was authorized to make written application for aid in the event of a riot or civil disturbance which municipal authorities could not handle. In this instance the mayor acceded to the company's demands, signed the necessary papers, and the military was put on alert at Fort Osborne Barracks. By all accounts, the strikers themselves were not involved in this violence; after being up all night at a union meeting and manning picket lines from 4:00 A.M., most union members were at home, sleeping peacefully in their beds.[30]

Throughout the strike the company's efforts to keep the streetcars running by the use of strikebreakers and private police were considerably hindered by widespread public support for the striking motormen and conductors. This backing was not only manifested in the streets but in meetings, on editorial pages, and in churches. The

Winnipeg Trades and Labor Council, while deploring the violence, supported the strikers and offered its services as a mediation agency. The *Free Press* attacked the company in an editorial and blamed the violence on its questionable tactics. The special agents brought to Winnipeg to "protect" streetcars were thugs, the paper charged, even though they had been granted a dubious authority by the provincial police magistrate.[31] Rev. Salem Bland, speaking at a meeting of the Young Men's Club of St. Stephens Church, attacked the company for refusing to arbitrate. He argued that the present actions of this civic-chartered monopoly pointed out once again the necessity to think seriously about public ownership.[32]

A peculiar story of quasi-official sanction for the company's actions was dramatically brought to light soon after. The *Free Press* revealed that Provincial Magistrate McMicken, who had sworn in the Thiel men at the request of the Electric Railway, had been placed under suspension by the attorney general because, the government claimed, he had acted improperly in granting official approval to private agents. McMicken defended himself by claiming he did not know Thiel was a private American agency or that the men he had sworn in were strikebreakers. He asserted that he had acted only after the company had requested the swearing in so that its facilities could be protected. The Electric Railway denied any of its men were Americans, but did finally admit that the "employees referred to [were] men hired in Toronto, Ottawa and Montreal."[33]

At this point the Electric Railway attempted to switch the blame for this incident on to the civic administration. They claimed their own agents had been hired when the city advised them that there were only enough regular police to protect six streetcars and suggested they obtain private guards. They produced a letter from Mayor Sharpe which said, in part: "The City will . . . expect your company to furnish the usual service required throughout the city . . . and the city . . . will do everything in its power to preserve order. . . ."[34] This letter, however, was dated March 30, a full day after the strike began and at least twelve hours after the Thiel men had appeared in the streets.

Violence reached new heights the second afternoon of the strike. The scenes of the previous day were repeated on a larger scale, with more people milling about and more damage to Electric Railway equipment. In one ironic incident a Thiel agent mistook the mayor for a strike sympathizer and assaulted him. The mayor nevertheless finally answered the company's demands for protection and called out the military. The Riot Act was read on Main Street and troops began to clear the broad thoroughfare, displaying open bayonets and a Lewis gun. The crowd quickly scattered, running down side streets to escape the expected fusillade, while many, not aware the Riot Act had been read, were swept up in the stampede. The soldiers, called out at 2.50 P.M., remained on duty for about four hours and retired at dusk.[35]

It is arguable whether the mayor's action was necessary for the restoration and maintenance of peace and order. What is clear, however, is that the summoning of troops made victory far less possible for the union. The crowds were present because they supported the strikers and were demonstrably angry at the company's attempts to operate car service with the aid of strikebreakers. With the crowds gone, the cars could run as usual and the union had much less leverage.

The strike continued amid mediation efforts of a committee of the Winnipeg Ministerial Association, a study and information group formed primarily of Presbyterian and Methodist ministers in 1904, and the mayor's promises to the company to protect their equipment. The city now undertook the responsibility to swear in special police, though this time American citizens were pointedly excluded. With this new group of agents the militia were no longer required and were dismissed from barracks on April 1, after being under arms for forty hours. Service was still curtailed, however, because the boycott continued in working-class areas and cars stopped running at 7:00 P.M.

On Saturday, April 7, the strikers returned to work, almost all of the men's demands having been met to varying degrees. All employees, including those under suspension before the walkout, were reinstated, the ten-hour work day was granted with higher wages, and men with seniority were given route preference. The union, however, did not gain recognition, except in the following clause: "Neither the company nor its men will discriminate against, or interfere with any employees by reason of their being or not being members of any street railway employees' union."[36]

The union claimed victory and had indeed gained much of what it set out to accomplish. Recognition, however, was still out of reach. More important, the civic authorities had set a poor example in placing their first priority upon maintenance of service rather than justice for the workers. In other cases this might have been easily understood, but here, with the widespread support the strike gained, especially from sources not generally friendly to organized labour, it might be concluded that the cause was just. Whatever the moral implications of the episode, one lesson stood out—the strikers received little sympathy or support from their own local government.

A short month after the settlement of the streetcar strike a second dispute developed in Winnipeg that was to have even more far-reaching consequences. Though this disagreement did not touch the public conscience as widely as the first, it was more significant in its effects upon the conduct of industrial relations in an industry soon known for its chronic labour difficulties. The Vulcan Iron Works strike-lockout of 1906 set a pattern for labour-management relations in the city's contract shops that was to be followed for the next thirteen years. As with the streetcar strike, both sides wanted a show-down; but in this case the union was not yet strong enough to take on this most obstinate of employers and suffered humiliating defeat.

In mid-May of 1906 machinists, moulders, and blacksmiths at-tempted to negotiate a collective agreement with three contract shops in the city: Vulcan Iron Works, Manitoba Bridge and Iron Works, and Northern Iron Works. The unions were aided by first vice-president Champion of the IAM, who had arrived in the city from Toronto to guide negotiations with the Grand Trunk Pacific in an-other dispute. The moulders began the strike on May 18, when approximately forty-five men walked out for an additional five cents an hour. The employers were inconvenienced but able to keep the plants in operation. Union leaders probably realized a strike for recognition at this stage would be futile, and therefore did not go after it directly. They chose, however, to make their demand for higher wages through the union, rather than a shop committee. Management's refusal to reply was, in itself, a challenge to the legiti-macy of the union and touched off the moulders' strike before the other metal workers were ready to walk out.

The machinists and blacksmiths were soon up to their ears in the fight and presented their own list of demands to Vulcan Iron Works, including a new wage schedule and a model working agreement. The unions added an ultimatum that if a reply was not forthcoming a strike would take place. The answer came three hours later when, as the men were leaving the shop at the end of the working day, they were handed notes informing them the factory would be closed until further notice.[37]

A long and frustrating story lay behind the union's ultimatum to the shop. The negotiations which had culminated in the moulders' strike had been dragging on for over six weeks. With this first walkout the possibility arose that management would attempt to bring in "scab" moulders sending non-union castings to the machine shops. Champion thus gave his and the International's consent and the IAM and the blacksmiths presented their demands. With the lockout the three unions became united in their aims and set up a joint committee to act for all the striking metal workers. They succeeded in having the Amalgamated Society of Engineers, a British rival of the IAM, call out its members and agreed informally among themselves that no worker would return to his job until all went back. The unions candidly admitted that this contest was a test of strength with Vulcan and inferred that its resolution would provide guidelines for action at other metal plants.[38]

Vulcan was chosen for this duel because its owners were the most intransigent of the metal shop employers. They were a formidable foe and showed their fighting ability only too well. On May 30 the injunction was used as an anti-strike weapon for the first time in the history of Winnipeg. On application from Vulcan Iron Works, Justice Richards issued a court order effective until June 6 to stop the unions from picketing and "watching." The document named approximately one hundred workers along with IAM Lodges 122 and 189, Blacksmiths' Lodges 147 and 335 and Moulders' Lodge 174. This order was to be effective for seven days and was to be argued in court on the date of its expiry. Although the injunction stopped picketing, thus allowing strikebreakers into the plant, the unions vowed to continue the fight.

Organized labour was well aware of the serious consequences that could ensue if injunctions became common in industrial disputes. The Winnipeg Trades and Labor Council therefore quickly involved itself in the dispute and took action to back the strikers. They passed a motion of unqualified support, promised to aid workers financially, and invited J. G. O'Donoghue of Toronto, legal advisor to the Trades and Labor Congress, to the city.[39]

The expected day in court was delayed. The postponement of hearings on the injunction continued the order and further hampered the fighting ability of the workers. To add insult to injury, Vulcan applied to have seven union members cited for contempt because they had allegedly violated the court order. At the same time Vulcan's boilermakers, not yet on strike, threatened they would stop handling all non-union materials inside the shop. Picketing had been stopped, but Vulcan had not yet succeeded in hiring enough strikebreakers to effectively increase production to pre-strike levels.[40]

On June 14, Northern Iron Works and Manitoba Bridge arrived at an agreement with their moulders, whereby the men returned to work with a 5 percent pay increase even though the unions was not granted recognition. At Vulcan, however, the strike-lockout continued while the plant operated at reduced capacity. By this time some strikers had begun to break ranks and these men, combined with strikebreakers, enabled Vulcan to begin processing orders delayed due to the dispute. Victory was now farther from the unions' grasp than before but they kept the strike going and succeeded in getting the boilermakers to join the walkout. By mid-June the injunction question had still not been resolved in court, and the company continued to insist it would only operate on an "open shop" basis. It was now obvious that the unions could not win, even though financial support from the Internationals enabled them to hold out and the strike dragged on until it finally petered out by the end of July. The unions had been thoroughly whipped and the men found themselves competing with strikebreakers to regain their old jobs.[41]

Vulcan licked organized labour in the shop and at the factory gate, but the defeat which proved the hardest to swallow came at the hands of the court. In a lawsuit against certain members of the unions, the company took action for a permanent injunction and $50,000 damages. The suit dragged on for three years and was finally judged against the men. The court decided that though the picketing had been peaceful, it was a common-law nuisance and assessed $500 damages when the company admitted that no actual losses had been suffered. The $500 figure was small but must be added to the tremendous expense shouldered by the unions in fighting a suit for three years. This strike, the ensuing legal action, and the bitterness generated were the key events determining relationships between the contract shop employers and the metal trades unions for the next sixteen years.

The trade unions learned several important lessons from the events of 1906 and in future governed themselves by their experience. They learned that local government would almost automatically make common cause with business in a showdown with organized labour. The city fathers envisioned a golden future for Winnipeg based on industry and trade, a future that could only be created if conditions conducive to the free operation of industry were established. This did not mean that a concerted campaign against trade unions was about to be launched, only that if labour challenged any of the essential components of the municipal-industrial relationship, it would draw upon itself the wrath of both.

In addition, labour unions were forced to realize that the legal
system, with its law codes and judicial processes, was loaded against
them. A combination of injunctions and damage suits could make
their existence costly and precarious, and an independent employer
willing to fight to the last legal and industrial gasp would probably
win in the end. The problem could therefore be posed in terms of
absolutes. What did workers aspire to? At the least, comfort and
financial security with full safeguards against industrial accidents,
and the knowledge that the way lay open for them to raise themselves
up by their bootstraps. The basics of these aspirations centred on
higher real wages, better working conditions, and job security. The
key to these essentials had become union organization and recognition. The obstacles to union growth could be found in the attitudes
of employers, the apathy of society at large, a legal structure centred
around a commercial law which developed in an era of free-trade
liberalism, and governments and politicians whose chief aim was to
preserve society as it was.

Organized labour's task was now clear. Basic social assumptions
which worked against union growth would have to be changed, allies
would have to be won, the legal structure would have to be modified,
and governments would have to be made sympathetic. Once these
were accomplished employers could be faced on equal terms. But how
to mount the battle? It was soon clear that the campaign would have
to be twofold, a combination of political and industrial organization,
the one to complement and strengthen the other. In fact, the first
calls to political action had been made by *The People's Voice* as early
as 1895 and in March of 1896 a Labor Party was founded.[42] This
organization had been supported by widely divergent groups among
Winnipeg unions and did not have any common foundation. The
party was wracked by ideological infighting between socialists and
non-socialists, and the foundation of a local branch of the Canadian
Socialist League in 1899 had served to increase the rivalries.

Labour's first and, for a long period, only success in politics came
with the federal by-election victory of Arthur W. Puttee in 1900.
Puttee had been born in England and emigrated to North America
in 1888. In 1891 he settled in Winnipeg and became an active member
of the International Typographical Union and a strong supporter of
the labour movement. He acquired an interest in *The People's Voice*
soon after its establishment and began to edit the paper in 1897. By
the end of the decade he had clearly become a leader of the labour
movement and was nominated to carry the Labor Party banner in

the by-election. Splits and rivalries within the Liberal and Conservative parties prevented them from fielding official candidates and Puttee scored a surprising victory.[43] The unusual circumstance of this election became apparent when, in the general election of 1904, Puttee lost his deposit in a fight against official representatives of the two major parties.

Political victories would have to wait until trade unions gained in organizational strength and sophistication. The desire for political activity was always present; the ability to conduct such activity came only after trade unions themselves developed into instruments for social change through industrial action. Unity and identity developed out of strikes, lockouts, disputes, and rejection by courts and governments. Political and industrial action did eventually complement and strengthen each other, but only after a foundation of trade union factory and shop activity had been laid.

The lockout at the Great West Saddlery Company in the fall of 1911 did not involve a large number of workers, did not prompt the call-up of the militia, and did not mark the beginning of a thirteen-year-long industrial war. It was, however, significant in two different but related ways: it gained valuable friends and sympathizers for the trade union cause and demonstrated to those who may have had illusions how completely an employer could control the lives of his non-unionized workers.

In October 1911, ten Great West Saddlery Company workers were locked out for their refusal to sign an agreement which stipulated they would not join or be connected with a union. These men were not union members. The "yellow dog" contract was standard procedure at the company; no union existed on the premises and any individuals who were inadvertently hired and found to hold union cards were summarily dismissed. The men applied to the Trades Council for aid and began to consider organizing a union to protect other employees of Great West. The company would brook no interference with its standard methods of operation and fourteen other men, some of whom had worked for Great West for as long as thirteen years, were dismissed for attending a protest meeting shortly after the original lockout. The employers would not explain their action in public other than to maintain that the service of these men was no longer required.[44]

The Trades and Labor Council supported the locked-out men and attacked the company through the press. They charged that these men and other workers had been imported by Great West from

Britain under false pretences and once in Canada were being forced to work under "immoral, vicious and medieval" conditions.[45] They organized public protest meetings, attempted to raise funds to sustain the jobless workers, and aided the men in the formation of a weak and short-lived Union of Leather Workers. Enough money was eventually raised to begin small and irregular payments of "strike funds" two weeks after the men were fired.

At this point the Winnipeg Ministerial Association became involved, when Rev. J. S. Woodsworth, sitting for the association on the Trades and Labor Council, brought the affair before the ministers for their consideration. At a meeting attended by some of the locked-out men Woodsworth urged the association to appoint a conciliation committee. His arguments were heeded and eventually he, along with Dr. Sinclair and Rev. J. L. Gordon, began to interview the management and investigate conditions at the plant. In their final report the ministers sided with the employees, condemned the company for violating the basic rights of the workers, and urged the association to contribute financially to the locked-out men.[46] The company, secure in the knowledge that its legal position was unassailable and that no union of its employees dared challenge its authority, ignored the pleadings of all.

Despite temporary setbacks, the trade union movement grew steadily in Winnipeg. Union membership increased as a result of the growth of industry, the expanding labour force, and intense organizing activity in certain key industries. By 1913, eighty-two local unions existed in the city, sixty-two of which were affiliated to the Trades Council, with a total membership of a little over eight thousand workers.[47] The 1911 census reported a total of 11,705 wage earners, making Winnipeg one of the most heavily unionized cities in Canada.

The first thirteen years of the century were a period of unprecedented boom in Winnipeg and the west. Some wage earners reaped lucrative benefits; economic conditions were good, construction placed a heavy demand on skilled labour, and wages climbed steadily in the better-organized crafts. Building trades workers were particularly blessed and found steady employment at high wages as their unions grew in numbers and strength. Even so, the basic problems of Winnipeg's rapid growth were not being solved; poverty was still widespread, the slums stood virtually untouched, unorganized labour was continuously victimized, the boom-inspired inflationary spiral continued unabated, and in many cases trade unions still had to fight bitterly to pry concessions from employers.

The prosperity of the era served to dull the most vociferous and systematic condemnations of the industrial system, but good times never last forever. At least a full year before the Great War the euphoria caused by full employment, fat pay envelopes, and optimistic expansion began to disappear. The leaves turning brown in the autumn of 1913 signalled the end of the expansionary period and ushered in two hard years of depression. This economic downturn was soon compounded by a new order of problems associated with the outbreak of war in August 1914, which was to bring even greater disillusionment to the working classes. It also brought home in a very real and personal way the inability of workers or their unions to defend themselves against the ravages of depression or the arbitrariness of some employers.

2. ❖ The Depths of Depression

The most direct cause of the depression of 1913 was the latest in a series of power struggles centred in the Balkans. The wars of 1912 and 1913 channelled the heavy flow of British investment capital away from Canada, and the millions of pounds sterling which had financed railways, towns, industries, and grain elevators were converted into machines of war. The escalator of rising prices and heavy demand halted abruptly, as rural and urban land values tumbled, construction sagged, wheat prices dropped, wages fell, and unemployment began to climb rapidly. The "boom or bust" mentality of Winnipeg and the west in the years preceding the depression left many a farmer, worker, and speculator high and dry and increased the effects of the economic downturn. Winnipeg was so hard hit by this depression that the nation-wide stimulus to the economy provided by the outbreak of war in August 1914 did not materially affect the bleak picture in the city until the fall of 1915.

Widespread economic slowdown combined with rising unemployment hit Winnipeg in the autumn of 1913. Prairie winters are harsh, and the snow and cold always signal the beginning of a high rate of seasonal joblessness, particularly in the building industry. That winter was different from previous ones, however, in that unemployment was experienced on a broad front, was higher than usual, and did not abate with the arrival of spring. In October 1913 the lack of work in the CPR yards forced the company to dismiss many unskilled workers and place about two thousand others on short time. By the following month the sight of four to five hundred men waiting in the cold for work at the yard became all too common.[1] Towards the end of January 1914 the company began to shut its repair shops for days at a stretch, and unemployment in some inside building trades reached as high as 90 percent.[2] Though conditions improved somewhat over the summer the depression continued, and while other Canadians became preoccupied with the war after August 1914, labour in Winnipeg continued to focus its attention on the more mundane matter of unemployment.

Organized labour suffered greatly from the economic downturn. Although various methods were used to encourage unemployed members to stay with their unions, most organizing activity came to a halt and membership declined. The Winnipeg Trades Council was in such bad financial shape in September 1914 that it sent only one delegate to the annual Trades Congress convention at Saint John, New Brunswick.[3] The two chief pillars of organized labour in Winnipeg, the building trades and the railway shop craft unions, were the hardest hit by unemployment and their inability to keep up their numbers was crucial to labour's continuing misfortunes in the city.

In the midst of this crisis the unions looked to the three levels of government for leadership and found it lacking. The civic answer to unemployment was traditional; make-work projects were started in which unemployed men cleaned streets, cleared brush, or laid sewers —an approach which had never endeared itself to workers in the past and did not during this crisis period. The one tangible gain earned from a reluctant civic administration was the Winnipeg Free Employment Bureau, founded in October 1913 to find jobs, free of charge, for the unemployed who registered with it. In the following twelve months over thirteen thousand applications were received, of which twelve thousand were successfully processed;[4] but the bureau was only a clearing house and could not create jobs where none existed.

The work of the bureau aside, the city government was both slow and reluctant to attempt any programs which might have significantly alleviated unemployment. Mayor T. R. Deacon, owner of Manitoba Bridge and Iron Works, had never been known as a friend of labour and was a steadfast opponent of unions. During this period of recession his stock tumbled still further in labour's estimation. *The Voice* wrote of him that "he still continues to manifest that contemptible dog-in-the-manger spirit towards his less fortunate brothers that has been so characteristic of him and so noticeable of late."[5]

Whatever little aid was forthcoming from civic authorities, not much greater consideration was given by the provincial government.

Sir Rodmond Roblin's Conservative administration reacted to the unemployment crisis not with a patchwork program of charity employment but by curtailing construction on several key provincial projects. Upon the outbreak of war work on the most important job in Winnipeg, the provincial parliament buildings, was stopped because the provincial government claimed it had run out of money. The halt was to prove temporary, and lasted only a few weeks, but the government made no effort to calm the fears of the unions while the ban was in effect.[6]

Organized labour's opposition to unrestricted immigration was a direct result of the fear that immigrants willing to work at lower rates of pay would push union members out of their jobs. When the unemployment rate climbed in 1913 and 1914, labour turned to the federal government to seek the type of effective action which had been lacking at the civic and provincial levels. In the summer of 1913 R. A. Rigg, secretary of the Trades Council, told the federal minister of labour, T. W. Crothers, that current immigration policy was the chief cause of the unemployment then spreading throughout western Canada. A great number of skilled and unskilled workers could not find jobs, especially in the building trades, but at the same time the federal government was bringing immigrants to Canada who would also have to find some means of livelihood.[7]

Rigg was one of the most articulate and outspoken labour leaders in the city and commanded much respect in both union and socialist circles. He was an Englishman, like most other influential union men in the Canadian west, who had abandoned the Methodist ministry to come to Canada. After settling in Winnipeg he took up the bookbinding trade and became increasingly active in labour affairs. He was elected president of his local union in 1910, president of the Winnipeg Trades and Labor Council in 1911, and secretary of the council in 1912. In 1913 he became the first nominee of the Labor Representation Committee, organized the previous year by the Trades Council to coordinate the electoral activities of trade union and socialist candidates, to win a seat on city council.

In the spring of 1914 the Manitoba Executive Committee of the Trades and Labor Congress made a direct plea for action to the Borden government. A telegram was sent to the prime minister, asking him to halt immigration to western Canada until the job market improved and to adopt active measures to relieve the situation and accept responsibility for immigrants who had already arrived in the country.[8] Labour gained an ally in their campaign when the city council appealed to Borden to stop the inflow of prospective settlers and to begin public works projects as soon as possible. Mayor Deacon opposed the move, claiming there were still thousands of acres of empty land in Canada that could easily support ten million people, but the motion carried anyway. The opposition to this resolution put up by the mayor and his supporters was duly noted among labour circles in the city and not soon forgotten.

The reluctance of all three levels of government to act on any but the simplest of organized labour's pleas was bound to further alienate workers from their elected representatives. Relations with the provincial administration of Premier Roblin were particularly frustrating. The Manitoba Executive reported to the 1913 convention of the Trades and Labor Congress that the problems encountered in getting favourable legislation adopted were surpassed only by the difficulty in having existing laws properly administered. The Shops Act, they reported, was ignored by the municipalities, and the Factories Act was inefficiently administered in Winnipeg. These complaints about the Factories Act were tragically borne out with the death of two workers in September 1913. *The Voice* commented: "These incidents ought to be of some effect in reminding the government that there is not a factory inspector in the whole province and that the factory act is thereby practically suspended."[9] One month later an inspector was finally appointed but, much to the dismay of organized labour, the new appointee was completely unknown in trade union circles, while the announced appointment of a female inspector was delayed. The smell of patronage hung heavily in the air.

The depression of 1913 created hardship among most of the city's workers. The building trades, however, suffered the most because the construction industry was very vulnerable in the city's rapidly expanding economy. Thousands of skilled and unskilled workers had gravitated to construction during the preceding decade as hundreds of factories, warehouses, homes, and apartment blocks were thrown up in Winnipeg. These workers profited from the unprecedented boom and earned good wages at steady jobs while their unions waxed fat. By 1913 the building trades were at least as powerful and influential as the railway shop craft unions. The depression was a severe blow, therefore, because a proud and powerful group of workers was humbled in a very short time. The plight of the building trades exemplified the difficulties of so many other workers and explains why radicalism developed so readily in a traditionally conservative trade.

Not that the building trades were without radical voices. George

Armstrong, for example, an acknowledged leader of the carpenters' union, was also one of the best-known socialists in the city. He was an Ontarian by birth, had been one of the founders of the Winnipeg branch of the Socialist Party of Canada, and was endowed with considerable talent for public debate. But Armstrong was a voice in the wilderness in a trade dominated by aristocratic and conservative stonemasons and bricklayers. These few years, however, changed the perspective of many workers in the building trades.

The depression almost killed the construction industry, and the priorities placed on spending by the war served to keep building at a very low level until after the armistice. The 1914 national rate of construction was roughly half that of 1912, while the 1915—18 rate dropped to roughly one-sixth of what it had been in 1913.[10] The depression in the building trades was thus nationwide in scope and lasted for the duration of the war. In Winnipeg, as elsewhere, a multimillion dollar industry shrank to almost nothing in a short space of time.[11] The physical effect upon the unions and the psychological effect upon the workers was catastrophic and traumatic. By January of 1914 nine out of ten bricklayers, six out of ten painters and plasterers, five out of ten carpenters, and four out of ten plumbers could not find work. Under these circumstances the Building Trades Council permitted its member organizations to withhold per capita payments because many of them could not collect dues from unemployed workers.

The decline in union membership during 1914 and 1915 bore a direct relationship to the increase of unemployment. John Bruce, organizer for the plumbers union, passed through Winnipeg in July 1915 and reported that not more than 5 percent of the union's Canadian membership was working and many locals in the west had lost as much as 80 percent of their men. J. A. Kinney, organizer for the carpenters, repeated this story with respect to his own union and claimed that unemployment had caused a great reduction in union affiliation in all western Canadian locals because, in many places, building activity had ceased altogether. Unemployment, still prevalent in the fall of 1915, caused the Manitoba Executive of the Trades Congress to report to the annual convention:

> The building trade is paralysed and in almost every other trade short-time has been the rule for many months. As a result of the complete and prolonged distress, financial exhaustion is inflicting upon the toilers and their families in this province, the most intense

misery. The saddest thing of all is that there is no gleam of hope for the future.[12]

There was, nevertheless, some reason for optimism because the need for manpower at the front tended to draw off many unemployed workers. Thus, although there was still little building activity in Winnipeg in 1915, the general secretary of the Winnipeg Social Welfare Association, Howard T. Falk, reported to civic authorities in December that unemployment had been greatly alleviated through enlistments, particularly among British and Canadian tradesmen. As union membership fell off the organized building trades retrenched and waited for renewed expansion.[13] By 1916 the period of continuing unemployment had passed and George Armstrong, carpenters' delevate to the Trades Council, reported that craftsmen were again finding work.

The depression was bound to create tensions between employers and employees. Construction companies were being squeezed by the rising cost of materials and the scarcity of contracts. Unions often found themselves at the mercy of employers at a time when strikes would have been foolish and costly. Contractors might renege on agreements and refuse to pay the annual increases that a contract provided for, or make unwarranted deductions from weekly wages for protections or services that had always been free in the past. On many job sites, union wage scales were ignored or undercut by employers who were trying to cut their own costs and knew well that building trades workers dare not strike when there were so many unemployed waiting to fill their positions. Under the circumstances there was little the unions could do but make vocal protest.

All was far from peaceful in the industry, yet the character of those disputes which did occur was not extraordinary. There was no concerted drive by management for an open shop. There was no refusal to recognize the skilled craft unions or to bargain with them. The building trades depression prompted some employers to campaign for lower wages, to renege on agreements, and to ignore the stipulations of the provincial fair wage schedule; the same conditions forced labour to fight to hold the line on its own living and working standards. The struggle, however, never degenerated into attacks on the very existence of trade unions—it was almost as though both sides recognized a set of unwritten rules which governed their working relationships. Regardless of how bitter the workers may have felt, they did not launch diatribes against the Builders Exchange and tended instead to concentrate their efforts towards getting protection from the provincial government.

The government of Manitoba was customarily the key stabilizing agent in the province's construction industry and during the depression it emerged as one of the chief sponsors of building activity in Winnipeg. While private work was slowing considerably, the most important single project in the city was the construction of the new provincial parliament buildings and this placed great responsibility upon the leadership of the Roblin administration. Prior to 1916 working conditions on government projects were regulated by a fair wage officer who, in consultation with unions and management, was supposed to draw up a schedule of minimum wages to be followed on all public works. These schedules tended to set the pattern for many private contractors as well. The provincial government could have used this machinery to stabilize labour conditions in the industry, but it became one of the worst offenders amongst those who attempted to lower their costs of operation at the expense of the workingman. Roblin's administration refused to demonstrate the leadership that was so necessary for the maintenance of tranquility in this depression-wracked industry.

Union complaints about the setting and enforcing of wage standards began in earnest with the onset of depression in 1913 when workers charged that schedules were either being ignored outright on some jobs or illegally modified on others.[14] To add to these difficulties, the Winnipeg Board of Control and the School Board tended to follow provincial government practices; once wage schedules were being altered on provincial projects changes tended to follow elsewhere. The unions' attitude was shown when R. A. Rigg, secretary of the Trades Council, complained that the fair wage schedule was not worth the trouble it was causing because it always worked to the benefit of non-union employees.[15] George Armstrong, member of the Socialist Party of Canada and a prominent figure in the carpenters' union, criticized the fair wage officer and attempted to have the Trades Council censure him for approving lower wages and longer hours than would have applied in normal circumstances.[16]

The issue came to a head in March 1914 when the fair wage officer drew up a revised schedule for carpenters which introduced a series of drastically lower rates. The new standard was approved by the Winnipeg Board of Control for all civic-sponsored projects, even though the unions bitterly opposed it. Representatives of the carpenters' union met the acting minister of public works, responsible for the fair wage officer, and complained that the lowering of wages was unfair and a violation of government policy.

Two months later, at a meeting between representatives of the unions, the Builders Exchange, and Fair Wage Officer Reeve, the carpenters were faced with a coalition of employers who supported the new schedule and refused to yield on any of its points. Reeve thus announced his intention to keep it in operation despite union opposition. As a result the carpenters declared their refusal to support a government which employed a fair wage officer whose actions were detrimental to their interests.[17] With an election drawing near, Roblin moved to defuse this politically dangerous situation. The premier called Rigg, carpenters' representative Harding, and Fair Wage Officer Reeve to a meeting where he asked union representatives to draft a change in the legislation to the effect that union rates would in future be recognized as the government standard. As a result an amendment was drawn up stipulating that "the wages and conditions of labor shall be those recognized by the unions of the Trades concerned." Roblin consented to this shortly after.[18]

The unions had apparently won an important victory. At the September 1914 convention of the Trades and Labor Congress the Manitoba Executive Committee announced that henceforth the unions themselves were actually setting wage and working condition standards on government projects. Their jubilation was premature, however, because the provincial government soon reverted to its old attitudes and ignored its promises to labour. The Manitoba Executive's report to the 1915 TLC convention summed up its sense of betrayal: "It is with more than corresponding disgust that your committee reports that these promises have remained unfulfilled."[19]

Roblin's war of attrition against labour was stepped up a few months after the 1914 provincial election when T. Kelly and Sons, the contractors on the new parliament buildings, began cutting wages. This arbitrary action was given official approval two weeks later by amendments to the fair wage schedule, when the provincial government instituted reduced wages for four classes of workers, including carpenters; this meant that pay was now considerably lower than that allowed in union schedules. Rigg and five delegates of the affected unions were told by government officials that Kelly's contract allowed him to add additional work classifications at lower wages. Where, for example, there was formerly only one rate for carpenters, the amended schedule allowed Kelly to pay lower wages for such jobs as

floorlaying and formwork. The delegation was unable to convince the
government to rescind the amendments.[20]

The Trades Council was incensed. They condemned Roblin for
breaking his promise to the carpenters, charged that the new system
was an obvious subterfuge to cover wage reduction, and promised to
aid the building trades in their campaign to maintain a fair rate of
pay. In early January 1915 they succeeded in getting the fair wage
officer to admit that the new schedule had been set by express order
of the government and had been drawn up by himself in consultation
with the provincial architect and Thomas Kelly.[21] This was clear
proof that Roblin and Kelly were working together to deprive the
workers of decent wages in order to increase Kelly's profits.

In February F. J. Dixon rose in the legislature to charge that Kelly
was now violating the new lower schedule with the full knowledge of
the government and was paying less wages than the contract allowed.
He pried an admission from Dr. Montague, the minister of public
works, that the fair wage schedule was "more often honoured in the
breach than in the observance." The new contract contained a stipulation that workers had to present grievances to the fair wage officer
forty-eight hours after receiving their pay, but the minister of public
works waived the provision under Dixon's prodding and over $960
in back wages was returned to the men.[22]

In March the Public Accounts Committee of the provincial legislature began to examine the financial relationship between the Roblin
government and T. Kelly and Sons. At the hearings the fair wage
officer testified he had changed the original scales of his own volition,
but Rigg, who followed him on the stand, claimed Reeve had written
the Trades Council a full account of the affair and admitted that the
amendments were drawn up at the direction of the cabinet. Kelly did
not help his own case with his arrogant assertion to the committee
that fair wage clauses were not worth the paper they were written on.
Dixon, meanwhile, speaking on the opposition's motion calling for a
royal commission to investigate the parliament building contracts,
kept the pressure on in the legislature. He charged the government
with "gross negligence, unwarranted extravagance and rank incompetence," and accused Kelly of raking in over $60,000 in profits
earned from the "sweat and blood" of the workers by tampering with
the fair wage schedule.[23]

In over two months of investigations that followed an incredible
story of graft and corruption was revealed. Aside from the main points
at issue—illegal and unjustified profits squeezed out of the contracts,

government mismanagement, and kickbacks—the investigations showed that Kelly had cheated his workers, juggled his wage books, and hidden his pay figures under elaborate codes. Since May 1914 Kelly had withheld over $6,000 in wages, most of it from common labourers who earned the princely sum of $27\frac{1}{2}$ cents per hour.[24]

Roblin's shady deals compounded the impact of the depression for one class of workers; but the inability or unwillingness of all three levels of government to do very much of substance to aid the working population was far more serious to most individuals than the illegal manoeuvrings revealed by the parliament buildings scandal. War eventually ended unemployment and by the end of 1915 the labour surplus had been replaced by a labour shortage. The situation had not, however, been rectified by the planning or actions of any government and trade union leaders knew this. Their endless appeals for action had been greeted with silence, and the attitudes of a man like T. R. Deacon, who told Winnipeg's unemployed to "hit the trail,"[25] struck at the roots of their pride and increased their suspicions and resentment of those who governed. Deacon, for example, believed that any young man who had lived in Canada with the conditions that had prevailed during the previous decade and could still not provide for himself did not deserve much consideration. His opinion was probably reflective of many politicians, businessmen, and administrators of the middle and wealthy classes.

Organized labour emerged from the depression of 1913–15 battered and bruised. The unions had lost members, wages had fallen, governments and employers had reneged on agreements, and the problems of welfare and unemployment had been all but ignored. The growth of war industry and the new demands for manpower exerted by the armed forces were about to reverse roles, however, and put organized labour in the most favourable position it had been in for many years. Unfortunately the unions' newly developing strengths would not prove sufficient to overcome the complex difficulties posed by full-scale domestic mobilization in the months ahead.

3. ❖ The Trials of War

Since the outbreak of war the central government had assumed an increasingly important role in the daily lives of most Canadians. Through its assumption of emergency powers under the War Measures Act the task of mobilizing the nation's industries, as well as its manpower, fell almost exclusively upon Ottawa. The distribution and separation of powers established by the British North America Act virtually disappeared. Under these circumstances many of the complex problems faced by workers throughout the country fell to the federal government to solve. Its inability to control the runaway inflation that began to erode most workers' living standards, and its unwillingness to reach any accommodation with organized labour over the regulation of working conditions in war industries turned many unions against the government and created disenchantment with the entire war effort.

The Canadian cost of living had climbed steadily during the years of expansion but declined from a highpoint in 1912 to a 1915 low, as unemployment increased, investment capital dried up, and demand for goods and services decreased. Once the economy began to mobilize for war, however, demand for raw materials, foodstuffs, clothing, and many other products began to pick up. There were millions of people to feed in Europe, an army to clothe and equip, and millions of dollars' worth of munitions to produce. Then, too, Napoleon's old maxim that an army marches on its stomach was no less true for this war than for any other. The result of these factors was predictable— a high and apparently ever-rising cost of living. The increase began soon after the outbreak of war and although it did not push the cost of living back to prewar levels until 1916, its beginnings did not go unnoticed. Inflation soon became a prime cause of social unrest affecting not only labour but almost every class of consumer in the country.

Many Canadian workers were caught in an intolerable squeeze by rising costs and were not able to maintain their standard of living. Those, such as construction workers, whose skills were not as necessary as they had been before the war, were particularly affected and were left far behind in the race with prices. This inability to make ends meet prompted many of them to think their lives were being ruled by food pirates and price manipulators.[1] But the belief which became prevalent by the end of the war that every worker had suffered a decline in his living standard was, in fact, a blanket generalization based on popular misconception, prejudice, and simple blind panic. That assumption, however, became a major factor behind much labour unrest in Winnipeg and throughout Canada.

It is impossible to state with certainty the exact rate of the cost of living increase in Winnipeg during the war; the statistical data of the period are simply too primitive to arrive at concrete conclusions or to prepare accurate cost-of-living indexes. It is almost as difficult to prepare statistics that would reliably reflect a rise or fall in real wages for any particular craft. A comparison of the October 1914 retail prices of thirty staples, five types of fuels, and two types of rents in the Winnipeg area with those of October 1918 indicate, however, that the overall rate of increase of these items for this period was no greater than 40 percent.[2] The costs of services such as transportation or durable items such as clothing are not included in these figures but probably followed the main price trends of the day. These figures, when compared with the 1914 and 1918 wages of some groups of workers, give a rough estimate of how various trades fared in the wage-price battle.

Some of the most accurate wage figures available for the Winnipeg area cover railway shop machinists. In June 1915 the hourly rate for this class of worker was 45.5 cents while the June 1918 rate was 68 cents—an increase over three years of 49 percent.[3] The average hourly wage for contract shop machinists in the city was 40 cents in 1914 and 65 cents in 1918, an increase of 62 percent. Other groups did not fare as well. Carpenters' wages increased a mere 9 percent from 1914 to 1918, electricians 22 percent, building labourers, earning low wages to begin with, received a 29 percent increase, while motormen and street railway conductors' wages climbed 14 percent.[4] Thus the greatest increases went to the very group who usually led the most militant strikes and provided the most radical leadership—the contract and railway shop machinists.

Fear of the unknown, panic, the ravings of misinformed agitators, and other factors ensured that inflation would become an emotion-charged issue. There is no doubt that many Canadians were adversely affected by rising living costs during the war, but to what degree was almost never discussed. Some workers not only kept ahead of the inflationary spiral, they actually improved their living standards. What is of prime importance, however, is that almost all workers *believed* inflation was ruining their living standards and destroying their wage increases whether it really was or not. Under these circumstances hysteria was almost unavoidable.

Even by the summer of 1915 many were convinced that the cost of living was going up and would continue to go up because of the war. In June *The Voice* attacked the federal government for attempting to cover up the causes of inflation and alleged that trusts, combines and high tariffs were clearly behind the current situation of low wages, scarce jobs, and an ever-increasing cost of living.[5] In fact, prices in the city in mid-1915 were clearly lower than they had been one year before. Costs of food, fuel, lighting, and rent in July 1914 totalled $17.72 per week but twelve months later the same items totalled $15.53 per week—a drop of approximately 13 percent.[6]

As early as the fall of 1916 the inflation debate had wallowed into a morass of wild charges and conspiracy theories. One Winnipeg Trades Council delegate spoke of huge profits amassed by certain corporations and the council solemnly appointed a committee to investigate his charge. A. W. Puttee cautioned against this approach and warned that facts, rather than conspiracies, should be examined to find the real reasons for the increasing cost of living; in his view currency inflation, higher tariffs, and a heavy European demand for North American foodstuffs were clearly at fault. He conceded that speculators and trusts may have been working to increase prices, but asserted that there was no proof to back these beliefs. When the price of bread increased it was pointless to level charges at millers and retailers because, he claimed, "the factors governing the cost of living are not capable of being controlled by a few petty bakers." Nine months later, however, Puttee was flinging his own charges at mysterious "behind the scenes" manipulators and the "illegitimate" profits of packers and cold-storage companies.[7]

The belief that dark forces were at work to rob consumers through illegal or unfair practices was buttressed by a general feeling that measures could have been taken to end inflation except for government reluctance. The true rate of inflation was distorted out of proportion and at the same time the fact that wages were also rising in many crafts was ignored. It was taken for granted that the government and the foodpacking industry were victimizing workers who were powerless to stop the robbery. Belief became reality and half-truths were accepted as gospel. The federal government's failure to control the rising cost of living ensured that Ottawa would become the chief target for much of organized labour's wrath. Although complaints were made to municipal and provincial authorities, labour leaders knew that Borden's administration bore most of the responsibility since it was the prime agent behind the national war effort. Ottawa's added inability or unwillingness to regulate working conditions or stabilize labour-management relations in war industry plants was viewed as further evidence of its lack of concern for the welfare of Canadian workers. The insertion of a fair wage clause in Canadian munitions contracts, for example, would have made little difference in the fight against inflation but might have won back much of the respect the government was losing in direct proportion to the daily increase in the cost of living.

Winnipeg was not important to the nation's war production, but war production was important to the relations of workers and management in the city's iron works and machine shops. From 1915 to the end of the war, $4,355,812.36 worth of munitions contracts were filled by eleven companies in the Winnipeg area. The city, the third-largest in the dominion, actually placed thirtieth among all Canadian localities in the output of war materials, although its total was second for areas west of Thunder Bay.[8] Western Canada was at a serious disadvantage in comparison with Ontario and Quebec since its industrial capacity was lower and it produced shells at higher cost due to the greater shipping distances.

The production of munitions on a large scale in Canada began shortly after the outbreak of war, when Ottawa conceived the idea of using independent railway and contract shops throughout the country to manufacture shells. At that time there was only one modern Canadian factory, in Quebec City, capable of producing the projectiles, but its 75-per-day capacity was inadequate to meet the demands of a major conflict. To expedite production the Shell Committee, an arm of the British Ministry of Munitions, was formed under the chairmanship of Lt. Col. Alexander Bertram to organize Canadian manufacturers, educate industry in the production of munitions, and distribute contracts.[9] By the end of 1915 eight companies in Winnipeg and vicinity were engaged in shell production: the Canadian Pacific, Canadian Northern, and Grand Trunk Pacific Railways, Strong-Scott Manufacturing, Transcona Shell Company, Vulcan Iron Works, Manitoba Bridge and Iron Works, and Dominion Bridge. Pay rates and working conditions were poorer in the non-railway contract shops because employees worked longer hours and were paid less,[10] although they were engaged in exactly the same type of work as the men in the railway shops. As a result the metal trades unions initiated a campaign to raise the working standards of these employees. The battle was in reality fought as much to gain publicity for the unions and to show that organized labour was capable of successfully pressuring governments and employers as it was to gain higher wages for munitions workers. Shell production was the lever to be used for wiping out inequities that had actually existed for years.

On the surface the unions' case was clear-cut and based on very real complaints. After shell production began in the city in mid-1915, railway shop wages were as much as 10 cents higher for munitions work. Under the surface, however, the story was more complex. Shell workers in Winnipeg's contract shops were usually paid on a piecework basis throughout the war, and when straight piecework alone was not the rule an hourly wage with bonuses was paid. At Strong-Scott, for example, it was possible for a man working steadily to earn, on a piecework basis, a wage equivalent to 70 cents per hour[11]—as high or higher than he might earn at CPR. Vulcan, which combined an hourly wage with production bonuses, paid over $1,000 apiece to some of its shop employees during the period from September 1915 to August 1916, and many earned much more than that.[12]

There were, therefore, two classes of employees in the contract shops—those who worked on shell production and often earned wages equal to or higher than those paid in the railway shops, and the men who worked on the usual kinds of jobs, did not benefit from war-production bonuses, and were paid much less. The unions' underlying aim was to raise the latter class of workers to a higher plane and at the same time to standardize the shell workers' higher pay rates by placing them on an hourly wage system. The unions were fighting against disparities in hourly wages for "men who are all doing the same class of work,"[13] but were just as interested in destroying the system of piecework and bonuses, "two of the greatest enemies of organized labor."[14] A victory in this campaign would gain them tremendous prestige and bring in hundreds of new members.

Organized labour initially tried to win by a fair wages clause in all munitions contracts awarded in Canada what they could not achieve through negotiations with management. By this time it was standard procedure for Ottawa to include a fair wage schedule or a fair wage clause in every public works contract it awarded. The practice had begun with a resolution of the House of Commons in 1900 and was designed to protect workers on publicly financed jobs by stipulating what wages an employer must pay to different classes of workers or by forcing him to pay wages comparable to those already prevailing in the district where his job was located. Union leaders expected this practice to be extended to munitions production and were unpleasantly surprised when it became obvious this was not the case.

In February 1915, even before any munitions work was under way in Winnipeg, the Trades Council, with the support of the machinists' union, asked the federal government to approach the appropriate British authorities to insert the Dominion Fair Wages Clause in all contracts for war materials awarded in Canada. This followed news from James Watters, president of the TLC, that Ottawa had no power to either insert the clauses themselves or compel Great Britain to do so.[15] In March the federal minister of labour, T. W. Crothers, and Lt. Col. Bertram announced that henceforth all contracts placed in Canada would contain a fair wage clause. Bertram further asserted that manufacturers who failed to adhere to the clauses would not receive any more work from the Shell Committee.[16] The matter was not settled so easily, however, because this promise was never fulfilled. The Shell Committee was riddled with corruption and war profiteering. When the Liberal opposition unearthed evidence that members of the committee were growing fat from phony contracts, payoffs, and other shady deals, the committee was disbanded and reorganized into the Imperial Munitions Board under the leadership of Toronto packing magnate Joseph Flavelle. Bertram's pledge to the unions was lost in the shuffle.

For the next two years the Trades Congress and the International Association of Machinists hounded the Borden government and when they continually failed to receive satisfaction from Ottawa, appealed directly to the War Office and cabinet in London. Borden did not oppose the insertion of fair wage clauses in Canadian war-supply contracts,[17] but the unions never received any satisfaction. The British realized they were dealing with a potentially sticky constitutional issue and avoided direct interference in the affair, but did tell the Canadian government that they saw little reason why the unions should not receive satisfaction in the matter, particularly since it would go a long way to maintaining peace in the munitions industry.[18] Even Borden's labour minister eventually supported the unions and gave the prime minister his opinion that since wages and working conditions would not really change, the insertion of fair wage clauses in munitions contracts was a small price to pay to keep the unions happy.[19] Every effort was a failure, however, because Flavelle opposed the move from the start and never budged from this position.

Flavelle had two reasons for his refusal to sanction the insertion of fair wage clauses in contracts awarded by the IMB in Canada. He thought that if the rules were changed in the middle of the game the IMB would be courting trouble. Workers in factories already producing shells under the old system would raise a great hue and cry until they too were covered by renegotiated contracts containing the clauses.[20] This, however, was not the fundamental reason for his opposition; his prime motive was simply that he was philosophically opposed to trades unions and what they were trying to accomplish.[21]

Flavelle must have been aware that the granting of fair wage clauses in war supply contracts would not change working conditions very much but would be a great psychological victory to the unions. At one point Mark Howard Irish, director of munitions labour for the IMB, plainly told Flavelle that a great deal of the agitation beginning to surface in war plants might be forestalled if Flavelle gave in. Irish maintained that the union leaders could then claim they had "wrenched" a victory from the IMB and would be happy with what they received. In the meantime unrest would die down in munitions factories and production levels would be maintained. This, however, was the very thing Flavelle did not want, because although his main responsibility was the unhindered and continuing production of as much war material as could be squeezed out of Canadian industry, he had no intention of allowing the board to become a vehicle for union advancement. By 1917 this had become obvious to the unions and they began to launch attacks against Flavelle, who they charged with continuing indifference to workers' grievances, and the IMB. In May of that year the Trades Congress asserted that the board had ignored sanitary requirements in plants and work camps directly under its control, lowered established wage standards, eliminated the eight-hour work day, introduced unskilled labour into munitions factories, and consistently refused "to recognize Trade Union representations in determining wages and hours in contracts let by them."[22]

The situation in Winnipeg shell shops was no less frustrating than the national one. Beginning in mid-1915, the unions tried to get men such as T. R. Deacon to pay the same wages as the railway companies for shell work, but met with no success. Their continuing failure to budge the contract shop owners, combined with the traditional hostilities which had existed in these shops for many years, pushed the Winnipeg Trades Council into the forefront of the national fight for fair wage clauses. Secretary Rigg was one of the leaders of the movement to go over the heads of Canadian officials and appeal directly to London, and Winnipeg representatives of the IAM continually accused the TLC leadership of dragging its heels on this vital issue.

The atmosphere of discord at the Vulcan Iron Works in mid-1916 was probably not untypical of that in the other contract shops in Winnipeg. The union had been completely ignored in its campaign to raise wage levels and began covert attempts to organize the workers. Management, for its part, hired labour spies to attend the secret meetings and report the names of prominent pro-union workers and the extent of the union's success in signing Vulcan employees. The grumblings from the Vulcan assembly line were loud enough to be heard in Ottawa and to prompt Flavelle to make a personal investigation into the labour problems in this one small plant.[23]

Union leaders in Ottawa or Winnipeg were not party to any of the secret dispatches between Ottawa and London and could not read the interdepartmental memos of Borden, Crothers, or Irish. They knew only that the Imperial Munitions Board, headed by an industrialist appointed with the consent of the federal government, which was the virtual arm of the British War Office and in the close confidence of the Borden cabinet on many issues related to national mobilization, was frustrating their desires and there appeared to be no redress from either London or Ottawa. On the national level this led to a further separation between Congress leaders and the Borden government, while in Winnipeg the inequities between conditions in the railway shops and the contract shops, combined with union efforts to wipe them out, increased the bitterness harboured by labour and management from as far back as the 1906 Vulcan Iron strike. By late 1916 and early 1917 industrial peace in Winnipeg and throughout the nation was fragile at best. Its prospects for survival were not improved by Borden's introduction of conscription for overseas military service in May of 1917.

Labour's fight against conscription began with the government's announcement of a national manpower registration program in the spring of 1916. When the TLC failed to receive assurances that this policy would not lead to conscription, Watters and his executive publicly fought against the program for many months. At a meeting in December Bordon finally assured them that registration was not a prelude to conscription and the executive, now satisfied, issued a statement signed by Watters, R. A. Rigg, P. M. Draper, secretary of the TLC, and Ontario labour official James Simpson, urging congress affiliates to co-operate with the government's scheme. This recommendation was vigorously opposed by many western Trades Councils, particularly those of Vancouver and Winnipeg.

Waters had trusted Borden but was forced to change his position with the prime minister's announcement the following May that compulsory military service would soon be introduced to Canada. Watters and the executive now attempted to place themselves at the head of a rising tide of opposition and, at one point, the TLC president went so far as to discuss a national general strike to protest conscription. At the September convention, however, after the conscription bill had been given parliamentary approval, the executive retreated to their customary moderation and told the membership that the law ought to be obeyed, though efforts should be made to repeal it. An amendment strongly supported by western delegates to challenge conscription by "direct action" was defeated.[24]

Much of organized labour's opposition to the measure was based on the conviction that war was a capitalist undertaking carried out at the expense of the working class. Leaders of the anti-conscription drive in Winnipeg were convinced the fighting was an outgrowth of the desire of war industries and munitions suppliers to amass large profits. Things were bad enough, they believed, when workers were being forced, under substandard conditions, to build the supplies of war, but compulsory participation in the fighting was intolerable. Leaders of the anti-conscription movement took particular exception to "being forced to take active part in any war between sections of any master class" in which they would be "compelled to shoot down and be shot down by other members of the International working class."[25] There was, however, another reason for their opposition to conscription based not so much on their love for fellow members of the working class as on a practical assessment of the current labour situation. Trade unionists believed, quite simply, that conscription was "a subtle means of robbing labor of its virility and power to defend itself."[26] As early as January 1917 the TLC had expressed the fear that industrial conscription might be introduced. Although seldom given priority in public discussions, this ghost continued to haunt labour's consideration of military conscription. Winnipeg IAM Lodge 122 condemned compulsory military service because the war was capitalistic and only "incidently" mentioned that the measure would also help management control "the boys in the trenches of industry." If military conscription were put into effect, they believed, industrial conscription would follow and workers would lose the right to strike. Labour, therefore, thought conscription of manpower for military purposes was connected with and would lead to conscription of manpower for industry.[27]

The Winnipeg Trades and Labor Council placed itself in the forefront of the opposition to the government's registration and conscription measures and challenged the TLC leadership's reluctance to take a strong, unwavering stand against the Borden administration. In December 1916 president Harry Veitch urged workers to refuse to fill out their registration cards, even though they were legally obliged to do so. At a meeting of the Trade Council executive in early January 1917, Rigg, who had signed the TLC executive's recommendation of the previous month, reversed his stand and told delegates that Borden's public speeches clearly showed he had gone back on his promise to the Congress executive. Rigg, in effect, approved Veitch's suggestion and repudiated the TLC executive report he was then in the process of presenting.[28] Two days later a special Trades Council committee report supported the recommendation that registration cards be ignored and was given enthusiastic endorsation by the full council. In this way the first serious division in years between the Trades Congress leadership and western labour was opened up, with Winnipeg playing a key role.

Western disaffection with the Trades Congress was not new and grew out of the fundamental differences between working and living conditions on the prairies and British Columbia and those of central Canada. Trade unions in the west were numerically weak, isolated from each other and isolated too from the leadership of the Congress and the American Federation of Labor. Westerners were always more inclined to organize along industrial rather than craft lines, to engage in independent socialist politics, and to attempt to organize the large numbers of workers in primary industries such as mining or logging. These efforts were often thwarted by a special breed of tough, individualistically minded owners and managers, who fought organization every step of the way. The very first unions in British Columbia, organized in the 1860s, ran into tough going when they challenged the coal empire of Robert Dunsmuir in the late 1870s. By the outbreak of World War One, British Columbia had become famous for its violent labour wars. Shootings, bombings, and mass demonstrations at Extension, Rossland, Ladysmith, and Cumberland in 1912 and 1913 were all too typical of labour-management "relations" in the area.

These experiences led westerners to believe themselves different and, as such, to complain about eastern and American ignorance of their problems. They felt dominated by the greater numerical power of eastern trade unionists, which was almost always exercised in the conventions of the Trades Congress to endorse cautious AFL-inspired policies. There had been a brief division in the congress following passage of a resolution ordering the TLC to organize itself into a series of industrial unions at the 1911 Vancouver convention, but because of its location, it was a meeting dominated by westerners.

The following year the resolution was watered down and the split patched over to the satisfaction of the TLC executive. The breach over conscription was more serious, however, and not solvable by weak compromise resolutions.

Borden's announcement of conscription in May was taken up by the Winnipeg Trades Council at a stormy meeting on the night of May 31, when delegates declared their unyielding opposition to the draft and called for a national referendum on the issue. By the end of June the Anti-Conscription League, led by prominent socialists and labour leaders, began to hold meetings, circulate petitions, and submit articles to *The Voice* attempting to drum up additional opposition. Sometimes league meetings ended in violence, broken up by members of the Returned Soldiers' Association or their supporters, and at one gathering in late June ACL speakers were chased off a platform. Outside the hall returned soldiers mobbed F. J. Dixon and other speakers and threatened to riot until police arrived to calm the situation.[29] While stories circulated that a civic-wide general strike was being planned the Trades Council polled its membership to discern the strength of anti-conscription sentiment. The full results were not disclosed and the confused wording of the resolution left the validity of the vote open to question, but of twenty-three lodges that did reply, 1,787 individual members opposed conscription while 736, approximately 29 percent of those voting, supported it.[30]

The daily press and the Winnipeg Board of Trade were strong

advocates of conscription and took exception to labour's participation in the anti-conscription drive. In January 1917 the board sent letters to MLAs Dixon and Rigg, Controller Puttee and labour aldermen W. Simpson and John Queen protesting their stand on national registration and expressing the opinion that this position did not represent the true beliefs of their constituents.[31] J. W. Dafoe, editor of the *Free Press,* also threw himself into the fray. He attacked anti-conscriptionists for defacing recruiting posters with stickers bearing the union label. This, he maintained, was abusing a symbol held dear by many men serving in the armed forces abroad or supporting the war at home. He continually and correctly pointed out that many trade union members had already volunteered for military service and claimed this was because they realized that their interests lay with the defeat of Germany, regardless of what their leaders were doing.[32]

The Board of Trade and the press were not the only ones who took an interest in the anti-conscription activities of labour leaders in Winnipeg. The army kept close tabs on the activities of those believed to be the most active in the anti-draft agitation. In a July 1917 report the commanding officer of Military District 10, General Ruttan, told his superiors that the anti-conscription movement was led by socialists and labour leaders and was heavily supported by alien enemies. Ruttan pointed directly at R. A. Rigg, F. J. Dixon, John Queen, A. A. Heaps, and George Armstrong, all British subjects, and pleaded that a quick and effective method of dealing with them be adopted under the provisions of the War Measures Act.[33]

In August Ruttan stepped up his campaign and warned Ottawa that the opponents of conscription were still capable of mounting an effective attack and might even use violence. Although he admitted this was unlikely, he requested that his ammunition be augmented and that no regular troops be removed from his area until conscription was well under way.[34] By March 1918 this crisis had apparently passed and his district intelligence officer reported that "everything is perfectly in order and going smoothly."[35]

The words are ironic. As far as organized labour was concerned few things were even close to perfect and almost nothing was going smoothly. The high cost of living continued to erode living standards, while the government's refusal to force the IMB to place fair wage clauses in war-supply contracts had poisoned relations between workers and their government. Organized labour was determined to build its strength in numbers and at the bargaining table and the co-operation or encouragement of the government and the IMB would have helped them considerably to do both. Where business was treated as a partner in the war effort, however, labour was a poor third cousin and union leaders were rarely heeded or consulted on important matters bearing on the welfare of their members. The coolness of both the government and the IMB towards labour was more than apparent, and the unions were forced to go it alone and win their battles unaided.

To compound labour's frustrations, Borden had seized on an unbeatable political issue with his introduction of conscription. By the time national elections were held in December 1917 the TLC's roars of the summer had turned into a whimper, and the independent candidates who took to the field, with the support of the unions, to campaign against conscription were demolished at the polls. On all three fronts, therefore, labour and the Borden government found themselves on a collision course and the unions were bound to lose. Even so, a chronic shortage of skilled labour enabled the organizing to continue despite the apathy or hostility of the IMB and the government, and the unions continued to grow in strength. It was only a matter of time before union leaders threw up their arms in disgust, gave up on lobbying and persuasion, and told their men to hit the bricks and tie up war industries for higher wages and better working conditions.

4. ❖ Injunction City

After eighteen months of war Manitoba, along with the rest of the country, began to experience a labour shortage. The recruiting campaigns, the general stimulus given to the economy by mobilization, and the increase of munitions production in Winnipeg melted unemployment away and put a premium on skilled craftsmanship. The unions were quick to feel the changing pulse in the labour market and knew that a shortage of industrial manpower would give them considerable leverage in their fight to organize Canadian workers.

Membership drives helped create a new militancy in labour circles. In the days before the automatic check-off and the closed or union shop, it took a more active personal commitment to join a union, particularly in the face of management opposition. A union, therefore, had to demonstrate the advantages of affiliation. It had to show prospective members that it could protect them from anti-union employers and that it could win real gains in higher wages and better working conditions. This created a tendency to demand more and to be reluctant to settle for less. The desire to force rapid upward revision of wage scales usually ran into higher prices of wholesale commodities and raw materials pushed up by the very same inflationary factors eating away at the workers' standard of living. Too often the result was like the meeting of immovable object and irresistible force.

The organizing drive in Winnipeg added hundreds of new members to the fold and brought in workers who never before had anything to do with unionism. Lodges were set up amongst civic office workers, provincial telephone operators, retail clerks, and even fire-fighters. The campaign was aided by the appointment, in 1917, of W. H. Hoop, member of the Socialist Party of Canada and the Letter Carriers' Union, as the Trades Council's first permanent organizer working on a salaried basis.[1] But most of the canvassing was conducted by part-time, unpaid, union members. The war had presented a golden opportunity for the unions to get off the ropes and they were not about to let it pass. One member commented: "Economic conditions favour our class about once in seven years, let us take advantage of this fact."[2]

The new Liberal government of Manitoba, headed by T. C. Norris, was not unaware of, or unsympathetic to, labour's difficulties. It had come to power in the summer of 1915 after the Roblin administration foundered on the parliament buildings scandal, and it was strongly backed by a variety of progressive groups whose ambitions had long been thwarted by the Conservatives.[3] The Liberals were determined to make a clean sweep of provincial politics and cement the important support of farm, labour, and progressive groups. Once in office they introduced legislation regarding temperance, granted female suffrage, instituted civil service reform and compulsory school attendance, and brought in a host of other measures to benefit farmers and workers. In addition, they passed the Initiative and Referendum Act in 1916 which introduced the American concept of "direct legislation" to the province. For the first time in many years a provincial government willing to listen to and act upon some of organized labour's more pressing problems was in power. The Norris administration could not do much about the rising cost of living or the regulation of working conditions in war-industry plants, but it did not ignore the unions and sought, often with their co-operation, to usher in a new era of protection and regulation.

Roblin had created a Bureau of Labor in March 1915 in a desperate bid for labour votes, but the Norris government made it work effectively. Soon after taking office the Liberals, at the urging of the Winnipeg Trades and Labor Council, reorganized the bureau and made it responsible for the enforcement of eight measures on the statute books, including the Shops Regulation Act and the Factories Act. A staff of twenty-five, headed by one-time Trades Council president Ed McGrath, took on inspection and enforcement duties throughout the province and were invaluable advisors to the government on trade union matters. Within a short time the bureau assumed even greater importance, as the scope of its activities was expanded with the amendment of, and addition to, existing legislation. The application of the Shops Act and the Factories Act was widened, the loopholes plugged, the maximum allowable hours of labour were lowered, and it became unlawful for any factory to remain open on a legal holiday without the bureau's permission.[4]

In January of 1916 the provincial minister of public works, T. H. Johnson, decided to bring stability to the relations of labour and employers in the still-depressed building industry and referred the problem to the Bureau of Labor for consideration. It urged abolition of the fair wage officer's position and the appointment of a board to meet once a year to prepare a schedule of wages and hours to be applied and enforced on all government building projects. It further suggested investing the board with the power to adjudicate labour disputes and giving the parties to those disputes the right to make appeals to the minister.[5] The legislation embodying these proposals was promptly drawn up, presented to the legislature, and passed in March.

The Fair Wage Act of 1916 established a three-man board with full power to investigate pay rolls and employers' records in order to arrive at equitable wage standards. One member represented employers, one acted for labour, and the third sat for the Department of Public Works. They were to meet annually to conduct regular business and draw up a schedule to apply on all public works projects within the province over the next twelve months. The act instructed the board to base its recommendations on "the wages and hours of labor commonly recognized . . . as prevailing in the district where the work is carried on."[6] The schedule arrived at was generally based on standards set by existing agreements, but where employer and employee had not been able to arrive at a mutual understanding the board moved to set its own minimum rate. Thus the board did not arbitrarily set standards for industry to follow; rather, it sought to legalize the best examples of wage and working agreements and thereby to regulate the government-controlled sector. It was aided in this by the fair and impartial approach of the minister of public works. Johnson in action was a far cry from his Conservative predecessor and sought to maintain strict neutrality in his dealings with management and labour. Where, for example, Montague and the Roblin cabinet had treated Thomas Kelly and Sons like a trusted family member Johnson scrupulously kept his distance from the new parliament buildings contractor, J. McDiarmid Company.[7]

The effect of the board's establishment was at once far-reaching and limited. Its final schedule applied to all public works in the province but only regulated minimum wages and maximum hours. Other public bodies tended to follow the schedule, although they were not legally required to, and thus the board's work directly affected City of Winnipeg municipal projects, Winnipeg School Board contracts, and Greater Winnipeg Water District work. The schedule was optional on private construction jobs and if applied was still not subject to board regulation and policing. In addition, the act only covered construction workers and no effort was made to widen the scope of the legislation to protect shop or inside workers in any industry.[8] For example, although the Manitoba Bridge and Iron Works produced building materials, none of its workers were covered with the exception of hoist engineers and structural iron workers actually on a construction site.

The board's decisions tended to set the pattern for agreements and settlements between private employers and their workers. In August 1916, shortly after the first wage schedule had been published, the Winnipeg Builders Exchange and the Winnipeg District Council of Carpenters arrived at an agreement which closely followed the board's guidelines and was one of the most progressive ever arrived at in the city up to that time. Wage provisions, grades, and maximum hours were exactly the same as those of the fair wage schedule; union members were given preference in hiring and a union agent, if given permission, was allowed on job sites once a week for purposes of furthering his organization's interests.[9] Although building activity was on the upswing, it had not increased appreciably at this time and impetus for the agreement could not have come from a great demand for the services of skilled construction workers. The board's influence, combined with a general stabilization in the trade and falling unemployment rates, was of prime importance and fostered a desire to draw up a general settlement to wipe the slate clean. With the beginning of the board's work and the conclusion of the August agreement, therefore, a chapter was closed on a painful period in Winnipeg's building industry.

While the Fair Wage Act was a new departure, the provincial government's most ambitious piece of labour legislation during its first year was the Workmen's Compensation Act. There was little such legislation on the books in Manitoba in 1915 and what did exist was primitive and offered workers almost no protection at all. The government was determined to rectify this situation and forced representatives of the Trades Council and the Canadian Manufacturers' Association to meet to draw up a draft compensation bill.

When no common ground could be found, Norris turned to a private members' bill proposed by J. W. Wilton with the support of legislators from other working-class ridings and treated it as government legislation.[10]

The bill, introduced in the legislature in February 1916, was in many ways a compromise. Unlike many compensation schemes in existence or being introduced elsewhere in Canada, it provided for coverage by private insurance companies rather than a state-administered fund and did not initially cover occupational diseases. In addition, a worker could only receive compensation if he was disabled for at least seven days.[11] The Trades Council was decidedly unhappy with the private coverage and Rigg maintained that labour would only accept this as a temporary measure;[12] but faced with the choice of this bill or nothing, labour's opposition soon caved in and the measure was approved.

The Norris government's 1916 compensation legislation was a rather timid step, but in August 1918 his administration broke new ground with the introduction of a minimum wage bill for all female workers in the province. In 1917 the Trades Council had asked for a minimum wage of ten dollars per week for working women. This request, along with other complaints about inadequate wages paid to women, prompted the Bureau of Labor to begin a study of the condition of female workers in factories, stores, offices, and restaurants. A special representative actually took jobs in different industries to compare her earnings with the cost of necessities, and as a result of her investigation the bureau decided that minimum wage legislation should be enacted as quickly as possible.[13]

Labour and management were poles apart on the issue. The Trades Council's arguments were vigorously opposed by the CMA on the gounds that minimum wage legislation during a period of labour shortage would impose artificially high wages and short hours on industry. Management and their employees, they maintained, should be left free to arrive at mutually satisfactory agreements. The CMA changed its position early in 1918, however; though still opposed to the Trades Council's demands for a blanket minimum of ten dollars per week, it supported the principle of basic wages for women and maintained that a provincial body should be established to set standards in each individual industry.[14]

Both sides formulated their proposals into draft legislation and submitted bills to the legislature's Law Amendments Committee which, after much discussion, decided to back the CMA's proposal.

The resulting Manitoba Minimum Wage Act established a board of five: a male and female representative of management and a male and female representative of labour presided over by a "disinterested person." The board was empowered to investigate and fix minimum wages for female workers in shops, factories, and mail order houses in Manitoba and could impose fines and imprisonment upon employers who violated the provisions of the act or the orders of the board.[15] The act was not all that labour wanted but it was a milestone achievement of the Norris government's progressive approach to the regulation of labour conditions.

The philosophy of McGrath, the bureau, and the government was virtually indistinguishable and reflected traditional progressive motivations in the attempt to impose regulation from above, use government to balance the power of capital to help protect the weak members of society, and bring a degree of stability to labour-management relations. By setting standards and minimums they hoped to build a foundation for the establishment of social justice and their efforts were welcomed by the labour movement. The record was admirable and innovative.

The basic issue which increasingly separated labour and management was not capable of being resolved by regulatory legislation, however. The unions were determined to reduce management prerogatives and gain for themselves an increasing share of power in the daily operation of plant and industry. This would mean placing checks on management's unhindered ability to hire and fire at pleasure and at will, to set remuneration arbitrarily, and to determine under what physical conditions employees would work. During the period of depression the unions were weak and little could be done, but now war had created conditions which allowed the fight to be renewed with greater vigour than ever before. The Norris government had created a better working environment for many employees in Manitoba, but it could not or would not help organized labour's assault on the fortresses of management power. The Liberals were supported by middle-class progressives and farmers and either did not understand or could not sympathize with the unions' fundamental aims. When labour's drive ran into the stone wall of judicial injunction in 1917 Norris's failure to help put him into the enemy camp.

In late January of 1917 450 workers of three Winnipeg packing plants struck over the alleged dismissal of a number of employees for union activities. This dispute dragged on for some months until the employers entered $25,000 damage suits and applied for perpetual injunctions against the union and several named members. The employers demanded that the courts order the union and its members to refrain from interfering with the conduct of business in any way; faced with this legal action, the strike collapsed.[16]

In May an intense organizing campaign conducted by the Winnipeg Women's Labour League among store clerks employed by the F. W. Woolworth Company culminated in a strike for higher wages and shorter hours. After the walkout had been in progress for one week, Woolworth entered a damage claim for $25,000 against the union and asked for an injunction to prevent picketing. The judge dismissed the damage suit but granted the injunction allowing Woolworth to bring non-union labour into its stores, resume operations, and force the collapse of the strike.[17]

The ability of an employer to resort to injunctions and law suits had been a sore point in Winnipeg since the initial use of such instruments in the 1906 contract shops' dispute. Now the reappearance of the injunction served to focus the attention of the Trades Council and its parent congress on labour's precarious legal position. The use of injunctions in these two disputes clearly demonstrated that labour's status in law had not changed at all in eleven years. The employers' demonstration that they could and would use the tactics of 1906 to defeat labour's aspirations forced unions to recognize that all their organizing energy was useless if the courts could destroy the gains of a decade in a single blow. The injunction, aimed directly at labour's only real lever of any consequence—the strike—was a serious menace to the drive for organization and recognition, and the unions were thoroughly alarmed by the ease with which the Woolworth's and packing houses strikes had been crushed. These disputes, however, were relatively minor affairs in peripheral industries. The contract shops, on the other hand, were almost always at the centre of attention in Winnipeg and the use of injunctions in a series of strikes here was particularly infuriating.

The Winnipeg contract shops were the "Balkans of the . . . labour world,"[18] as much because of the personalities of the antagonists as the physical nature of the industry. Buildings and machines do not espouse philosophies. A company becomes a symbol and takes on a personality when guided by the firm hands of strong-willed men. The contract shops, led by Manitoba Bridge and Iron Works, Vulcan Iron Works, and the Manitoba branch of Dominion Bridge, became fortresses of conservatism because of their owners' attitudes to industrial relations. The strong views of these barons of industry presented a challenge to unions which was accepted time and again.

Thomas Russell Deacon, one-time mayor of Winnipeg, council

member of the Winnipeg Board of Trade, executive member of the Prairie Provinces Branch of the Canadian Manufacturers' Association, and owner and chairman of Manitoba Bridge and Iron Works was a complex man with definite views on almost every subject relating to the nation's industry and his own corporation. He was born on a small farm in Ontario and at eleven years of age was forced to leave a country school to assume part of the burden of supporting his family after his father died. He then worked as a labourer and lumberman in the logging camps of northwestern Ontario, becoming foreman of a log drive at an early age. From the bush he graduated to work in a sawmill but by saving his small earnings was able to gain his matriculation and enter a course in mining and civil engineering at the University of Toronto. By the time he was thirty, Deacon had one of the largest private engineering practices in the province and was earning, by his own estimate, over $7,000 per year. At this point he closed his office and took his capital west to Winnipeg to establish what eventually became Manitoba Bridge.

It is clear that Deacon's views were as complex and rough-hewn as his personality, but were consistently based on what one-time Trades Council President F. G. Tipping called "the old paternalistic Ontario 'bush culture' of that period."[19] He insisted on his right to run an open shop and consistently refused to recognize trade unions although he had no objection to his men joining such organizations. Deacon implicitly believed that capitalism stimulated individual initiative and that its abolition would produce stagnation; but he was ready to admit that free enterprise was not perfect.[20] Human nature was always going to be a deciding factor in any system, he claimed, and Deacon believed this had not changed "since the time that Jacob tried to steal his father-in-law's cattle."[21]

Deacon did not shy from the thought of government participation in the economic affairs of the nation and was ready at times to advocate such schemes as unemployment insurance and workmen's compensation. In fact, he participated in a 1907 Manitoba royal commission which drew up provincial compensation legislation and though he finally agreed with his fellow commissioners that a private system would be best he did put forward a proposal for government operation. In January 1917 he told a convention of the Prairie Provinces Branch of the CMA that government participation was essential for the maintenance of a healthy economy at the conclusion of the war: "The establishment of industries requires large sums of capital —in many cases the Government should arrange to loan them money or credit, protect their home market with a high tariff and in return should control prices and profits, allowing the private capital only a reasonable and safe return for its use. . . ."[22] Deacon was the philosopher par excellence of private enterprise and anti-trade unionism and he rarely failed to grasp the opportunity to explain his views to anyone who would listen.

The owners of Vulcan Iron Works, the Barrett brothers, were primitive by comparison. At Manitoba Bridge, Deacon's strong hand was tempered by paternalism, but at Vulcan no such considerations interfered with what the Barretts believed was their God-given right to operate in any manner they wished.[23] Where Deacon would talk to his workers in his frequent inspections of the shops and at times demonstrated the correct method of operating a piece of equipment or performing a difficult job, the Barretts stayed aloof and did not mix with their employees. They had beaten the union soundly in 1906 and would not countenance any form of organization in their plant.

N. W. Warren, manager of Dominion Bridge's Winnipeg operations was a temporary figure in the city's manufacturing world. He was a company man, a technician, rather than a philosopher or dictator. He arrived in the city in 1914 and left in 1921 and although he participated in local organizations such as the Prairie Provinces Branch of the CMA, his plant responsibilities were delegated from the head office in Montreal.

The powerful combination of ownership and capital known as the contract shops faced a growing challenge from organized labour throughout the war. In mid-1915 Canadian manufacturers, attempting to fill some $200 million worth of war contracts, awoke to the realization that they were facing an acute labour shortage with respect to skilled craftsmen.[24] The IAM's membership in Canada had declined from 5,000 in 1913 to 4,643 in 1914 and other unions in the metal trades experienced similar difficulties; but now the opportunity arose to increase organizational activity and strengthen the union movement. In November 1915 the Winnipeg CPR shop craft unions launched a concerted and successful drive to attract new membership and turned their attention to the contract shops, labour's Achilles heel.[25]

The railway unions took an active interest in the independent metal works because of the relatively poor working conditions which prevailed there. Contract shops workers were chided for working longer hours at less pay, while it was generally held that the lower standards set by these shops tended to hold the other metal trades back in their attempts to improve their position.[26] The international head office of the machinists' union aided the drive by providing financial assistance, and by March 1916 increasing numbers of men were being signed up in all the contract shops, with the notable exception of Vulcan Iron Works. The Barrett brothers fought the unions down the line, and stamped out any attempts to sign up their workers.[27]

It was not unusual for officials of the railway shops unions to attend contract shops meetings, but the one man who worked hard on every organizing drive, speaking at union meetings and outside factory gates, was Robert Boyd Russell. Russell was Scottish born and came to Canada in 1911. He had already undergone his political and industrial baptism by the time he arrived in Winnipeg and was an accomplished machinist. He served his apprenticeship in Glasgow and joined the Amalgamated Society of Engineers and the Independent Labour Party. Russell became active with socialist groups such as the Clarion Scouts and went to Glasgow Square every weekend to hear fiery orators harangue the crowd on questions of current left-wing interest. His father was a socialist while two uncles were ministers, and the constant doctrinal arguments which took place in his home trained the young machinist in the principles of socialist debate.[28]

Bob Russell became active in union affairs almost immediately after his arrival in Canada. There was no local branch of the Amalgamated in Winnipeg in 1911 so, when he began to work at the CPR, he became a member of the International Association of Machinists. In April 1914 Russell became Lodge 122's correspondent to the *Bulletin,* the official journal of the IAM in Canada, and spiced the usual shop news with liberal amounts of socialist and pacifist rhetoric. Six months later Russell received wide attention with a controversial anti-war column in which he announced that he personally had nothing against the Kaiser and was not going to join the army to fight a capitalist crusade. He paraphrased Edward Carpenter, socialist poet and philosopher, in blaming the war on "insane commercial and capitalistic rivalry, the piling up of power in the hands of speculators and financiers, and . . . trading for dividends in the engines of death. . . ."[29] The piece caused a tremendous uproar and prompted an attempt by the paper's editor to stifle all contributions which did not bear directly on union news.

Russell actively supported the drive within the IAM, led by the Grand Lodge officers in St. Louis, for consolidation of all the metal trades craft unions into one organization. Craft exclusiveness in the shops was irksome and dangerous, and these same divisions on an international scale divided and weakened the labour movement. The workingman's worst enemies, Russell asserted, were those who encouraged and defended craft unionism, a system which segregated skilled workers from the rest of their class. He actively supported the amalgamation movement in the IAM and forecast that eventually all workers would be members of "one big army."[30]

Russell's rapid rise to a position of power and authority in the union demonstrated his increasing popularity as well as his considerable ability. By the fall of 1915 he had been elected to the executive board of Section 1, the CPR unit of the IAM in Canada, and in December 1916 he became chairman of that section. In this capacity he was an ex officio member of the Canadian executive board of the union. His climb to the top reached a climax in the spring of 1918 when he became secretary-treasurer of the IAM in Canada,[31] holding this position in addition to the chairmanship of Section 1. Over the years Bob Russell, more than any other man, personified the Winnipeg metal unions, in much the same way as Deacon was a symbol for many of Winnipeg's employers.

Almost every element traditionally contributing to open warfare between workers and management could be found in the contract shops; they were a microcosmic picture of much of Winnipeg's industries. Here unbending and self-made men were determined to build their relatively small shops (Manitoba Bridge never employed more than three hundred workers during this period) into major factories producing for national markets. They treated their employees in arbitrary fashion, paying what the labour market dictated, and ruling over their industrial domains like feudal barons. Their workers were skilled tradesmen, proud of their craft and their abilities, who had come to western Canada from England, Ontario, the United States, or central Europe to improve their position in life. They were led by hardworking, tough, and able men such as Bob Russell, dedicated to socialism or unionism, who were determined to bring equally tough men such as Deacon or the Barretts to the bargaining table, and eventually, do away with society's need for such men altogether. The fight in the contract shops, therefore, was not only about wages and hours, nor even recognition, it was also a struggle of will.

By the spring of 1917 tension in this industry had reached a new peak. Workers were still being denied wage parity with their brothers in the railway shops and the unions had given up hope of ever seeing fair wage clauses inserted in munitions contracts. The organizing drive continued, fuelled by the workers' belief that inflation was "taxing the shirt off [their] back"[32] but the owners were as determined as ever to deny recognition to the unions. In April the machinists attempted once again to pry a wage increase from the contract shop owners but were completely ignored. Finally, on May 1, members of IAM Lodge 457 left their shops and workbenches and the first contract shops strike in eleven years was on. The machinists' leading antagonist were Manitoba Bridge, Vulcan, and Strong-Scott and the strike soon settled into the pattern of mistrust and hostility that had become typical of the industry.

T. R. Deacon took the lead in the anti-union fight when he hired the Thiel Detective Agency to supply strikebreaking machinists from Montreal.[33] This move backfired, however, when seventy non-union workers in the munitions department walked out in protest and forced Deacon to retreat. He was not to be defeated so easily, however; he applied for an anti-picketing injunction and entered a damage suit for $50,000 against Lodge 457 and eight of its members. Strong-Scott followed with another injunction application and a $25,000 damage suit. These moves added an unnecessary and dangerous element to an already explosive atmosphere. Deacon had not been the first city employer to use the damage suit–injunction combination—he was not even the first in 1917—but his move inflamed labour more than any previous manoeuvre because it was so reminiscent of Vulcan's similar action in 1906.[34] The Trades Council began a campaign against the injunction and urged union members throughout Canada to support their drive; nevertheless, Deacon and his fellow employers held the upper hand and used it to blackmail the union out of continuing the strike. On July 4 the walkout was called off in return for management's promise that all legal proceedings would be dropped.[35] The contract shops then extended small wage increases to their workers almost as a gesture of contempt for the men and the unions who had tried and failed to defeat them a second time.

The unions had suffered several important defeats in 1917, but the Trades Council could still take solace in the work accomplished in the formation of new unions and the strengthening of lodges which had been weakened through enlistments and unemployment. Labour was now more powerful and more willing to flex its muscles than it had been for a long time, perhaps stronger than at any time. But it was still all but ignored, or worse, misunderstood, by the provincial and federal governments and strongly and successfully challenged by local industry through the courts. When it could not find redress of grievances or achievement of fundamental aspirations through governments it resorted to action of its own. Workers believed they were falling behind in their fight against inflation and this led to strikes for higher wages and union recognition. In 1917 more man-days of labour were lost in Winnipeg due to strikes and lockouts than in the previous four years combined. The trend was to increasing numbers of strikes of greater length as union leaders warned that it may be necessary in future "to adopt stringent measures to force a recognition of [labour's] rights."[36] In the coming months Winnipegers would learn exactly how severe these might be.

5. ❖ The Triumph of Radicalism

In April 1918 teamsters, electrical workers, water works employees, and office workers of the city of Winnipeg approached the municipal administration for wage increases. Civic authorities held that a new schedule would freeze inflated wartime pay scales at an artificially high level but offered a bonus designed to tide their employees over until peacetime, when new wages could be negotiated. This proposition was totally unacceptable to the unions even though the grants came close to matching the workers' financial demands. The bonus itself became the main issue and neither side showed any desire to compromise. On May 7 the electricians, teamsters, and water works employees ordered their men to strike. City council thought their offer reasonable, if not generous, and prepared to fight the workers down the line on the bonus question. They were strongly supported by the *Free Press,* when the editor, J. W. Dafoe, asked "whether, when labour has to deal with the . . . duly constituted representatives of the people . . . a resort to strike is justifiable."[1] The readiness of many businessmen as well as members of city council to adopt this mode of thinking assured that the very right of civic employees to strike would also become a major issue in the dispute.

Amid rumours that a general strike vote was about to be conducted by the Trades Council, a mass meeting of Winnipeg union members was held on the evening of May 8. Ernie Robinson, who had replaced R. A. Rigg as council secretary, urged the delegates to keep a solid front and force a victory both in the dispute and at the polls in the next civic election. Alderman John Queen pointed out that the refusal of less than one hundred men to work had thrown the whole employing class into a fit. Labour's power was great if it would only wake to its potential, he said, and the present strike must be won to "make Winnipeg safe for democracy." A. W. Puttee, elected to the Winnipeg Board of Control in 1916, then outlined his position and declared that the strike was ill-advised because the unions had rushed into a confrontation without seriously considering the city council's position. He charged that this kind of action was of the type resorted to by the Industrial Workers of the World (IWW), a radical American-based revolutionary union, and that strikes should only be used as a last resort.[2]

The clash between Puttee and Queen revealed a fundamental difference in the two men. Both were British-born, but there the similarity ended. Queen had been trained as a cooper, had come to Canada in 1906, and had involved himself in socialist activities and the Social Democratic Party almost from the beginning. Puttee's reputation was derived from his devotion to the cause of trade unionism and reform in any of its guises, as well as his generally moderate style. Queen, on the other hand, believed that reform could only come through socialism and that unions must be in the vanguard of that movement. He was a large and genial man with a great sense of humour, and had succeeded in winning a seat on city council under the Social Democratic Party banner in 1916. Now, two years later, his star was clearly waxing in labour circles while Puttee's was on the wane.

The meeting was in no mood to listen to Puttee and passed a resolution which endorsed the actions of the striking workers but fell short of the call for a general strike which some people had expected. The gathering did serve to polarize feeling in the city, however, because many individual unions rushed to support the strikers and began to conduct strike votes of their own members. Within forty-eight hours rumours circulated to the effect that all municipal employees, including officers and men of the fire department, would soon join the walkout. Throughout the rushing tide of events the only calm voice to be heard among labour ranks was that of Puttee, who maintained that a strike against the public would destroy any sympathy for labour that might exist and continued to call upon union leaders to arbitrate their grievances.[3]

With a strike of civic firemen a distinct possibility, the time had arrived for city council to act. After much fencing between labour aldermen and their opponents, council decided to form a negotiating committee consisting of Puttee (acting as chairman), the mayor, and aldermen Fisher, Sparling, Hamlin, and Heaps to deal directly with the strikers. Heaps contacted the leaders of the striking unions, notifying them that the committee had been formed and signifying its willingness to hold immediate discussions. By Saturday morning, May 11, the committee and the unions had hammered out the rudiments of an agreement. This quick action impressed the firemen, who decided to postpone their strike, and stimulated a mood of optimism in the city. The *Free Press* reported the following Monday that a settlement had been reached and indicated that striking civic employees were already returning to work.[4]

The man whose motion had resulted in the establishment of the Puttee committee was Abraham Albert Heaps, Social Democratic alderman who had come to Winnipeg from Leeds, England, in 1911. Heaps was an upholsterer by trade and had gravitated to the city's labour movement within a few months of his arrival. In 1912 he was elected to the Trades Council and became its official statistician. Heaps was a close friend of John Queen but was very different in attitude and manner. He was a careful, almost meticulous, man who preferred behind-the-scenes negotiation to flamboyant public rhetoric and who was instrumental in working out the settlement which appeared to have ended the strike.

Hopes that a quick solution to the city's labour troubles had finally been found were dashed in the city council that very night. The report of the committee was amended by a vote of nine to eight when the council added, over the heated opposition of labour representatives and the non-labour councillors who were members of Puttee's committee, a proviso that all civic employees undertake to pledge they would not strike at any time but would instead have their grievances settled by arbitration. In addition, the amendment specified that all questions arising out of the current strike be settled by a board of conciliation which should be appointed immediately.[5] In effect this "Fowler Amendment," named after its chief sponsor, Alderman Frank O. Fowler, put the city council on record opposing any right to strike for civic employees.

This attempt to put out a fire with a shower of gasoline was indicative of a growing mood of toughness in certain quarters. The Winnipeg Board of Trade endorsed the Fowler Amendment and Dafoe asserted that the unions should signify their acceptance of the principle of compulsory arbitration for civic employees before any meaningful negotiations were begun. The question at issue, Dafoe reiterated the day after the amendment had been approved, was whether or not civic employees should have the right to strike.[6]

The recommendations of the Puttee committee had indeed been liberal but had been drawn up by a group of six city office-holders of whom only two were Labor Party representatives—Heaps and Puttee. They had sponsored a settlement which would give the unions official recognition, replace the bonus system with new wage schedules, and make provision for a sixty-day period of arbitration in any future labour disputes before strikes or lockouts could be instituted.[7] This had been accepted by the unions and once approved by the city council would have ended the dispute right there. Instead the council, by approving the Fowler Amendment, threw down the gauntlet and challenged the unions to a battle over the question of the right of civic employees to strike.

At this point the labour movement in Winnipeg was not about to shy away from a fight on so fundamental an issue. The effects of the Fowler Amendment's approval were immediate and electrifying. Tuesday morning, May 14, the city's firemen walked off the job. Within the next ten days ten other unions joined the strike while the city government, strongly supported by the Board of Trade, confidently assumed that they could carry on the operation of essential services without their employees.[8] At this stage neither side had yet been chastened and the municipal authorities' views found a vocal champion in J. W. Dafoe, who wrote that only natural catastrophes should put an end to essential services such as water, light, and protection from fire.[9]

Thursday, May 16, witnessed a turn for the worse in an already critical situation. Telephone operators in Winnipeg joined the strike and city yardmen and CPR machinists announced they too were ready to walk out. The municipal government made plans to staff the light, power, and water departments with volunteers from the "Public Service League" and to recruit temporary staff for the firehalls. The officers and men of the fire brigade maintained an emergency force to save lives, but would not fight fires which threatened only property because, they explained, they were fighting "capitalism" in the city.[10] By Monday, May 20, freight-handlers and non-municipal teamsters had also joined the strike, while street railway employees, typographers, stationary engineers and Canadian Northern Railway shopmen had signified their willingness to enter the fray.

Dafoe now backed down. He pointed out that the city was no

longer fighting four unions but was facing a general sympathy strike and that labour's position had been considerably strengthened by the actions of unions not involved in the original dispute. The conduct of both parties thus far had been irrational, he claimed, because neither side had realized the strength of the other, and the only possible solution to this dispute was through mutual concessions. Dafoe was willing to concede the right to strike for municipal employees, with the exception of firemen, if it were coupled with compulsory conciliation.[11] This was almost the same provision contained in the recommendations of the Puttee committee. The city government had proceeded arm-in-arm with the Board of Trade and the *Free Press* thus far, but now they lost Dafoe's vigorous and important support.

The Trades Council's campaign continued and its successes were becoming increasingly apparent. By the evening of May 22 eleven unions were off their jobs, including the street railwaymen, and the dispute was beginning to take on the proportions of a complete general strike of the city's industry and government. By Friday, May 24, two more unions had joined the work stoppage bringing the estimated total of strikers to more than 6,800 from thirteen trades, including such crucial municipal services as fire, water, light and power, and public transportation.[12] At the massive marshalling yards the running trades, as always, remained aloof but carmen, storemen, freighthandlers, and shopmen stayed away from work. The head offices of the International Typographical Union and the Brotherhood of Railway Carmen of America were strongly against their members joining any sympathetic strikes, but the carmen disobeyed their leaders and struck anyway.[13] In this way labour met Fowler's challenge.

The week following city council's approval of the Fowler Amendment saw the formation of an ad hoc group of private individuals who aimed to raise volunteers to staff essential civic services and also attempt to bring about a negotiated settlement of the strike. The impetus for the formation of this group came from the Board of Trade, the Citizens' Alliance (an informal discussion group which talked about industrial relations problems) and G. W. Allan, Conservative Unionist M.P. for the federal riding of Winnipeg South. On Tuesday, May 14, the Board of Trade had approved a recommendation of one of its members to form a small committee to seek volunteers for the city's fire halls. Two days later Allan wired from Ottawa with a suggestion that "various Winnipeg organizations . . . directly affected and the citizens generally" approach the city and provincial governments to act together in solving current labour problems.[14] That night the Citizens' Alliance met with other interested parties and passed a series of resolutions demanding the outlawing of strikes and lockouts for the duration of the war and suggesting the Industrial Disputes Investigation Act be made applicable to municipal corporations. The next day the new Citizens' Committee of 100 was formed which promptly endorsed the resolutions passed the previous night.[15]

The primary purpose of this group was the manning of civic facilities abandoned by strikers and the first business conducted by it was the organization of volunteer workers to staff power, light, water, and fire departments. The parent Alliance, however, had also announced its intention to work for a negotiated settlement, and consequently discussions were initiated on Sunday, May 19, between a subcommittee of the Committee of 100 and a subcommittee of the General Strike Committee, formed by the Trades Council.[16]

On Wednesday, May 15, letters had started to pour into Ottawa urging federal action to end the strike. Such local luminaries as financier A. M. Nanton, A. W. McLimont, of the Winnipeg Electric Railway Company, the president and secretary of the South Winnipeg Unionist Committee, and the Prairie Provinces Branch of the CMA wired to demand various courses of action such as outlawing strikes and lockouts for the duration of the war. Until May 20, however, the federal government played a limited role in the dispute, despite the pleas for intervention. Prior to that date, the strike prompted federal labour minister T. W. Crothers to appoint Winnipeg lawyer D. Campbell to bring the two sides together, but Campbell was completely unsuccessful in reaching a compromise. He could not get city council to budge from its position of May 13, and was undoubtedly hindered by a lack of any official federal weight to back him up. Borden, for instance, took the position that his government could not get involved in the labour troubles of a municipality. He wrote A. L. Crossin, of the Citizens' Committee, that the provincial government was directly responsible for the conduct, rights, and obligations of municipal employees. If the province were to pass legislation outlawing strikes of civic workers, then the federal government could intervene under Section 164 of the Criminal Code.[17] In Manitoba the provincial government had adopted no such legislation and until it did, Borden was implying, no federal action would be forthcoming. Winnipeg, however, was vital to the nation's communications, and as the strike intensified and the clamour for intervention increased, the prime minister was forced to look for solutions outside the strict formalities of the law; he accordingly sent Senator Gideon Robertson to the city to help settle the dispute.

Gideon Robertson was relatively new to government. He had been appointed to the Senate in 1917 and was a former vice-president of the Order of Railway Telegraphers. He was described by one labour paper as "a big good-looking clean-shaven Canadian, one of the statesmen among the ranks of the railway labour officials," and was considered trade unionism's representative in Parliament. Robertson was of a conservative cast and a friend and admirer of Samuel Gompers and was thus readily accepted by supporters of the AFL's brand of conservative, exclusive craft unionism. In 1918 he was called upon with increasing frequency by the Borden government to act as its industrial relations troubleshooter and was appointed minister of labour in the late summer of that year.

On Monday night, May 20, the senator boarded a train for Winnipeg with specific instructions to bring about a negotiated settlement. He made up his mind before his arrival that he was entering a difficult situation and would weigh all sides of the issue before taking any precipitate action. He did decide early, however, that the Fowler Amendment had been a bad mistake and was the root of the current troubles in the city.[18] The representatives of the Citizens' Committee and the strikers had been meeting continuously since May 19 and by the time Robertson arrived had reached agreement on all points except the right of fire department officers to belong to a union. Robertson's immediate task therefore, was to settle this one outstanding issue and persuade city council to accept the compromise worked out by the two committees. Shortly after his train pulled in, he met with civic officials and strikers' representatives, strongly criticized the Fowler Amendment, and chalked up the strikes to misunderstanding and hasty action. He asserted that the workers believed they were fighting for the right to strike and that a settlement now would lay the basis for amicable relations in future. He told the city council that workers in at least five other cities, watching developments in Winnipeg, might strike if a settlement were not reached and this would be disastrous to Canada's war efforts. Robertson persuaded the council to accept the Citizens' Committee report and at the same time convinced the strikers to agree to a stipulation that fire brigade officers were henceforth to be excluded from any union.[19] A basis for accord had been laid and settlement followed almost immediately.

The agreement was signed Friday night, May 24, and was substantially that which had been proposed by the Puttee Committee twelve days before. New schedules with higher wages were provided for civic electricians, water works employees, teamsters, and firemen. All employees on strike were reinstated in their former positions and rank without prejudice and the Fowler Amendment was withdrawn. Thus city employees, with the exception of fire brigade officers, were given the right to strike, and a conciliation process was outlined which stipulated that sixty days must pass after notification that a new agreement was desired before a work stoppage was possible. The city began to return to normal and by the end of the month all workers were back at their jobs.[20]

The settlement was a clear victory for the unions but spelled defeat for the man who, more than any other, had fashioned the agreement that was ultimately accepted on May 24. A. W. Puttee did not fall from grace, he was pushed, and his waning authority was evidence of the increasing power of the radicals on the Trades Council. By May, 1918, Puttee, as editor and publisher of *The Voice,* as a federal M.P., and as a controller in the city government, had served labour in Winnipeg for over twenty years. In several past elections his paper attacked the SPC for its opposition to F. J. Dixon and R. A. Rigg and had pledged to fight any group which set itself up in opposition to the Labor Representation Committee and its parent Trades Council. His outspokenness had created many foes, and now his enemies saw a chance to put him out to pasture because he had made the grave mistake of opposing the sympathetic strike that had proved to be a great success. Puttee had urged moderation while the negotiations were still going on in April, and had risen at Trades Council meetings during the strike to attack "strike first, negotiate later" tactics. His stand earned him kudos from the wrong people. After the strike was settled Dafoe told the readers of the *Free Press* that Puttee was the one man who came out of the episode looking good. He had taken an unpopular stand with his colleagues, had stuck to his guns through the strike, and had been vindicated when the final settlement adopted the report of his committee almost verbatim. Events had proven his wisdom, Dafoe wrote, and he had shown great moral courage throughout.[21] These congratulatory words were not enough to halt the anti-Puttee onslaught.

Former Trades Council president Harry Veitch launched the campaign against Puttee's newspaper, *The Voice,* at a May 16 council meeting. "I did at one time think we had a labor paper in the city," he said. "Now I know we have not." He then raised the possibility of starting up another paper to reflect the true attitudes and positions of the Trades Council rather than the personal ideals of A. W. Puttee.[22] Puttee's sin was that he had urged moderation from the start and continued to do so even after the city council had passed the Fowler Amendment, which *The Voice* charged had greatly aggravated the situation by putting the city government in direct opposition to the best interests of organized labour.[23] As a result of the disagreements *The Labor News,* an ad hoc organ of the Trades Council and Strike Committee, made its appearance on the streets of Winnipeg.[24]

After the strike was settled a special press committee of the Trades Council, headed by Veitch, urged publication on a weekly basis of a new newspaper devoted to the "economic or trade union side of labour," with columns open to all working-class political parties. Final arrangements were then made to end publication of *The Voice* and on August 2, 1918, the *Western Labor News* made its first appearance, edited by Rev. William Ivens.[25] *The Voice* had been laid to rest and with it one of the SPC's strongest opponents. Perhaps the most accurate, if not final, assessment of this situation was made by Trades Council solicitor T. J. Murray: "I am sincerely hoping that labor will realize what an awful mistake it would make if it retained its recent grudge against Puttee. He was right and they were wrong and they were sore because he told them publicly that they were wrong. It took some courage, but looking back on it it was by far the best thing to do."[26]

The founding of the *Western Labor News* brought another important figure to prominence in a growing field of radical labour leaders. William Ivens had been born in England and came to Canada in 1896. For several years he worked as a farm labourer until he entered Wesley College in 1905. Three years later he became an ordained minister in the Methodist Church and he earned an M.A. degree from the University of Manitoba in 1909. In these years Ivens came under the influence of social gospel proponents Salem Bland, J. S. Woodsworth and A. E. Smith. He developed a marked sympathy towards labour and socialist causes and was a confirmed pacifist. In 1916 Ivens was put in charge of McDougall Methodist Church in Winnipeg and created considerable controversy because of his pronounced anti-war views. In June 1918 he requested and was granted permission to leave his position and shortly after founded the Winnipeg Labor Church.

Ivens' Labor Church met Sunday evenings and was designed to be a forum for reform-minded Christians. The services and hymns of the new church were basically Methodist but were supplemented by classes and discussion groups covering topics such as Marxian economics, anthropology, sociology, and politics. Ivens' views and activities, as well as his struggles against the established lay leaders of McDougall, had brought him close to the labour movement in the city and his talents for organization, combined with his eloquence, made him the natural choice to edit the new paper. His passionate belief in the necessity for change made him and the *Western Labor News* decidedly more radical than Puttee and *The Voice*.

The demise of *The Voice* parallelled and was not unconnected with an increasingly militant approach to labour questions by union leaders in Winnipeg in the weeks following the conclusion of the sympathetic strike. Dafoe hailed the settlement as a sign of things to come and predicted the end of serious labour difficulties on the question of civic employees' bargaining rights. Strike leaders had ceased exalting or justifying the use of the strike, Dafoe maintained, because such talk was too anti-social to be tolerated;[27] but his assessment of the situation could not have been more wrong.

R. J. Johns, writing in the *Bulletin,* official journal of the IAM in Canada, drew conclusions directly counter to Dafoe's as he reflected on the lessons of the strike. There were only two groups in society, he wrote, and Fowler had merely acted as the mouthpiece of the propertied class. The workers of Winnipeg had met Fowler's challenge in high style by exhibiting a new "proletarian morality" in their solidarity during the sympathetic strike.[28] Johns was a militant member of the Socialist Party of Canada but even T. J. Murray fell under the spell of victory. Trade unionism emerged stronger than ever as a result of the strike, he wrote to Rigg, who had recently joined the army, and had "Certainly . . . proven its strength."[29] Ominously, almost every observer recognized that the strike had only been won because other unions had rushed to the defence of the original striking trades. Murray believed that "the several unions would probably have been beaten had it not been for the extent of the sympathetic strike," and the *Free Press* pointed out that the city experienced little difficulty running the water, power, and light departments when those employees had walked out, but had been stopped short by the general support demonstrated by the rest of labour in the city.

The lesson was not lost on the radicals. In June an article appeared in the *Bulletin* which claimed that the ability of individual unions to achieve their economic aims was growing less because "the master class" was uniting to present a solid front to labour. In future, workers would have to organize themselves along industrial lines to protect their individual and collective interests. Such organization, it was claimed, would ultimately give workers the power to achieve their complete emancipation through "the abolition of the wage system."[30]

The mood of unrest manifest in the sympathetic strike and its aftermath was not confined to Winnipeg but was a national phenomenon. In every part of the country workers were reacting to the strains and restraints placed upon them by the war effort in the only manner calculated to win results—strikes and the threat of strikes. The industrial disputes of 1918 were different from those of the previous year, however, in that they were often widespread, involving thousands of workers in vital industries and, like the sympathetic strike, brought unprecedented victories. Many of these strikes or near strikes greatly affected the attitude of workers in Winnipeg because the city figured prominently in several of them. Even those that did not touch Winnipeg affected it, however, because every union victory was taken as proof that the time for moderate discussion was over and the time for mass industrial action had arrived.

In the third week of July national postal service was paralysed by Canada's first post office strike. Since January 1917 postal workers had tried to pry higher wages from Ottawa but were continually thwarted because, in the prime minister's words, there was a war on and the administration did not have an unlimited supply of cash on hand. The government was willing to grant the men a $100-a-year war bonus, but even this small concession was poorly handled and interminable delays held up its distribution. The postal workers grew more impatient with each passing month and finally struck on July 22 when their request that an arbitrator be appointed under the provisions of the Industrial Disputes Investigation Act was turned down.

The strikers received aid and sympathy from several unexpected quarters. The Winnipeg Board of Trade told Ottawa to stop quibbling and grant the union's requests for an arbitrator,[31] while the city council reflected the prevailing mood of public sympathy and added their support to the board's demands. Even J. W. Dafoe, long-time enemy of strikes in the public service, sympathized with the walkout: "The offer of the government does not, in view of the undoubted strength of the postal employees case, err on the side of generosity." The public were supporting the postal workers to a degree unusual in an ordinary wage dispute, he observed, and even those who generally questioned the right of such workers to strike were admitting that this dispute was an exception to the rule.[32]

In the east, the executive of the Letter Carriers' Federation exacted a promise from the Borden government that a cabinet committee would investigate the labour trouble in the post office and, as a result, asked its members to return to work on July 25. Western members of the union, led by the Winnipeg local, rejected this solution and charged it was a manoeuvre to evade the demand for a board of arbitration. On July 25 city postal workers voted 355 to 2 against returning to work and continued the strike alongside other western locals. T. W. Crothers and Postmaster General A. K. McLean travelled to Winnipeg to meet the leaders of the insurgency and promised that their grievances would be investigated by the Civil Service Commission. On Wednesday, August 7, the western letter carriers returned to work and were granted full pay for the time they had been on strike.[33]

Once again, militancy was rewarded. The western postal workers held out after their eastern brothers returned to work and were able to exact much better terms from the federal government than they might otherwise have obtained. This buttressed the feeling that militant action was likely to bring victory, even though the postal workers were greatly helped by a friendly and sympathetic public. In fact, it is hard to explain the government's granting of pay for the time the workers had been on strike, a highly unusual move, without pointing to the support offered by the Board of Trade, the city council, and the *Free Press*. The men recognized that this outside help had been valuable but believed it had followed as a matter of course because of the justice of their cause. This was no doubt true but clouded the crucial fact that militancy alone would not have been enough. The workers, nevertheless, drew their own conclusions from the postal strike and became more convinced than ever that the lessons they had already learned in the May sympathetic strike should be taken to heart.

If the experience of the postal workers was not sufficient to prove this point, then the stunning victory achieved by railway shop craft workers throughout Canada was. In October 1917 the Canadian Pacific, Canadian Northern, Grand Trunk Pacific, and Canadian Government Railways had joined together at the urging of the federal government to form the Canadian Railway War Board in an effort to promote more efficient rail transport for the duration of the war.

The board was composed of representatives of the managements of the constituent roads and worked closely with government officials in co-ordinating railway policy and activities. At first there was no intention to use the new organization to present a solid front to the unions for bargaining purposes, but in early 1918 a negotiating function was forced on the board with the formation of Division 4, Railway Employees Department of the American Federation of Labor.

The formation of the Canadian Railway War Board laid the foundation for the fulfillment of an old union dream that there should be one joint set of negotiations between all the shop craft unions and all the transcontinental railroads. The unions were spurred by management's new unity and decided to build one nation-wide federation to represent and bargain for every railway shop worker in Canada. At a Winnipeg convention in late February 1918, representatives of all the different shop craft unions formed Division 4 with R. J. Tallon of Calgary as president, Frank McKenna of Vancouver, first vice-president, and Charles Dickie of Montreal, secretary-treasurer. Winnipeg became headquarters of the new federation and westerners dominated the executive. Following the founding convention, the division conducted a vote of its entire membership to obtain authorization for a nationwide rail strike if the War Board refused to meet it at the bargaining table. Union members gave their overwhelming approval and, armed with this authorization, Tallon approached the combined railways, who agreed to a summit bargaining session.[34] The railway workers had won an important concession, undoubtedly with the tacit approval of the federal government, and bargaining began in Montreal on April 29, 1918.

The discussions, extending through July, were protracted and difficult. The unions were determined to win large wage increases and standardized pay scales throughout Canada, eliminating the existing system of separate rates for eastern and western shop workers. Management was willing to increase wages and meet other demands if they could get government permission to raise freight rates.[35] In May the negotiations were complicated by the actions of the United States Railroad Administration under the direction of William McAdoo, which granted American shop craft workers a substantial wage increase on all U.S. railroads with its General Order No. 27, known as the McAdoo Award. The Canadian Railway War Board seized upon the award as a solution to its employees' demands and offered Division 4 exactly the same wages, conditions, and stipulations as General Order No. 27. The division was reluctant to accept the award at first and continued to press its demands for even higher wage scales; but under pressure from the government and its international presidents, it agreed to forego strike action and accept the offer.[36] The move was given official federal approval with the promulgation of orders-in-council P.C. 1743 of July 11 and P.C. 1768 of July 16, 1918.

In one move Canadian railway shop workers received wage parity with their American counterparts, but a large number of western union men were left embittered. The federal government, fearing the disastrous consequences of a national shop craft strike, had told the executive of Division 4 that, in the event of a walkout, all railway men would be conscripted and forced to work on army pay.[37] In addition, the presidents of the shop craft unions, meeting in Washington in mid-July, threatened to revoke Canadian union charters in the event of a strike—they were following AFL president Samuel Gompers's "no strikes during war" policy.[38] Under this combined pressure, eastern locals voted overwhelmingly to accept the offer despite the disapproval of their western colleagues. Western members of the negotiating committee walked out of bargaining headquarters in disgust and boarded a Winnipeg-bound train on the evening of July 20.[39] The bitterness ran so deep that Winnipeg lodges of the IAM stopped all per capita payments to their international headquarters in Washington for several months.

Although western shopmen were convinced that they had been sold down the river by their eastern brothers and by their American leaders, their unions had won substantial wage gains, a single pay scale for all of Canada, and had achieved recognition, by management and by the government, of Division 4. None of this had come about through lobbying or petitions, or even through strikes or threats of strikes against one or two railroads or in one or two rail centres. The victory had come about because of the threat that the fifty thousand shop craft workers who kept all transcontinental rail traffic in Canada moving would walk off their jobs. The running trades, it is true, would probably have continued working; but without proper maintenance it would not have taken long for all rail traffic in Canada to grind to a halt. The shop crafts had actually created one large union of railway maintenance workers and the consequences of a strike could have been disastrous to the economy and the war effort. That is why the government, which had allowed the negotiations to take place, could not allow them to fail and was walking a tightrope. In this situation two facts had been made crystal clear: the massed power of fifty thousand workers threatening to strike had achieved an undeniable victory, and the threats of government intervention and the actions of eastern and American union leaders had denied a potentially greater success. Winnipeg, the headquarters of Division 4 and home to thousands of shop craft workers, was bound to be affected; indeed, the fortunes and struggles of Division 4 in the summer of 1918 formed a backdrop for labour's second assault on the contract shops in two years.

In the spring the railway shop craft unions had begun yet another attempt to organize the city's iron and bridge works and machine shops. Spurred on by their defeat in 1917 and a belief that victory would only come through total organization, they aimed to sign up every worker and win union recognition. After an intense period of preliminary activity, during which leaflets were distributed and speeches made at factory gates, a mass meeting was held in late April which signalled the founding of the Winnipeg Metal Trades Council, designed, like Division 4, to impart unity to the desires, aims, and activities of the contract shop workers. The concept was not new and such councils already existed in eight cities, including Hamilton, Toronto, Victoria, and Vancouver. Winnipeg's Metal Trades Council contained representatives from six unions and was led by J. R. Adair with R. B. Russell as secretary.

In early June of 1918, following a successful organizing campaign, the Metal Trades Council submitted a draft agreement to forty-five contract shops and automobile repair establishments containing demands for higher wages and improved working conditions; but the companies, led by Manitoba Bridge, Vulcan, and Dominion Bridge, refused to sign or discuss these draft agreements. Once again rebuffed in their attempt to gain wage parity with the railway shops, the unions set June 10 as a strike deadline if negotiations were not entered into by that date.[40] The unions' aim, as stated by the Metal Trades Council, was the achievement of higher wages, but recognition was the actual objective. The council asked for a 75-cent per hour minimum wage for Winnipeg machinists at a time when other such workers in the country were earning considerably less. The unions undoubtedly asked for these high rates only for negotiation purposes and were probably willing to settle for less after bargaining with management. If management bargained they would have had to recognize the unions; if they did not they would be struck. Instead of openly demanding recognition as they had unsuccessfully done so many times before, the unions tried a flank approach through the Metal Trades Council.

The federal government, already burdened with a threatened nation-wide rail strike and well-versed in the contract shops' troublesome history, bent every effort to force a settlement. The unions, stalled by management, postponed the walkout for five days. Before the shutdown occurred T. W. Crothers appointed R. S. Ward, formerly of the machinists' union, mediator and asked the Metal Trades Council to put the strike off. The unions, led by Russell, agreed and Ward began his efforts to find common ground for settlement. He met with no success and was replaced by an ad hoc committee of Winnipeg's three federal M.P.s, G. W. Allan, Major Andrews, and Dr. Blake. This committee was also unsuccessful and urged Crothers to appoint a royal commission to conduct a full-fledged investigation into the dispute.[41] The minister agreed, and on June 26 he appointed Justice T. G. Mathers to preside over a commission of three with George Fisher, city alderman and F. G. Tipping, president of the Winnipeg Trades and Labor Council, as members. Fred Tipping came to the labour movement by a circuitous route. He was a slightly built, scholarly looking Englishman who had entered the Baptist ministry to become a circuit-riding preacher shortly after his arrival in Canada in 1905. Tipping had always been receptive to the ideas of social reform and eventually drifted away from religious fundamentalism and the established church. Eventually, in Winnipeg, he began to teach woodworking in the school system and used his position as justification for joining the carpenters' union against the opposition of his employers and with the dubious acquiescence of the union's leaders. Tipping became a moderate socialist and joined the Social Democratic Party. His eloquence and his obvious devotion to the cause of unionism earned him much respect in labour circles and he was elected president of the Winnipeg Trades Council in late 1917.

The commission began its study on June 29. Russell, chief representative of the Metal Trades Council, presented a large number of contracts from different parts of Canada to show that the refusal of Winnipeg employers to negotiate or sign agreements was unreasonable and not in line with practices elsewhere. Russell and the unions were determined to achieve recognition and pressed this point above all others. But they made a grave miscalculation. The agreements presented to the commission uniformly showed contract shop wages all over Canada to be lower than railway rates, which in essence proved management's point that Winnipeg wages were not unduly low. As Deacon asked Tipping, why should he pay wages equal to those of the railways when no one else did?[42] Moreover, management maintained that the wages demanded were much too high, beyond their capacity to pay, and not justified by the performance of the employees. They charged the unions with slowing production, filling their ranks with unskilled men, and making exorbitant demands. They declared they would rather shut down than meet the Metal Trades Council's conditions.[43]

After a series of closed meetings and private discussions, both sides arrived at their final positions. The employers, with the exception of the Barrett brothers, agreed to recognize and negotiate with individual committees representing each craft in their shops, provided these committees had no connection whatever with the Metal Trades Council. The unions insisted that these committees must contain representation from all the crafts in a given plant and should act under the direction and control of the Metal Trades Council.[44] Both sides remained far apart and no compromise appeared possible on this most important issue.

After two and a half weeks the restless metal workers, who had the mistaken impression that the royal commission had no authority to make recommendations in its final report, moved to set a final strike deadline. Unless management abandoned its position and entered into negotiations with union representatives, they threatened, the contract shops would be closed on Monday, July 22. Russell and other union officials met the commission and representatives of management on July 20 and pledged to head the strike off when it was explained that the commission would make definite recommendations to the minister of labour. But Russell returned the next day to tell Mathers that he could not hold the rank and file any longer.[45] The mood among the metal workers in the city was already electric because of the serious differences that had surfaced between eastern and western shopmen in the railway negotiations and the decision of shop craft union members in Winnipeg to support a national strike if necessary to back their original demands. Russell held great power in the metal unions by this time and this inability to control his own men was probably due to a steadily weakening desire to avoid confrontation. On Monday morning, as threatened, the contract shops were struck; the dispute quickly developed ominous overtones when the Trades Council decided to conduct a general strike vote unless there was an immediate settlement. Militancy was now running at an all-time high.

The royal commission's report, containing little of solace to the unions, was submitted to Crothers on August 2. The commissioners agreed on four key points and made one major recommendation. They concluded that the most important issue separating employers from their workers was the role of the Metal Trades Council. They had tried to find some common ground on this, had not been successful, and had gone on to consider other issues. They discovered that pay rates were not unreasonable nor unduly low in the shops, and concluded that the unions insisted on uniform scales while the employers were determined to pay each man what they believed he was worth. The commission was deeply disappointed when the strike began and asserted that the Metal Trades Council had, by their action, tended to confirm the employers' contention that unions had no respect for contracts or agreements. Finally, the commissioners pointed to the bitterness and hostility in the industry as a prime factor in the dispute: "In the larger contract shops there exists an atmosphere of suspicion and distrust between employer and organized labour. . . . The real purpose of the movement on the part of the men is, we believe, to secure recognition of the unions, but until the present deep-seated distrust . . . is removed . . . we believe the purpose to be unattainable." They recommended that employers, as a first step, abandon their objections to meeting factory committees, and suggested that the unions allow these committees to function unhindered and independent of trade union or Metal Trades Council control.[46]

The report itself was a shocking surprise and Tipping's signature on a document that contained far more criticisms of labour than of the employers was the signal for a series of bitter attacks led by Bob Russell and the Metal Trades Council. The report was released to the public on the morning of August 8 and that night, at a packed meeting, Russell gave his most militant speech of the campaign thus far. The Winnipeg Trades Council would back the metal workers to the limit, he maintained, and there was even a chance of a nationwide sympathy strike on the railways. He urged the metal workers to hold out at all costs, to go into the fields at harvest time if they must, but to keep firm until union recognition was won. The Metal Trades Council, he asserted, would never accept the report of the royal commission without a recommendation of union recognition.

Tipping had signed the report in the hope that a basis for agreement might be laid which could be accepted by both sides.[47] The recommendations, however, irritated an already explosive situation.

The spectre of a general strike, which had already been raised several times in 1918, was raised again when the contract shops owners reverted to their usual methods of handling labour relations and applied for an anti-picketing injunction. A large and enthusiastic Trades Council meeting of August 15 passed a motion calling for the second general strike vote in four weeks to counter the employers' and court's anti-labour activities. The general strike was being waved about as the solution to all of labour's difficulties and was going to smash forever the destructive power of anti-union injunctions and lawsuits. The vote in favour of a general strike was heavy and might have forced a city-wide tie-up if the contract shops strike had not actually petered out. The workers were long on confidence and rhetoric but, in late summer of 1918, short on tenacity. They began to drift back to work in mid-August, and by the end of September were at their jobs, with nothing more to show for their efforts than a small wage increase. The strike, by Russell's own admission, had been lost.[48]

The waning strike formed the backdrop for Fred Tipping's fall from power in the early weeks of September. He had signed a report which appeared to many to stab the metal unions in the back during a period of crisis. Russell challenged Tipping, a moderate left-winger and member of the Social Democratic Party, while the Trades Council became judge and jury. Tipping angered many delegates and compounded his own difficulties by his continued refusal to explain his actions to the council until he had first discussed the situation with the metal trades. This may have been the proper thing to do, but since Russell was in obvious control of the Metal Trades Council, it was a useless gesture. They refused to listen to him and, as a result, Tipping tendered his resignation. Once he had removed himself from office, however, he strongly criticized Russell and the Metal Trades Council for their failure to control their own men despite promises to Justice Mathers to head off a strike. He explained that he had signed the report because he was certain the strike was doomed and the Metal Trades Council would never win recognition. The men, in his opinion, should have tried to use the report to gain what they could instead of immediately attacking it.[49]

Russell had had a frustrating summer and was in no mood to accept a rebuke from Tipping. He charged that the former Trades Council president had been appointed to the royal commission as a direct representative of organized labour and should not have strained to play an objective role. Tipping was a failure as a labour man and a socialist and had been wrong about the Metal Trades Council's ability to win the strike. They could have prevailed but had lost because "organized labour did not back [them]."[50] The fault, he was implying, lay not with the metal unions or their leaders but with the Trades Council which had failed to carry through with its plans for a sympathetic strike.

As summer faded into fall radicalism was firmly in the saddle. Three influential and moderate leaders of the labour movement in the city were no longer at the centre of power. R. A. Rigg was now a corporal in the army; A. W. Puttee had been shoved aside and his newspaper replaced by the militant *Western Labor News;* and Fred Tipping had been ousted from power. At the same time, new faces and names were becoming prominent. Rev. William Ivens and R. J. Johns would become well known in coming months but the militants were still not strong enough to replace Tipping with a left-wing president, even though their presence was felt much more often.

In two key strikes out of three in the spring and summer of 1918, militancy had paid off. Russell, in fact, had chalked up the defeat of the third to the lack of outside support, as though it had become an accepted fact that individual strikes fought in isolation no longer had any chance of being won and that the only way to impose terms on the employer was to face him and society with awesome and overwhelming power. The general strike, called for and voted upon twice in three months, had become fully accepted as a new weapon in the workers' arsenal. It was to be used along with political action, lobbying, and strikes in individual trades. The general strike was discussed with increased frequency as a natural development in the daily confrontation with management, but little or no time was devoted to a serious consideration of its political and social consequences. It was now thought of as another and more effective weapon but nothing more. This, if nothing else, signalled the triumph of radicalism.

6. ❖ Socialists and Soldiers

The thirty-fourth annual convention of the Trades and Labor Congress of Canada opened at Quebec City on September 16, 1918. The meeting witnessed a mounting assault by western delegates against TLC policies and its connection with international unions and the American Federation of Labor. Western representatives, armed with resolutions expressing concern over government censorship, the jailing of war opponents, and Congress war policies were beaten back again and again. Resolutions calling for a reorganization of the Trades Congress along industrial lines met a similar fate; and to add final insult, James Watters, socialist and westerner, was ousted from the presidency by Tom Moore, a representative of the carpenters' union from Ontario and close friend of Samuel Gompers. The westerners, fired by long-felt grievances, were too few in number and, more important, too disorganized and divided amongst themselves to achieve any results. Their defeat in September started events in train which eventually led to secession.

The west's long-smouldering resentment against the east had boiled up quickly as a result of several factors. The negotiations that summer between the Canadian Railway War Board and Division 4, complicated by interference from American head offices, had ended with violent disagreements between east and west and a walkout of western delegates. In July western members of the Letter Carriers' Union had broken with their eastern co-workers to reject a government-offered compromise. Both situations showed that western workers were willing to split with their eastern brothers rather than accept settlements they considered unsatisfactory. They were giving notice they would not sit quietly any longer and be dictated to by eastern or American leaders whom they considered too moderate or too cosy with government or management. In the unsuccessful fights against conscription and in favour of fair wage clauses in munitions contracts westerners had taken the lead in attacking the government and the alleged "weak-kneed" attitude of the congress executive. Resentment ran ever deeper against the Borden government, the leaders of the international unions, and the strength in Canadian organized labour of Gomperian policies and attitudes. The Winnipeg Trades Council was in the vanguard of the western assault and was propelled by the strong anti-eastern and anti-international bias of certain of its constituent members. Motions had been prepared by the council weeks in advance of the convention emphasizing the need for immediate action in reorganizing the TLC and wresting its leadership from AFL-dominated "choreboys."[1]

Every one of these resolutions was swept aside at Quebec City. Six motions calling for an immediate referendum on the question of reorganizing the congress were killed by the committee on constitution and law. A resolution proposing a change in the policy of automatically expelling unions which had been banished from the AFL suffered a like fate. Later, in a roll-call vote, a resolution from the Winnipeg Trades and Labor Council calling on the government to temporarily release conscientious objectors to work on farms was defeated by 99 votes to 90. Resolutions which formed the core of Winnipeg's demands and served as rallying points for western delegates were snowed under by eastern votes.[2]

The inability of western delegates to press their case prompted a number of them to meet in caucus one lunch hour in the Château Frontenac. The meeting was presided over by a British Columbian representative of the United Mineworkers, David Rees, and was well attended by western delegates and other "progressives." The idea had occurred to several men that continual differences of opinion between east and west forestalled any progressive change and that many workers in the Maritimes, Quebec, and Ontario might be inclined to support the west if they were fully appraised of its policies. Rees attempted to squelch secession speculation at the outset by telling those present that he had no intention of participating in such a move and that the meeting had been called solely to "tone up the Trades Congress general policy." The assembled delegates elected a committee to be responsible for arranging a conference of westerners before the next TLC convention with a view to working out a united program. Chosen were David Rees, chairman, V. R. Midgely, secretary, and Frank Wheatley, H. Perry, and Ernie Robinson.

Constant defeats on the floor and in committee rooms at Quebec City greatly increased western disaffection. Rees may not have had secession in mind, but the idea was clearly spreading within a month after the delegates had gone. Ivens, for example, wrote in the *Western Labor News* that the easy remedy which suggested itself was for "the west to shake off all the shackles and associations of South and East," but that this would be a retrograde move. There were, nevertheless, great differences between east and west: "Western Canada is composed wholly of the adventurous spirits who have left the more effete East because of the restlessness of their nature and their passion for justice. Naturally, therefore, the atmosphere is tense and charged. . . ."[3]

The atmosphere was tense, not only because of events within the labour movement, but also because of the Borden government's decision to impede the normal collective bargaining process and to move against those elements in society it considered seditious and conspiratorial. By late June 1918, strikes and lockouts had reached epidemic proportions throughout Canada and were causing serious interruptions in some areas of war production. The trouble was being caused by several factors, according to the minister of labour, including inflation, low wages and long hours, refusal of employers to recognize unions, and a general labour shortage. The Industrial Disputes Investigation Act was being ignored, he warned, and the walkouts would undoubtedly increase if nothing were done to stop them.[4]

The Imperial Munitions Board's director of munitions labour, Mark Howard Irish, was also acutely aware of the deteriorating industrial situation. He believed that if the government expected munitions production to continue at its then current pace the cabinet should take steps to force all labour disputes to go to compulsory arbitration.[5] Crothers and Robertson were equally impressed by the gravity of the situation and were designing a new war labour policy along the lines Irish suggested. Crothers, in fact, responded to Irish that he, too, believed the situation was growing intolerable and would recommend a "general policy for the whole country." His plan was soon submitted to the cabinet and on July 11 became law as Order-in-Council P.C. 1743. It was a drastic departure from the previous labour policy of any Canadian government.

The new legislation applied to all industries engaged in war production or covered by the Industrial Disputes Investigation Act, with the exception of railways. The order was a declaration of "principles and policies" and contained no penalty clauses for failure to abide by its provisions. Nevertheless, it put the government on record in support of a new status quo in Canada's war industries by declaring that for the duration of the war there should be no strikes or lockouts, and that disputes which could not be resolved by negotiation should be settled by recourse to the IDI Act. All employees were declared to have the right to join unions, to work for a decent and adequate wage, and, if possible, for no more than eight hours per day. Employers were declared to have the right to form associations but not to dismiss workers simply for their membership in unions. The order sought, in addition, to spell out adequate wage and working standards and urged labour and management to spare no effort to settle their disputes peacefully so that war production could continue.[6]

The legislation had no teeth and, in the words of Senator Robertson, was "permissive rather than compulsory." Crothers informed labour leaders in a private communication that there were no legal obligations attached to the order-in-council, although he did not send any such message to employers. Robertson also indicated that this was only the first step of the new campaign and explained the lack of penalty clauses with a hint that the cabinet believed they should "advance by one step at a time."

The Borden administration had ample evidence that the causes of the current industrial unrest were many and deep rooted. Not only had Crothers outlined some of the problems to the cabinet in July, but a committee headed by Senator Robertson reported two months later that the rise in the cost of living was outpacing wage increases and causing the bulk of labour unrest. Robertson's Labour Committee of the Cabinet's Reconstruction and Development Committee suggested wages be increased and that curbs be placed on rising prices. But the government had more immediate and pressing problems. An attack on the root causes of unrest may have been more beneficial in the long run, but it was the short run that counted where munitions production was concerned. On October 11, 1918, therefore, the cabinet issued Order-in-Council P.C. 2525 which completely forbade the use of strikes or lockouts in industrial disputes.

This order was different from its predecessor in that it covered all industries falling under the IDI Act, including the railways, and provided fines or imprisonment for violators. Boards of conciliation now became final boards of compulsory arbitration. The order prohibited employers from dismissing employees for membership in a union and barred workers from using "coercion or intimidation" in efforts to organize their colleagues.[7]

The policy was immediately and vigorously protested by TLC officials in Ottawa. The new president of the Trades Congress, Tom Moore, issued a statement to the press decrying the action and pointing out that the good will of Canada's industrial workers could never be obtained through coercion. On November 8 he was informed by Robertson, now minister of labour, that the government would soon alter the legislation in view of the rapidly improving military situation in Europe. On November 19, seven days after the armistice, the government rescinded the order.[8] For one short month the labour movement had been deprived of the right to strike, but that deprivation had lasted long enough to become yet another wartime grievance.

In Winnipeg, the Trades and Labor Council reacted to the order as though it were a direct challenge to itself alone. The month witnessed a strike of Canadian Pacific freight handlers at Calgary which was beginning to paralyse western shipments of foodstuffs and merchandise. On October 16 the Trades Council decided to support this walkout by taking steps intended to lead to a city-wide general strike.[9] By the following week 92 percent of the ballots distributed had been returned backing the council's hand. Messages were then sent to other councils across Canada urging support for the campaign, while the Winnipeg unions threatened to proceed with their general strike if the government prosecuted five of the Calgary strike leaders arrested for defying the anti-strike order. When the government decided not to pursue the prosecutions the *Western Labor News* declared that the Borden administration had backed down.[10] Once more radical approaches to industrial problems appeared to pay off.

The government's policy was ill-timed and mistakenly conceived, because the very unrest they hoped to stamp out contributed to the militant response. The government's own advisors knew the causes of industrial disputes were complex and deep-rooted, yet Ottawa did little to attack the main problems. In addition, the short period these orders were in effect did not give the government enough time to demonstrate their utility. Industrial strife was not averted for any significant length of time, but the psychological ramifications of the orders did not soon disappear. Things seemed bad enough when employers appeared to conspire with courts to destroy the right to strike, but when the federal government itself was behind the move the situation could not be much worse.

Government by order-in-council was not restricted to labour-management problems. The Borden administration also attempted to regulate and limit the distribution of foreign-language publications and ban suspected revolutionary or radical organizations. As early as March 1918, the Intelligence Branch of the Department of Militia and Defence in Ottawa had attempted to ascertain how widespread was membership in the Industrial Workers of the World in Canada. In August of that year the chief of the Dominion Police informed the head of the General Staff in Canada, General Gwatkin, that municipal, provincial, and dominion law-enforcement authorities were all co-operating to stamp out "the activities of the I.W.W. root and branch."[11] In September the federal government swung behind the effort and curbed the civil liberties of political and ethnic groups it believed were seditious or supporters of the enemy. Order-in-Council P.C. 2381 of September 25, prohibiting the use of fourteen languages claimed to be "alien enemy," was strongly protested by the Trades Congress because, it was claimed, this measure would severely restrict union activities in areas where English was rarely used. Three days later Order-in-Council P.C. 2384 declared fourteen alien organizations unlawful and announced heavy fines and imprisonment for persons belonging to these groups, supporting them, or attending their meetings. The proscribed list included the IWW, the Social Democratic Party and twelve other ethnic and political organizations representing socialist or Bolshevik ideologies.[12]

In December the Winnipeg Trades Council again discussed possible use of the general strike as a reaction to the orders-in-council. The executive declared that labour must stand together to increase its power in industrial disputes and that delays in calling a general strike would reveal the weakness of the workers' position. The main point now at issue was whether a general strike should be called upon a clear majority vote of all union members in the city taken together, or upon a majority or two-thirds vote within each union. The matter was decided when a resolution was passed with only two dissenting voices that all future ballots be pooled and "a clear majority of the whole" be sufficient to call a general strike.[13] The question of who controlled strikes in the city was thus decided; henceforth the ultimate power lay not with the local alone, nor with international headquarters, but with the combined membership of the Winnipeg Trades and Labor Council.

The left wing was thus growing more powerful but it still lacked the support necessary to take over formal leadership of the council. In elections held in mid-December Bob Russell was defeated in his try for the presidency by James Winning; Ernie Robinson retained his position as secretary, beating off a challenge from R. J. Johns; and A. C. Hay defeated W. Coburn for the vice-presidency. It was announced at this meeting, however, that the executive, in conjunction with the Socialist Party of Canada, had completed arrangements for a mass meeting on Sunday, December 22, at the Walker Theatre.[14] Thus, although Russell and his colleagues had failed in their bid to capture the council, their effectiveness did not suffer and they continued to receive the co-operation they required from the moderate majority. The Socialist Party of Canada had remained somewhat outside the pale of organized labour in Winnipeg for many years. Their attacks on the Labor Representation Committee, the Social Democratic Party, and individual Trades Council members contributed to a degree of alienation not experienced by other labour political groups. Russell, Johns, and Bill Hoop, were well known and respected in Winnipeg labour circles, but the party they were members of had always been viewed with a certain amount of suspicion. That situation began to change in the late fall of 1918. Labour in Winnipeg was angry and growing more militant in its approach to politics and industrial relations, and the SPC became more acceptable than it had been in the past.

The SPC in Winnipeg was a small elitist organization which placed a premium on its members' knowledge of Marxian theory. In late 1918 the membership of the Winnipeg branch of the party was rarely greater than fifty, and only twenty to thirty of those were active. It was not easy to join the SPC; a member had to demonstrate both a solid grasp of socialist theory and the purity of his motives. The party was heavily dependent on the donations of a few private individuals and its most active adherents were usually members of trade unions.[15] Towards the end of 1918 the SPC became very active in the city, holding meetings on street corners and vacant lots, distributing leaflets and selling pamphlets whenever the opportunity presented itself. During this period its members, priding themselves on their knowledge of Marxian economics, were in great demand as speakers all over the city. In December the party began to hold gatherings in several small Winnipeg theatres and succeeded in drawing large crowds.

The now-famous meeting of Sunday, December 22, at the Walker Theatre was only one in a series of assemblies called or participated in by the SPC. There is still dispute as to whether the party was acting alone or in conjunction with the Trades Council. Alderman John

Queen, the opening speaker, was not a member of the Socialist Party and was clearly under the impression that this was, at least in part, a Trades Council effort though it has also been suggested that the SPC summoned the meeting without the co-operation of the Trades Council.[16] There seems no doubt, however, that the audience and other interested parties were under the impression that the council was deeply involved.

The "Red Letter Day" opened to a packed house at 2:30 P.M. Alderman Queen told his audience the meeting had been called by the Trades Council and the SPC to protest government by order-in-council, the continued incarceration of political prisoners, and allied intervention in Russia. Six speakers addressed the crowd; Hoop and Armstrong put forward the motion against orders-in-council, Ivens and Dixon asked for the release of political prisoners, and Russell and Sam Blumenberg denounced allied intervention in Russia. The order-in-council, Hoop declared, was the "sum total and reflex of the doctrine of property," while Ivens charged the government had forgotten one of the basic precepts of Christianity—forgiveness. Russell's speech introducing the resolution demanding withdrawal of allied troops from Russia drew applause when he referred to the accusation that Bolsheviks were recipients of German money. The same tactic had often been used in Canada, he exclaimed, when Canadian workers themselves were charged with accepting "German gold." In fact, their main trouble was that "they don't get gold of any kind." The troops sent to Russia, he declared, were there only to protect the interests of the capitalists in allied countries.[17]

The radicals held stage centre and James Winning, president of the Winnipeg Trades and Labor Council, said not a word. Winning was a moderate union man. He, like Russell, was Scottish-born and had supported socialist causes in his youth. Winning was a bricklayer and when he came to Winnipeg in 1906 and joined the local union he ceased to support radical causes. He was respected by governments and employers, rose to a position of prominence in the bricklayers' union and the Building Trades Council, and was elected to succeed Fred Tipping in early December 1918. But Winning was a stolid figure and not charismatic like Russell or Ivens. He could not fire a crowd, like Queen or Johns, and though he was president of the Trades Council, he was out of his element. James Winning was simply not capable of rallying the moderate majority to put a check on the activities of the radicals.

The Walker Theatre meeting was considered a great success. Ivens later declared that if gatherings such as the one of December 22 were held once a month, "a bloody revolution may be averted." The meeting was, in his opinion, a great opportunity to blow off steam and at the same time create "a sane policy of reconstruction."[18] The secretary of Winnipeg's local No. 3 of the SPC, W. Breeze, was also elated. The meeting had attracted at least 1,700 people, over $220 had poured into party coffers, and many new applications for membership were being received. He hoped for another similar meeting in the near future, but the projected second gathering was never held.

In the early months of 1919 veterans of the Canadian Expeditionary Force began to play a greater role in the political and industrial life of the city and in those months, at least, their aspirations and beliefs were hostile to the Socialist Party of Canada and organized labour. The intervention of the returned men in the affairs and activities of the Socialist Party and the Trades Council was compounded by the presence in Winnipeg of thousands of "enemy aliens" who, the soldiers alleged, had taken their jobs during the war. They wanted their old positions back, demanding that enemy aliens be deported, and at the beginning they believed the socialists and the unions stood in their paths.

On the afternoon of Sunday, January 26, a large group of veterans advanced on Market Square, site of an intended Socialist Party open-air rally. The party had not planned to hold this meeting outdoors but they had been unsuccessful in their bid to rent the Walker Theatre. Undaunted, several members acted on their own initiative to distribute leaflets announcing the Market Square gathering. As the returned soldiers began to move into the square, party officials decided discretion was the better part of valour and circulated word among the crowd calling the meeting off. The veterans were incensed at the cancellation and several of them began to rough up suspected aliens. The milling continued for several minutes until suddenly an exhortation was heard above the noise of the crowd calling for a march on Socialist Party headquarters. The veterans, now an angry mob, began to move through the streets.[19]

The SPC's main hall was located on Smith Street, opposite the Marlborough Hotel, and above a restaurant and a drug store. The offices were sparsely furnished except for a well-stocked socialist library and a piano. The soldiers stormed up the stairs, broke into the hall, smashed the furniture, pushed the piano through the window onto the street, and began to shower the pavement with books, leaflets, and pamphlets. The paper and the piano were then set ablaze,[20] a fiery monument to the veterans' wrath.

Ex-servicemen had been trickling back to Winnipeg since the beginning of the war but the armistice of November 11 gave the promise of a far heavier flow in the near future. What was to be done with these men? The president of the Winnipeg Board of Trade, A. L. Crossin, ridiculed the idea that they could be placed on farms and suggested the government would do far better to set up schools to train them in the trade or business they were best suited to. Many veterans, however, were not willing to wait for special training; they wanted jobs and they wanted them immediately. In Winnipeg, for example, the local branch of the Great War Veterans' Association demanded that enemy aliens be fired and deported. The attack on Socialist Party headquarters was, in fact, merely the first move in a campaign to oust aliens from employment. The day following the abortive SPC meeting, groups of soldiers visited several establishments in Winnipeg demanding that non-Canadians be dismissed, and on Tuesday, January 28, more veterans visited the packing plant of Swift Canadian to repeat these exhortations. In the meantime, attacks on individual aliens increased throughout the city.[21] Some of the soldiers were in an ugly mood.

In early February the provincial and municipal governments decided to come to grips with the situation and called upon the aid of returned soldiers' associations, the Prairie Provinces Branch of the CMA, the Board of Trade, and the Trades Council. Premier Norris was concerned over the developing agitation and suggested to the interested parties that a solution lay in registering all enemy aliens in the province. The Trades Council was subsequently asked to name a representative to a three-man commission to investigate the citizenship of aliens.[22] The council did not object to this proposition, but insisted the onus of proof should lie with the government and its commission. As A. A. Heaps put it, the Trade Council could not take it upon itself to stand between the soldier and the alien.[23] The Trades Council knew they were dealing with an explosive issue and were attempting to avoid involvement. By sending a delegate to sit on the three-man board with a veterans' representative and a county court judge they were avoiding the possibility of angering the soldiers by doing nothing. Both Russell and Hoop were anxious to establish contacts between organized labour and the returned soldiers' associations, and this was a golden opportunity to show the soldiers they sympathized with their aims. If forced to choose between aliens and soldiers, the Trades Council would clearly pick the latter.

The veterans were a disillusioned lot and the socialists knew it. J. W. Wilton, responsible for the provincial government's compensation bill in 1916, returned to Winnipeg from the fighting in late 1918 and clearly saw that fellow veterans were discontented and might furnish fertile material for "radical labour agitators."[24] Something of the mood then prevalent in many quarters can be gained from an editorial published in the *Ontario Labor News:*

> . . . in 1914 the great war broke out . . . men who had never seen each other before rended, maimed and slew each other. . . . In the workshops men and women worked 10 to 12 hours each day, producing the wherewithal to fight . . . the workers slaved and slaved until exhaustion. All this was done without complaint, and glowing promises were made of a New Jerusalem after the holacaust of blood.[25]

Royal North West Mounted Police officers were also concerned that the returned men might fall easy prey to "Bolsheviks." Late in January 1919 Commissioner A. B. Perry was warned that all efforts must be made to get returned men "on the right track" and away from radicals and agitators since "it would be hard to tell what would happen."[26] Perry agreed that "the returned soldier must not be allowed to drift into the hands of the Bolshevist and Socialist elements" who were actively attempting to secure their support, and thought the Great War Veterans' Association would be valuable in this. The Mounties were aware, therefore, of a disturbing possibility that those returned men who had destroyed the Winnipeg Socialist Party headquarters in January might think twice the next time or might even soon be found passing out SPC literature.

The fears of these officials were partially confirmed in late March by an intelligence report emanating from Military District 10. The document noted that the party had cancelled most public meetings after the January riots until they felt that trouble with returned soldiers could be avoided. Now, the report estimated, at least half of the veterans in the city had become sympathetic to the socialists and the party therefore planned to recommence street-corner activity about June 1.[27] Three weeks later General Gwatkin ominously warned a colleague in the Naval Branch that it would be possible for a revolution to succeed if a considerable number of returned soldiers joined the insurrection. Labour agitators realized this and were hard at work among the veterans, he wrote, making it imperative that everything be done to deal with the "reasonable grievances" of returned soldiers.

To a degree these sentiments reflected over-reaction. A definite tendency had emerged in the months following the armistice to see revolution in every disturbance and a Bolshevik behind every strike. The trend to hysteria was particularly strong in the United States and developed into the "big Red scare." Police and government officials worked themselves into a panic fearing imminent revolution carried out by bushy-headed, bomb-throwing anarchists or Bolsheviks. In April 1919 bombs were sent through the mails to several important individuals, including Attorney General Palmer, convincing many that their worst fears were close to realization. In Canada, officials were now beginning to doubt the loyalty of the very men who had so recently offered their all for country and empire. The socialists knew of the discontent among returned veterans and attempted to enlist their support. The army and RNWMP were also aware that these veterans were unhappy and feared the inroads radicals were so obviously beginning to make.

Winnipeg and western Canada were thus obviously not immune to the radical feeling and social unrest so evident in other countries in the period following the armistice. In fact, Canadian military and government figures believed these months to be fraught with danger. They saw revolutions toppling governments from Petrograd to Berlin and general strikes breaking out from Scandinavia to Seattle. They misunderstood, or could not empathize with, the motives of moderate socialists, trade unionists, and returned soldiers who sought changes that would reform social inequity; instead they tied these people to anarchy and revolution. Thus the creation in western Canada of the One Big Union, an obviously Marxist and syndicalist trade union centre, in the spring of 1919 was bound to be interpreted as another sign of the imminence of catastrophe. For this reason alone the OBU was destined to become a factor in the events leading to and deciding the outcome of the developing industrial tensions in Winnipeg and the west.

7. ❖ The One Big Union

A grey and sombre atmosphere hung heavily over the Russian capital of Petrograd in the first days of November 1917. The weather, damp and cool, robbed the city of its colour and provided an appropriate setting for the foreboding which permeated the capital. The government of Alexander Feodorovitch Kerensky, which had come to power upon the abdication of Czar Nicholas II in March, was on the verge of collapse. The Bolshevik section of the Russian Social Democratic Party, led by a small group of determined revolutionaries including Vladimir Ulyanov, known to the world as Lenin, and Lev Bronstein, who used the name Trotsky, was readying itself for the last push to topple the government. On November 6 the Bolsheviks and their allies, using the armed assistance of the Red Guard and allied with soldiers and sailors from the Kronstadt naval base, fanned out through the city to begin their takeover of power. During the evening they seized the offices of anti-Bolshevik newspapers and used these presses to publish their own propaganda. In the early morning hours of November 7 they took control of the telegraph agency, the post office, the military hotel, the telephone exchange, and city hall. By 10:00 A.M. they had thrown a cordon of troops around the Winter Palace, home and last refuge of the Kerensky government.

Wednesday, November 7, was a day of eerie and unrealistic calm in the city. Life continued as usual in many quarters while the now almost powerless cabinet continued to deliberate inside its massive white stone mausoleum. Kerensky, however, was not in the city. He had slipped out in a vain attempt to rally loyal army units to the rescue of his government. Around the Winter Palace Bolshevik troops and Red Guards, supported by armoured cars with slogans or party initials newly daubbed on their sides, waited for the final moves. The guns of the Fortress of Peter and Paul, situated on an island in the River Neva together with those on board the cruiser *Aurora* were ready to add their power to the final assault. After the delivery of a surrender ultimatum in the early evening, several attempts were made to capture the building. Supported by intermittent shelling from the fortress and the cruiser, the Bolshevik forces mounted their last attack in the final minutes of November 7. Within two hours they had penetrated to the innermost depths of the palace and put the Kerensky ministers under arrest. Though many months, and a civil war, marked by the deaths of thousands of people, stood between them and final victory, the Bolshevik revolution had begun.[1]

Lenin's success fired the imagination and spurred the efforts of socialists throughout the world. Even those in violent opposition to armed uprisings, who deeply believed in the necessity of revolution through the ballot, looked to Russia as the first successful attempt to establish a socialist government in modern history. The effects of the Bolshevik revolution began to sweep, wavelike, through Europe while government after government stood in the path of the revolutionary and socialist tide. Wartime conditions had greatly aggravated the unrest which gave the Russian Bolsheviks their foothold of power and these conditions existed in almost every nation participating in the First World War. Russia had suffered grievously because of the massive defeats of her armies and the frail structure of her economy; but inflation, commody shortages, authoritarianism, and mounting casualty lists created war-weariness in almost every belligerent country, victorious or defeated. People throughout the world desperately hoped for a new world order to rise from the ashes of war and radicals of almost every stripe were determined to hasten the arrival of the millennium.

Although social unrest in many forms gave rise to rioting, mutinies, and minor uprisings in many European nations in the months following the Bolshevik revolution, one of the most serious challenges to authority materialized in Germany. It is somewhat ironic that the same German government which had allowed Lenin to travel by sealed railway car from Switzerland to Russia, to lead the Bolsheviks who had pledged to take Russia out of the war, should have been toppled by a Social Democratic revolution in early November of 1918. The pressure of an allied offensive on the western front created confusion and dismay in the Kaiser's government and forced them to open their ranks to members of the German Social Democratic Party which held a majority of seats in the Reichstag. This allowed some semblance of representative government to be established and, at the same time, held out the promise of an imminent peace.

Late in October 1918 sailors of the German fleet balked at orders to prepare for a final battle with the British and began to revolt in their North Sea ports. By November 5 most of the fleet was controlled by sailors' revolutionary councils, while workers were taking similar action ashore. Troops sent to suppress these outbreaks had no desire to shoot their comrades and began to join them instead. The crisis mounted and forced the moderate leaders of the Social Democratic Party, under Freidrich Ebert, to demand the abdication of the Kaiser. On November 8 the monarchy was declared at an end, a provisional government under Ebert was appointed, and a republic was proclaimed.

Ebert, however, was not to have clear sailing; he was bitterly opposed by the revolutionary wing of the Social Democrats, the Spartacists led by Karl Liebknecht and Rosa Luxemburg. They were determined to create a "socialist republic" and bring in the rule of "proletarian dictatorship" as in Soviet Russia, and they tried to undermine the regime. Early in December the first violent confrontation occurred when Spartacist demonstrators in Berlin were fired upon by troops loyal to the provisional government and sixteen were killed. This was only the first blow, however, and provided Ebert's more radical opponents with the opportunity of accusing him of being a class traitor and a murderer of fellow socialists.

At the end of the month the Spartacists met to found the German Communist Party. A majority of the delegates decided that the time was ripe to launch a revolution and convinced Luxemburg and Liebknecht to go along with the plans. On January 5 they issued a manifesto calling for armed revolt against the government and large crowds of workers and soldiers began to move through the streets of Berlin. Spartacist forces occupied several newspaper offices, even though it quickly became apparent that their action was only supported by a small minority. By January 11 the leaders of the revolt were isolated in the offices of *Vorwarts,* a Social Democrat newspaper, and surrendered when government troops began to shell the building. Several party members were shot after they surrendered. Liebknecht and Luxemburg were clubbed to death by cavalry officers several days after their arrest.[2]

Europe seethed with upheaval and rumours of revolution and was increasingly split into two camps: those who supported the Bolsheviks and revolutionaries and those who opposed them—the Reds and the Whites. Lurid stories of the "terror" rule of the revolutionaries were splashed across the front pages of North American newspapers while several governments, including those of Britain, Canada, Japan, and the United States, intervened directly in the Russian civil war to throw money, arms, and men behind various White leaders in a desperate attempt to stamp out Bolshevism on its home ground. Socialists and radical trade union leaders in the democracies of western Europe, North America, and Australia did not look dispassionately at these massive struggles for power between traditionalists and radicals being fought in the streets, towns, and steppes of central and eastern Europe. Although they often scarcely understood the aims and methods of the Bolsheviks and their other European counterparts, many made no secret of their admiration of and support for the socialist revolutionaries.

Europe's wave of unrest was reflected in similar, though less drastic, upheavals in North America. The northwestern and western United States were particularly affected by political and industrial strikes which were sometimes led or influenced by the militantly syndicalist Industrial Workers of the World. In the United States growing labour unrest caused by inflation and reaction to attacks upon the unions' newly won gains by powerful employers created serious social divisions. This unrest was played upon by cynical employers, conservative politicians, and anti-union newspaper publishers to spread the fantasy that the Bolshevik revolution was being secretly imported into the United States.[3]

The most active radical labour groups in the United States, led by the IWW, did not need the example of the Russian revolution as justification for their own efforts and neither did their enemies. In 1917 and 1918 the IWW led strikes against metal mining and shipbuilding concerns on the west coast, in Arizona, Washington, and Montana. They opposed the war and conscription, and were persecuted for these views as pro-German agitators and traitors. In July 1917 two thousand vigilantes rounded up twelve hundred alleged members of the IWW in Bisbee, Arizona, loaded them aboard cattle cars of the El Paso and Southwestern Railroad and, with a minimum of food and water, deported them across the state boundary. The following month another group of vigilantes hanged IWW organizer Frank Little from a railroad trestle in Butte, Montana. Beginning in

September, the anti-IWW campaign was capped by widespread arrests of "Wobbly" leaders and by the end of the year every first-line IWW leader was behind bars.[4]

IWW agitation was only one indication of the tumult developing on the American scene even before the armistice of November 11, 1918. Strikers increasingly met with violence in city after city and town after town, not only in the west but throughout the United States. Newspapers derisively attacked workers for demanding higher wages when they were allegedly driving their own cars and wearing silk shirts and the general public appeared more and more willing to accept military and police intervention to end walkouts. The last vestige of the prewar progressive era was melting away in the desire of many citizens to "return to normalcy." One of the key events contributing to the fear of Bolshevik activity and the development of the "big Red scare" in the United States was the Seattle general strike of February 1919, North America's first true general strike.[5]

The strike in Seattle was touched off by a walkout of 35,000 shipyard workers on January 21. These men were attempting to win higher wages from their employers but struck two months before their contract expired. For this reason Charles Piez, director of the government's Emergency Fleet Corporation, refused to discuss working conditions with the men and ordered them back to work. The Seattle Central Labor Council, led by James A. Duncan, was incensed over Piez's attitude and decided to support the shipyard workers by calling a city-wide general strike. On Thursday morning, February 6, 60,000 workers from almost every industry left their jobs. The walkout was led by a General Strike Committee which was itself directed by a Committee of Fifteen under Duncan's leadership. They realized that essential services had to be provided for the city's population and thus permitted garbage trucks, laundry services, and milk trucks to continue to operate and also arranged for food distribution, light, heat, and water. Despite the fact that Seattle was not being denied the necessities of life, Mayor Ole Hanson, blessed with a sharp eye for political issues that might place him in the limelight, set out to break the strike and forestall the "revolution" that was threatening his city.

Hanson hated the IWW and charged that the general strike was organized and led by the Wobblies. He requested and secured federal troops to patrol the streets of Seattle and personally led them into the city with his own flag-decked car. He then called on the strikers to end the walkout or he would use the troops to break the strike and operate essential services. These flamboyant gestures secured the solid support of many of the city's non-union citizens as well as the daily press. This increasingly hostile public opinion, coupled with great pressure applied by the leadership of the AFL unions participating in the walkout, forced the Central Labor Council to back down and call the strike off by February 10.[6]

These events in Europe and America formed a backdrop for the emergence of Winnipeg radical union leaders and socialists from the intellectual isolation of decades. If *The Voice* and its successor, the *Western Labor News* and Trades Council meetings are an accurate reflection of the mood of Winnipeg workers at this period, it is apparent that a great change occurred in mid-1918, almost exclusively as a result of domestic industrial unrest. This was reflected in their attitudes towards the radical and revolutionary events that were then beginning to occupy the world stage, vying for headlines with the closing battles of the war.

In November 1917 there was scarcely any reaction to Lenin's seizure of power; a worker who confined his reading to *The Voice* would not learn for months, and then only incidentally, that it had occurred. Events involving the IWW and other radical groups in the United States were also ignored—even the murder of Frank Little and the Everett Massacre. *The Voice* was almost exclusively concerned with conscription and the federal elections, as though European and American influences didn't matter and had no bearing on Winnipeg or western Canada.[7]

All this changed with the appearance of the *Western Labor News,* which not only grew progressively more radical but paid a great deal more attention to events in Russia, Germany, and the United States. Stories began to appear with increasing frequency about the efforts of socialist and labour movements throughout the world. There was, for example, news of the suppression of the IWW in the United States and of the arrest and trial of the great American socialist, Eugene V. Debs. Eventually the *Western Labor News* began to include a regular column keeping readers up to date with the revolutions, general strikes, and other forms of industrial and political unrest occurring throughout the world.[8] Winnipeg workers were becoming fully awake to the ebb and flow of the revolutionary tide, even though many probably did not understand what some of these movements aimed to accomplish. At one point in April 1919, for example, the *Western Labor News* published a diagram claimed to be the "blueprint" for the "Russian Soviet System" which was actually a design for the "ideal" workers' government as postulated by Daniel DeLeon and the IWW in 1905.[9]

Other western workers were less insular to begin with but followed the same paths as their Winnipeg brothers. The influential west coast labour paper *B.C. Federationist* reflected world radical and revolutionary events to a much greater degree than *The Voice* in the period prior to mid-1918. This paper concentrated on the western United States, however, devoted only a few inches of space to the Little murder and Bisbee and was as much in the dark about Lenin's seizure of power as other labour papers in western Canada. Such coverage was undoubtedly the result of a lack of concrete information, rather than disinterest. West coast workers were always more aware of the outside because of their proximity to the turbulent northwestern United States. Socialist politicians in the province had played important roles in the passage of legislation beneficial to labour just after the turn of the century but here, too, workers became more interested in the growth of Bolshevism and other international revolutionary movements in the spring and summer of 1918.

Western Canadian and Winnipeg workers were not radicalized by events such as the Russian revolution—more immediate and close-to-home concerns and considerations were responsible for their new mood. As they grew more radical, however, they began to take note of groups with similar ambitions taking like action in other parts of the world. Once they began to identify with those challenging the established industrial and political order in Russia, Germany, Hungary, the United States, and other countries they became more certain than ever that they themselves were part of a great world tide of change.

Thus world events played a definite part in the further development of western radicalism, but domestic experiences and problems most occupied their thoughts. The Seattle general strike was barely noted in Winnipeg, although it received some attention on the west coast, and there was almost no attempt to study the methods and procedures of the Seattle strikers or their leaders until several months later.[10] Even then Winnipeg labour paid attention to this event in a cursory and superficial manner and never pondered some of the very difficult situations which a general strike such as the one in Seattle necessarily created. Seattle hardly rated space, whereas the Calgary freight-handlers strike had been given much attention because it involved a problem (the order-in-council banning strikes) that directly concerned their lives.

It was important to their cause and their sense of self-confidence that western radicals look upon themselves as the Canadian vanguard of the revolutionary and leftist forces trying to change the world. They adopted much of the rhetoric of these revolutions and even some of the titles and trappings. The "brother" of trade union parlance became "comrade," while radicals began to refer to themselves as "Reds" or even "Bolsheviks." A letter from one union leader to another was often signed "yours in revolt." Sometimes platform speakers, such as those at the Walker Theatre meeting, let their emotions run away with their reason and threatened that blood would flow if changes were not soon forthcoming. All these things were not indicative of secret revolutionary desires, but of the need to identify with others who were fighting and dying for the cause of "the working class."

In this atmosphere, some westerners began to reject the notion that what was necessary for change was a revitalized Trades Congress. The idea developed, instead, that nothing short of western secession and the creation of a new and radical union centre would be sufficient. Once this idea took hold, many radicals, especially members of the Socialist Party of Canada, began to work behind the scenes to turn the proposed conference of western labour into a forum for a virtual declaration of independence from the conservative, craft union, policies of the AFL-dominated Trades Congress.

Bob Russell had been a believer in industrial unionism for many years and had constantly supported efforts to reform the craft structure of his own organization from within. In later life Russell maintained that the reasons for this had nothing to do with politics but were rooted in the daily job situation. Narrow trade and craft restrictions made life in the shops more difficult if not dangerous, he maintained, and introduced divisions where none need occur.[11] In fact, this kind of support for industrial unionism was traditional in western Canada but increased during the war because the existence of autonomous crafts made negotiating difficult in many industries. The railway shop craft unions, for example, had wrestled with separate negotiations for years but had finally united to form Division 4 to expedite discussions and bring more leverage to bear at the negotiating table.

What exactly did Russell, Johns, and others mean by the term "industrial union"? The idea had been clear enough in the past, but in September 1918 the *Western Labor News* used it to describe a form of syndicalism then beginning to emerge halfway around the globe. In an article entitled "Industrial Union Under Way in

Australia," the paper reported the founding of "one big union" and reprinted its draft constitution.[12] Later, the Australian One Big Union's constitutional preamble was published; it asserted that there were only two classes in society, that conflict between those two classes was inevitable, and that the capitalist system must be wiped out.[13] In the weeks that followed, the *News* continued to keep track of the OBU's progress down under.

The name One Big Union had been used by the IWW in the United States for many years. It was not until its adoption by the Australian Workers International Industrial Union in South Melbourne, however, that it became widely known in western Canada. This organization espoused industrial unionism, but took the traditional concept further and advocated one great union of industrial unions which would have, as its main aim, the abolition of private ownership of the means of production. The Australians were not too clear about how they would accomplish this, other than to assert that they repudiated industrial sabotage or other forms of illegal action and were attempting to organize the future system of "industrial democracy" within the shell of existing "capitalistic society." At some point not specified, they planned to take control of industry and reorganize the government along industrial lines.[14] This latter aim closely followed the ideas and concepts already advanced by the IWW, although the mystical and millennialist nature of the Australian movement was closely akin to Robert Owen's Grand National Consolidated Trades Union which had existed for a brief period in Great Britain in the 1830s.

Wherever the idea of one big union originated, whether in the United States, Great Britain, or Australia, it soon caught on in Winnipeg. When the term "industrial union" was used in early 1919 it was being applied to "one big union." It is quite clear the concept had undergone a change. When Russell and the IAM leadership had spoken of amalgamation of the metal trades in 1915 they were talking about one union covering all workers within a given industry, a concept followed by groups such as the United Mineworkers of America and later adopted by the Congress of Industrial Organizations. This was very different from the type of all-embracing "one big union" Russell was discussing in 1919. The latter concept was, in fact, nothing less than syndicalism. That this change had developed should not be surprising when the events of the past summer are recalled. It was during and after the civic and metal trades walkouts that the idea of general strikes became more widely accepted; what better body was there for calling and carrying on such a strike than one big union of all workers? The concept of one was a logical extension of the other. The original idea may have been of foreign origin, but the impulse to apply it to the Canadian experience grew out of purely local conditions.

As the date of David Rees's proposed Western Labor Conference approached, the more vocal element in Winnipeg was already leaning towards secession. Ivens reflected the mood when he wrote of the "effete East," and heralded the approach of a "new day" for western labour.[15] At a special conference Trades Council meeting delegates approved resolutions demanding the institution of the thirty-hour week, suggesting a referendum be held on the question of industrial organization, and calling for creation of a "Central Industrial Committee" to co-ordinate strike action in the west.[16] The connection, in many minds, between general strikes and reorganization along "industrial" lines was demonstrated at this gathering. A resolution calling for abolition of craft unions explained the necessity for industrial organization by asserting that the existence of many unions in a single industry made the conduct of strikes very difficult. The proposed Central Industrial Committee was supposed to "more effectively work out the plan of the sympathetic strike in Western Canada."[17]

The Western Labor Conference opened at Calgary on March 16, 1919. David Rees, chairman of the conference planning committee, addressed the 237 delegates and reiterated his desire to forge a united policy for presentation to the next TLC convention. There was, however, little possibility at this point that the convention was about to follow his suggestions. The British Columbia Federation of Labor, meeting the previous three days in the city, had just opted for a program of unmitigated radicalism. Over Rees's and other moderate delegates' objections, the federation registered its approval of the one big union idea, attacked the federal government for allowing censorship and imprisonment of political prisoners to continue, and sent greetings to the Bolshevik government in Moscow. In addition, delegates decided that in future the federation would cease to conduct lobbying activities and would stay clear of elections.[18]

Rees addressed the conference and then departed to attend to UMW business in the United States. His place was taken by R. J. Tallon, vice-president of the Calgary Trades and Labor Council, who was elected presiding officer, and Victor R. Midgley of British Columbia, who was chosen secretary. Although neither of these two men was a member of the Socialist Party of Canada, adherents of the SPC played leading roles at the convention.[19] The forty-six Manitoba delegates hardly took part with the exception of Russell and Johns, who were influential at several points. The resolutions passed, however, accurately reflected opinions put forward in the Winnipeg Trades Council during previous months.

Briefly, the Western Labor Conference declared itself in favour of polling all Canadian trade unionists on the question of secession from the AFL-TLC and adherence to a new centre to be organized as an "industrial" union. The conference's committee on policy, headed by Johns, suggested the new body be called the One Big Union and that a five-man committee be elected to popularize the proposed OBU, raise funds, and organize the referendum. The men chosen at the convention were R. J. Johns, W. A. Pritchard, J. Knight, J. Naylor, and V. R. Midgley. In addition, provincial executives were elected to act in conjunction with this central organization and delegates from Manitoba elected Russell chairman of their committee.[20]

The referendum decided upon was not to be a simple poll of all union members in Canada, since the ballots were to be divided into those from the east of Port Arthur and those from the west. The question was to be decided by majority vote of organizations considered to be "vital" trades—transportation, metal trades, mining, and construction. Locals of other trades were also to be polled, with those members not voting to be counted in the affirmative. In addition, a vote was to be taken in conjunction with the referendum to determine if Canadian workers favoured a nationwide general strike on June 1 to draw attention to their demand for the thirty-hour week.

The Western Labor Conference did not actually launch the One Big Union, but it was a declaration of intent to do so. It reflected the mood of militancy which had been growing in the west for some time. Resolutions sending greetings to the new Soviet government in Russia, demanding allied withdrawal from the Soviet Union, and an end to government restrictions on civil liberties[21] were only the outward manifestation of the new radicalism. The significant part of the three-day proceedings was the delegates' decision to take secessionist action.

Russell returned to Winnipeg to begin working for the OBU. He set out to popularize the idea and raise money for it, and at the end of March 1919, won a significant victory. A boycott conducted by Winnipeg unions against the *Winnipeg Tribune* in retaliation for the newspaper's attacks on the Calgary convention and the OBU resulted in a peculiar compromise. The *Tribune* offered to print the verbatim report of the Calgary proceedings if the unions would call off their campaign. The Trades Council's press committee, realizing that this was a golden opportunity to rush the convention proceedings into print, accepted the *Tribune's* offer, but only if the paper would print an additional 20,000 copies as supplements for the *Western Labor News*. In Russell's words, there was an "awful scrap" about this, but the newspaper finally agreed.[22] The convention, therefore, received a great deal of publicity at very little cost.

The Trades Council and the *Western Labor News* lined up almost automatically behind the One Big Union. In early April the council's executive and educational committees were given authority to arrange special meetings to spread the OBU message. The *Western Labor News* urged its readers to cast an affirmative vote on the question of secession from the TLC, while the council began the highly unusual move of assessing its membership to raise money for the One Big Union. Thus, although the OBU had not yet formally been founded and the Trades Council still held a charter from the Trades and Labor Congress, the council and many TLC-affiliated unions were now openly working for withdrawal.

The Winnipeg unions did not hold a formal vote on secession until July, but the One Big Union began to come alive in the city many months before the final split. Russell's campaign for OBU funds was successful and netted over one thousand dollars from Trades Council affiliates before the end of April.[23] Under these circumstances it was unavoidable that the One Big Union issue, complicated as it was by the call for a June 1 general strike for the thirty-hour week, would be injected into the Winnipeg industrial scene.

The Trades Council's increasing enthusiasm for secession signified a great deal more than a simple desire to change the organizational structure of Canadian unionism. It demonstrated that many western labour leaders now looked at society through polarized glasses and were leading their followers along the radical paths they deemed appropriate to protect their class interests. It was not simply a choice between "industrial" unionism and craft unionism, it was also notification that labour was moving towards mass organization, general strikes, and continual confrontations with government and business.

In taking this road western labour leaders cast their eyes to the United States, Hungary, Great Britain, Germany, and the Soviet

Union and were reassured that they were part of a great world tide of social change. Most realized their situation was different from that of European workers and advocated the ballot as the most powerful and effective weapon in labour's arsenal. Those who demanded an immediate rush to the barricades were few and ineffective. There were, however, a great many who desired immediate change but were unsure of the best method of bringing it about. These men fell all too easily into the trap of advocating devices such as the general strike as the all-powerful weapon which would force governments and employers to melt before labour's irresistible onslaught and allow the working classes to construct the New Jerusalem. There was, therefore, uncertainty not only about the shape the new society might take, but also concerning the means of bringing it into existence. Thus the One Big Union was in large measure a political union, whether admitted or not, while the general strike, by its very nature, was a political strike.

This, however, many workers failed to see or understand. To them the OBU was a larger and hopefully more effective type of trade union, but trade union it was. The general strike they thought, was a greater, more widespread work stoppage, but still just another, larger, strike. True, the scale of confrontation would now be greater than before but, after all, hadn't it been demonstrated in 1918 that lesser action was not effective enough? Fortified by these beliefs and fired by a sense of holy mission, Winnipeg union men prepared to do battle to protect their rights, assert their newly discovered strengths, and do their part in the global struggle to build a new postwar world.

8. ❖ Towards the Brink

By January 1919 the tremors of social upheaval were shaking a significant part of the globe. The western democracies were not immune to fears and hatreds that had set almost half a world aflame with execution, assassination, and revolution. The end of the Great War had not ushered in the New Jerusalem that many had worked and fought for but, instead, unleashed pent-up forces seeking rapid changes in the world order. In Canada events which had begun the previous year were yet to reach their fruition. The increasingly serious nature of industrial confrontation forced men to seek new solutions to time-worn problems in a desperate search for eleventh-hour respite. Their failure, rendered almost inevitable by the rancour and suspicion of motive on the part of both capital and labour, set the stage for one of the most trying periods in the history of the city of Winnipeg.

In early 1919 the Norris government embarked on its most ambitious attempt to date to regulate working conditions and dispell industrial unrest. Spurred by the belief that industrial relations had deteriorated to the point where it was "tragically necessary" to attempt some sort of intervention to keep capital and labour from each other's throats, they decided to introduce the principle of compulsory conciliation to labour disputes within the province. The Trades Council also believed the time was ripe for action, but of a different kind, and chose to bring their campaign for the abolition of injunctions and anti-union damage suits to fruition by presenting a bill to the legislature for government consideration. This divergence of interest, now increasingly apparent in almost everything government, business, and labour did, doomed both campaigns to failure and probably served to increase tension and bitterness rather than quell it.

In mid-February delegations from the Trades Council and the Manufacturers' Association met Norris and J. W. Wilton, who had rejoined the Liberals after a hitch in the army, in Winnipeg. The premier attempted to persuade labour that industrial peace was absolutely necessary for the future development of the province and that his government's proposed new conciliation act was the best way to assure that tranquillity. He hinted at plans to spend millions of dollars on industrial development in Manitoba, but claimed the banks were reluctant to provide financial backing until the labour question was settled. The Trades Council discussed the government's proposals but, at this point, disagreed on what action to take.[1]

In the first week of March the government introduced its bill proposing the establishment of an Industrial Disputes Commission with sweeping powers to investigate labour disputes, the cost of living, unemployment, and unfair profits. The commission was to consist of a neutral chairman, two representatives appointed by employers and two by labour and would have power to enforce compulsory arbitration, declare sympathetic strikes illegal, and fix the conditions and limits of strikes and lockouts. The original bill made no provision for prohibition of injunctions or the legalization of picketing, but a rider was added giving the commission power to extend or withhold the right of picketing in an attempt to make the legislation more palatable to labour.[2] As proposed, however, the legislation had the opposite effect and stimulated even greater opposition to the government's actions. The Trades Council was not, at this point, interested in this kind of legislation. They only wanted to see injunctions wiped out and urged the government to pass the anti-injunction clause alone, without the commission bill. When this request was ignored they decided to destroy the very foundation of the commission by calling on their member unions not to make any nominations to the five-man board. Without the co-operation of the Trades Council and the appointment by any official labour organization of two delegates to the Industrial Disputes Commission, it could not function. The unions thus rendered the commission impotent five days before the act was finally assented to in March 1919.[3]

In the weeks that followed the government tried unsuccessfully to secure labour's co-operation. By early April the act had been officially proclaimed, and the government had approached the unions asking for nominations out of which the two labour representatives would be chosen. Labour's attitude had not changed, however, and the council reaffirmed its refusal to recognize the legislation. Two weeks later Ed McGrath, chairman of the provincial Bureau of Labor, appeared before the Trades Council to urge it to reconsider its position. He warned the delegates the government would go ahead with its program without their co-operation if necessary, and would be forced to choose labour representatives from outside union ranks. The council discussed the matter but decided to stand on its original ground.[4] By the end of April the Manufacturers' Association had submitted their nominees to the government but the Trades Council continued its steadfast opposition.

The manufacturers went along with the legislation but were scarcely more satisfied. J. B. Hugg, counsel for the Prairie Provinces Branch of the Canadian Manufacturers' Association, attacked the government and the legislation in the April issue of *Industrial Canada*, the CMA organ. Hugg scorned the government's attempts at compromise and pointed out that dodging vital issues had not satisfied anyone. The manufacturers objected to the inclusion of the anti-injunction stipulation because, they claimed, its invocation by the commission would deprive them of the protection of the law. The CMA called upon the government to "assert the authority of the state and . . . repress all unlawfulness no matter by whom committed."[5]

Norris's attempt was a failure, possibly the most significant since his government began to enact labour and social legislation when it came to office in 1915. It had made an attempt to come to grips with some of the fundamental issues causing most industrial unrest. It had tried to regulate the process of collective bargaining, prepare labour and employers to meet each other as equals, destroy the law's built-in bias against picketing, and provide unions with some legal protection. The effort, however, was a timid one and ignored the unions' belief that the simple abolition of injunctions was all the protection needed. In thus moving to bring some peace and harmony to the industrial scene, the government incurred the wrath of the unions by not bending to their demands to have injunctions abolished. The result was almost predictable in the volatile atmosphere of pre-general strike Winnipeg; Norris and his government, with its admirable record of progressive labour legislation, was shifted into the enemy camp.

The provincial government was not the only party trying to pour oil on very troubled waters. Winnipeg's manufacturers were aware of the growing discontent in the ranks of organized labour and what this dissatisfaction might mean in future. In January the Prairie Provinces Branch of the CMA appointed a five-man committee to investigate current industrial relations problems. The committee's chairman was Edward Parnell, vice-president of the branch, and included J. B. Hugg, L. R. Barrett of Vulcan Iron Works, W. G. Fraser, and W. Martin. Barrett's credentials as a potential bridge of reason were somewhat tarnished by his attitudes towards his own employees, and Hugg's beliefs were hardly more progressive. In his opinion, Winnipeg's "responsible" British and Canadian labour leaders had all gone into the army during the war and their places had been taken by "unskilled workmen of alien origin, permeated with . . . socialistic and anarchistic theories." Current union leaders were "violent extremists" who aimed to convert the Trades Council into a "true Russian Soviet."[6] Parnell's attitude was somewhat different. He believed two groups of leaders were vying for the allegiance of organized labour—the "bolsheviks" and the true trade unionists; the former wanted nothing less than the total destruction of the system, the latter were unhappy about specific problems and honestly believed they were being robbed by their employers. Manufacturers must prevent union members from falling under the sway of extremists, Parnell maintained, and in future employers would have to be more conciliatory towards their employees.[7]

Parnell proposed a series of round table conferences between representatives of capital and labour to discuss problems with an immediate bearing on the industrial situation. Profits, cost of living, wages and hours, and land values should all come under scrutiny, he suggested, while a scheme of employee respresentation in the factories, based possibly on the British Whitley Report, might be worked out. This Report provided for joint employer-employee representation named by trade unions and employer associations on councils which provided a forum to enable the parties to deal with the crucial ongoing problems of industrial relations. However, when Parnell approached the Trades Council with his suggestions, his insistence that "the interests of employer and employees were identical" caused roars of laughter in the Labor Temple.[8]

The spring of 1919 also witnessed an attempt by the federal government to explore the causes of the current industrial unrest. At the urging of the Labour Committee of the cabinet's Reconstruction and Development Committee, a royal commission to enquire into industrial relations in Canada was established in early April. The commission's members were Chief Justice Mathers of Manitoba, chairman, Tom Moore and John Bruce, representing labour, Senator Smeaton White and Charles Harrison, M.P. representing the public, and F. Pauze and Carl Riordon representing the employers.

The Mathers Commission opened hearings at Victoria, British Columbia, on April 16, and completed its work in Ottawa on June 13. In the interim it held 70 sessions in 28 industrial centres and heard 486 witnesses. The commission arrived in Manitoba in May and sat to hear testimony in Winnipeg on the 10th, 12th and 13th. It provided an opportunity for Deacon and Hugg, as well as other interested parties, to present their views of labour-management problems, but it was completely ignored by the Winnipeg Trades and Labor Council.

Four days before the commission arrived the council decided simply to ignore its presence. Congress president Tom Moore offered to address a council meeting while in Winnipeg, but the delegates gave the offer short shrift, and decided not to pay official attention to him either. The Trades Council's reasoning was that the federal government, through the royal commission, was investigating "effects of which they are and have always been a party to the cause." The council asserted that the chief factor behind labour unrest was the system of "production for profit."[9] The only prominent member of the labour community to appear before the commission was Rev. William Ivens, but he sat only as a private person to rebut Hugg's testimony.

Unlike the Trades Council, the Manufacturers' Association took advantage of the commission's sittings to put forward a scheme for "Joint Plan Councils" as a solution to industrial relations problems. J. B. Hugg, representing one hundred Winnipeg employers, presented and explained an idea based on Mackenzie King's Colorado Plan, which provided for internal factory councils representing both employers and employees to be in charge of all matters directly affecting workers in shops. The scheme envisioned union and non-union workers electing representatives to sit on a plant council with management or its representatives. The councils were charged with dealing with problems such as health and safety, wages, and grievances, but left the crucial power to hire and fire in the hands of management and thus offered only an illusion of industrial democracy. This plan also proposed formation of councils on provincial and national levels to take care of problems in larger and more widespread industries.[10] Thomas Russell Deacon also appeared to give his version of the ills affecting manufacturing in western Canada. He complained his company was losing money and had incurred a total deficit of $11,000 as of May 1. Manitoba Bridge was not receiving outside orders, Deacon asserted, and was also losing money on the inventory in stock. He claimed he had not turned a profit since November 1918 and, though he realized he was not paying his workers enough to live on, asserted it was all he could afford to avoid bankruptcy. The picture he painted was all doom and gloom unlit by any hint of improvement in the future.

Deacon's pessimism must be taken with a grain of salt. If the situation was as bad as he described and if his company had not turned a profit in six months it would have been poor business sense to embark on a major expansion of plant and facilities. That, however, is exactly what Deacon and Manitoba Bridge were contemplating and had been pursuing since the previous December. In the last days of 1918 Deacon had approached the Department of Customs in Ottawa inquiring if there was any existing provisions that would allow his company to import duty-free materials for metallurgical development. The following month he wrote Arthur Meighen, minister of the interior in the federal government, and asked for fifteen minutes of the minister's time on his next trip to Winnipeg. At this meeting Deacon outlined plans to introduce a radical new metallurgical development process which would do away with the necessity of importing thousands of tons of expensive high-grade American coal. The new operation would allow Manitoba Bridge to produce quality steel from low-grade scrap iron using a system of pulverized Souris Lignite coal blown like oil into the furnaces. Deacon discussed the installation of a new open-hearth furnace and related facilities based on this new process, and estimated that total costs for building and equipment alone would range from $150,000 to $200,000. This was a gamble of major proportion, he claimed, because it would be financed with borrowed money.[11]

Several times over the next few months Meighen went to bat for Deacon with the customs department. He forwarded his letters and kept urging him to provide the detailed lists so necessary for a final ruling.[12] In late February Deacon wrote the deputy minister of customs, at Meighen's request, to ask his department to place a "generous interpretation" on what was allowable under tariff item 460. In Mid-March he finally received the assurances he had been seeking for the previous four months, when the commissioner of customs wrote Manitoba Bridge that his department "would not object" to the import of materials necessary for the metallurgical conversion process Deacon had outlined. The battle was won, expansion could now go ahead.

The plans are not of themselves indicative of the size of Manitoba Bridge's profits. They are, however, a sign that Deacon was gearing up for a new period of increased postwar business and wanted to be ready when the orders began to pour in once again. Although his requests mentioned the great benefits that could accrue to Canada if the experiment was successful, Deacon's first obligation was to Manitoba Bridge. An expansion program that could, with the addition of labour costs, total one-quarter of the entire capitalization of the company was certainly ambitious. Deacon must have been optimistic about the future.

While Deacon was engaged in discussions that would eventually lead to an expansion of the metal working industry in the city, trouble was brewing in the building trades. After failing to draw up a new wage schedule for 1919—20 the Manitoba Fair Wage Board decided in early April to adjourn to give labour and management a chance to work out their own settlement. This was a serious mistake because it passed responsibility for the determination of new pay rates to parties incapable of arriving at a mutually satisfactory settlement. The Fair Wage Board had been founded to provide a model for working agreements in the province and had served its purpose well. Now, when its leadership was so greatly needed, it failed to fulfill its functions.

The Winnipeg Building Trades Council had taken on a new task in the spring of 1919; henceforth it would be responsible for negotiating working agreements directly with the Builders Exchange. The new arrangement was initially welcomed by all, since it meant both sides would be unable to take advantage of disunity in their respective opponents. The builders were particularly pleased because the new arrangement allowed them to conclude one agreement for the entire industry.[13] Negotiations were proving difficult because the workers were determined to make substantial new gains. They had been forced to settle for very small increases throughout the war and now demanded a straight 20 cents per hour raise for all trades amounting, in some cases, to increments of from 20 to 50 percent. The employers, on the other hand, offered increases of only 10 cents per hour—exactly half the demands of the workers. The builders realized their offer was not high and in fact admitted that their employees' demands were fair, but asserted they could not pay if they were to avoid bankruptcy. Half a loaf was better than none, they pointed out, and a strike would only mean no wages at all going into workers' pockets.[14]

The Building Trades Council knew their demands were high but believed them justified under the circumstances. They claimed that the cost of living had increased at least 75 percent since 1913, while their wages had only gone up 18 percent in the same period. The builders, however, were not experiencing a boom in the early months of 1919 and were probably not in a position to pay large increases. Construction permits granted in the city of Winnipeg in the first four months of the year amounted to $402,350, actually less than in the same period of 1918 and only some $18,000 higher than the first third of 1917, hardly a sign of better times. Employers were doing no more business than they had the previous year and yet were being asked for large wage increases. The impasse was complete and, as a result, all construction activity in the city ceased Thursday morning, May 1, as building trades union members walked out.

April also signalled the Metal Trades Council's second attempt to open discussions with the city's contract shops. The council repeated its approach of the previous year by not demanding union recognition in its initial correspondence; it presented draft schedules asking only for higher wages and the forty-four-hour week. The contract shops also repeated their previous tactics by refusing to discuss anything with the council although they told their men they were prepared to consider implementation of the nine-hour day.[15]

On Tuesday, April 22, each employee of Vulcan Iron Works received a letter explaining the view of management. The Barretts maintained they had agreed to meet individual workers or a committee of their employees but would not, under any circumstances, negotiate with the Metal Trades Council. They were running "an absolutely 'open shop' " and refused to meet with any group which, in their opinion, contained representatives of employees of other companies.[16] Aside from this letter no word was received from any of the major contract shops, and only three of the smaller concerns indicated their willingness to negotiate.

The Big Three were determined to keep up the fiction that they were willing to meet and had been negotiating with shop committees freely elected by their own employees. J. B. Hugg told the Mathers Commission that metal workers had elected committees to negotiate new agreements with management and had been perfectly satisfied with the results. The strike against the contract shops, he explained, had occurred because "some people told [the workers] they had to go out."[17] One example of what the contract shops meant by negotiating with their own employees was the shop committee set up at Dominion Bridge. There a group was appointed from among the workers to bring grievances or other matters of importance to the shop superintendent. Half of the committee was selected by the employees, half by the superintendent, and a neutral chairman was then elected.

On Wednesday night, April 30, members of the various unions connected with the Metal Trades Council crowded into the Labour Temple on James Street to hear a report from their executive. The council's negotiators told them they had submitted twenty-eight schedules to various shops in Winnipeg and had received answers from only three. These small shops had agreed to pay higher wages on the basis of the eight-hour day and would grant further raises if the railroads did. The Big Three, however, had completely ignored the council, leaving the executive little choice but to hand the matter over to the rank and file. The members then voted unanimously to begin their strike the next morning but were persuaded by their executive to stay at work for one more day to see if the Big Three would agree to negotiate. The extra day of grace did not bring any response and on Friday, May 2, at 11:00 A.M., Winnipeg's third metal trades' strike in three years closed the factories down. The issues were distressingly familiar; union recognition, wage parity with the railway shops, and the eight-hour day.[18]

At this point, many union members in the city of Winnipeg were ripe for a call of support for the striking trades, since several were involved in disputes of their own. In the last week of April a strike of telephone operators was narrowly averted when the government met demands for a pay increase scant days before a union deadline ran out. At the same time, the policemen's union was involved in its own negotiations and had a great deal of trouble squeezing higher wages out of the civic administration. The men had voted overwhelmingly to strike but received a new contract with higher wages in the final days of April. The street railway employees had initiated negotiations with their employer on April 21 and, after reaching an impasse, voted 900 to 79 to strike. They held off, however, until receiving the report of a conciliation commission appointed under the Industrial Disputes Investigation Act.

When delegates entered the Labor Temple for the weekly Trades Council meeting on May 6 there was already widespread labour unrest in the city. Two trades were on strike, one was threatening to strike, and two were just emerging from bitter negotiations. The hall was therefore crowded as representatives of the Metal and Building Trades councils reported on the progress of their disputes. W. H. Lovatt, of the Building Trades Council, told the meeting that union recognition had never before been an issue in the construction strike but that the Builders Exchange was now threatening to withdraw its recognition of the Building Trades Council unless their offer was accepted. They still maintained they could not pay the higher wages and Lovatt charged that the banks were behind the impasse. The Building Trades Council as now constituted was really an industrial union which had not been sanctioned by the international union, Lovatt claimed, and there would be no strike pay for those who had walked out. They would need help to win this strike.[19]

As the meeting progressed a note was handed to secretary Robinson which he promptly read to the delegates. A worker of German origin, who had been visiting metal trades shops at the instructions of his local, had been arrested. A number of delegates immediately volunteered to form a committee to go to the police station to investigate and returned some time later with the worker in tow. His speech, charging government-employer collusion and maintaining he was the victim of labour spies and *agents provocateurs,* was a sensation. It was nothing, however, compared to Russell's effort. The fiery Scot was the centre of attention as he put forth one of his finest efforts. He outlined the progress of other metal disputes across the country and charged that Barrett was behind stiffening employer opposition. Winnipeg must stand firm for the sake of labour everywhere. The present strike was due to the partial defeat of the previous summer and there must be no more defeats.

Finally, Harry Veitch told the delegates of the great progress that had been made in previous weeks in organizing non-union workers in the city, thus assuring that a general strike would completely tie up everything in Winnipeg. These words added the final argument. The council voted to start the general strike machinery rolling with a distribution of ballots to every local in the city and asked that all results be returned prior to a special meeting to be held Tuesday evening, May 13, when the date and hour of the strike would be decided upon. In accordance with the decision reached by the council the previous December, a simple majority of all unionized workers would suffice to instruct delegates to call the strike. This decision was made amidst "tumultuous applause and scenes of the greatest enthusiasm."[20] In the jubilation, more than one delegate must have experienced a twinge of disquiet but remained silent in the face of apparently massive pro-strike sentiment. Those supporting the walk-out may have thought of words published in the *Bulletin* not too many months before: "We in Winnipeg . . . had the honour of pulling off the first general strike on this continent and through the swiftness and unexpectedness of our action we beat the capitalist class of this city handsomely."[21]

The next few days were feverish with activity, as Robinson arranged the printing of 18,000 ballots and their distribution to union members throughout the city. In a few cases, such as that of the letter carriers, the vote was taken by an open show of hands, but in most instances the slips were simply filled out during work and returned to Robinson. Ballot boxes were rarely used and votes were added up as they came in to the Labor Temple. In some instances the general strike ballot was distributed the same time as the OBU referendum and strike ballot, which led to much confusion. The typographical union was the only organization in the city to refuse to participate in the voting and was bitterly attacked by several Trades Council members, who charged that they were afraid to lose their funeral expenses and old-age homes and demanded their suspension from the council.[22]

On Tuesday evening, May 13, excited delegates again jammed the Labor Temple to hear reports on the progress of the building and metal trades disputes and the results of the vote. Lovatt told the gathering that the Builders Exchange had reorganized itself, refused to deal with the Building Trades Council, and would only sign agreements with individual unions. Delegates were also told that Premier Norris had met with the contract shop employers and the Metal Trades Council earlier in the day to work out a compromise arrangement. The contract shop owners told him they were thinking of forming a united organization of their own in the coming year and might then deal with the combined metal trades but for the moment would not. Norris, undaunted, appointed Russell and Trades Council solicitor T. J. Murray and two representatives of management to an ad hoc committee to work out a settlement. The idea of independent arbitration at this late date was ridiculed, however, because union recognition was considered a must before any agreement could be considered. Secretary Robinson then read the results of the voting to a jubilant crowd, and announced that union members in the city had given overwhelming support to the general strike—over 11,000 in favour with a mere 500 opposed. As a result the council announced that the strike would begin at 11:00 A.M. Thursday, May 15.[23]

One final attempt was made late Wednesday night to postpone the strike. Mayor Charles F. Gray, Premier Norris, and the provincial attorney general conferred in the premier's room in the Royal Alexandra Hotel. At approximately 11:00 P.M. Gray placed a telephone call to Trades Council president James Winning and asked him if there was any chance the strike would be abandoned if the ironmasters could be persuaded to adopt a more reasonable approach. "Well, it might help," Winning answered, "but it is too late to discuss that now."[24] Gray put the receiver in its cradle, picked up a blank telegram form and began to compose a night letter to Acting Prime Minister Sir Thomas White in Ottawa. At 6:35 A.M. the next morning, Ottawa time, the message was delivered:

> General strike of all trades except typographical takes place here eleven o'clock tomorrow (Thursday) morning, all efforts at reaching a settlement having failed. . . . Situation extremely critical. . . . Fully 27,000 workers involved in strike. Fullest co-operation of government required toward effecting early settlement. . . .[25]

Everything was now ready. The great confrontation was finally at hand. The principle of the general strike, the resolve of the workers, the patience and neutrality of all three governments, and the intransigence of the contract shop owners was about to receive the most difficult of tests. In the weeks ahead many would be found wanting and rationality would succumb to hysteria all too often. As darkness fell over the city on Wednesday night who could possibly have known what lay ahead?

9. ❖ Battling for the Lord: May 15-29

The Winnipeg general strike began quietly in the early hours of Thursday, May 15, 1919. Most of the city's population was sleeping as five hundred telephone operators in Winnipeg's five central exchanges left work at the end of each shift. There was little unusual about their departure, except that no one came in to replace them at the switchboards as the night wore on. When the last shift punched out at 7:00 A.M. Thursday morning, no one was left to operate the telephone system in Canada's third-largest city. It was almost as though Alexander Graham Bell had never existed.

Aside from the absence of telephone services there were few other outward signs of the strike to come. By 9:00 A.M., most of the working population of Winnipeg, with the exception of those in the striking metal and building trades were at their jobs. At McDougal and Company, a small machine shop located near the corner of Portage and Main, Alex Shepherd, secretary-treasurer of IAM local 457, was still at work. McDougal had been one of the few contract shops in the city to come to terms with the Metal Trades Council, and Shepherd and his fellow employees had stayed at work after the other shops were closed May 2. At 11:00 A.M., Shepherd, wearing a bowler hat with the letters "OBU" written on front, walked out the door with several other men. As they headed for the corner of Portage and Main people began to pour out of shop doors and factory gates along the way. Crowds began to gather as workers made their way towards the corner of Winnipeg's two main thoroughfares.

As the hour of the strike approached, streetcars paused momentarily as motormen reached above their heads, placed "To Barn" signs in the route window and began to head for the yard. Passengers already in the cars were dropped off along the way and few new ones were picked up. By noon all the streetcars were in their barns and the tracks were deserted.

Over 22,000 workers answered the strike call within the first twenty-four hours. The atmosphere was almost festive, the belief in ultimate victory strong. Few among them believed they were starting on a long hard road because, after all, how long could the employers stand up to the united power of the working class? Thus ninety-four of ninety-six unions joined the strike; only the typographers and police remained at work. Firemen left their stations, telephones were shut down, the city's electrical workers left turbines and transmission equipment unattended, telegraphers and others responsible for keeping a modern city in touch with the rest of the world refused to work. At the waterworks, a skeleton staff remained behind at the urging of the Trades Council to provide the meagre 30 lbs. pressure which was deemed sufficient for single-story dwellings. Commercial establishments of every sort, from moving-picture houses to restaurants, were closed in the first flush of enthusiasm. Significantly, many thousands of the strikers were not members of any trade union; the long years of war and sacrifice, pent-up frustrations and anger, had taken their toll.

At the sprawling railway marshalling yards and repair shops in and around the city workers obeyed the strike order and walked off their jobs. Approximately 3,000 workers at the Canadian Pacific Railway's Weston shops joined in the strike, along with hundreds of men employed in Union Station. At the Canadian Government Railway's Transcona yards, 1,500 men poured out of the shops and boarded a special train which carried them into Winnipeg. The running trades, however, did not join the walkout. Most of them were in complete sympathy with the strikers, but they were not represented on the Trades and Labor Council and did not participate in the strike vote. Although they had to contend with great pressures from their international officers compelling them to stay at work,[1] several of their representatives went to the Labor Temple to register their complete support for the strike.

Thus, by the evening of May 15, Winnipeg was paralysed. There were no streetcars, no elevators in service, no sanitary facilities on the higher floors of the city's office buildings. Garbage lay in its cans fouling the air in apartment house hallways. Moving-picture theatres, stores, and restaurants were all closed. Inside the many factories, machine shops, slaughter houses, streetcar barns, garages, all was silence. No one ran the lathes or the boring mills, no one tended sewing machines or band saws. The post office was deserted, mail lying unsorted in bins and sacks. In the marshalling yards, repair shops and roundhouses, great black monster locomotives stood untended, in need of repair. In express company offices crates of produce piled upon one another, large cans of cream and milk waited for delivery rigs which were not coming. The great day of reckoning was finally at hand.

The Winnipeg city police was one of the few groups of unionized workers to remain on the job in the days following May 15. Winnipeg's finest, sworn to uphold law and order in the city, were members of a union affiliated to the Trades and Labor Council, and had voted overwhelmingly to join in the sympathetic strike. This posed a serious problem for the General Strike Committee who realized that the absence of police in the city's streets would undoubtedly lead to disorders and a breakdown of the social fabric. The committee believed this would play into the hands of their opponents and there was some hint that troops would be called in if the police walked out. They therefore decided to keep them on the streets, and after several consultations with Mayor Gray, asked the members of the policemen's union to remain at work.[2]

The strike of Winnipeg's commercial telegraphers put federal officials in a difficult position. It was imperative that lines of communication be kept open between militia commanders in the strike-bound city and their superiors in Ottawa. The general officer commanding Military District 10, H. D. B. Ketchen, worked with the CPR in Winnipeg while E. J. Chambers, Chief Press Censor for Canada, carried on negotiations in Ottawa and Montreal. With the full co-operation of railway officials, they were able to link Ottawa to Winnipeg, by way of Montreal, with a direct quadruplex wire system operated by trusted management personnel, which, Chambers believed, could not be intercepted en route by unauthorized persons.[3]

Major General Herbert D. B. Ketchen was faced with a situation no Canadian army man had ever had to cope with before. As commander of the military district in which the strike-bound city was located, the responsibility for organizing and maintaining a militia force to be at the disposal of the federal government fell exclusively to him. Ketchen was well suited for the job. Born in India, he had attended the Royal Military College, in Kingston, Ontario, and

Sandhurst, in England. He had served in the North West Mounted Police from 1894 to 1900 and saw action in South Africa in the final year of the Boer War. Though he was a member of the Manitoba Club, and hard pressed to sympathize with the strikers, he tried hard to fulfil his commitments to his superiors while avoiding any obvious public bias against the strike. Throughout the next six weeks he continued to be the perfect professional soldier.

The federal government was not alone in attempting to set up emergency communications procedures in the first few days of the general strike. At noon on Saturday, May 17, the Canadian Press's six wire-services operators in Winnipeg walked out after twelve hours' notice. This cut the press's transcontinental transmissions until direct communications could be established between Fort William and Regina. This did not end the difficulties, however, because telegraphers west of Winnipeg often refused to handle items with a Winnipeg dateline or took it upon themselves to alter strike stories as they came off the wire. In Winnipeg, the Strike Committee informed Canadian Press it would permit them to resume operations if all news items were first passed to a special committee for approval, but the proposal was rejected out of hand.[4]

The strikers' campaign against the press was not limited to the wire service. As early as February the Winnipeg Trades and Labor Council voted to exclude newspaper reporters from its meetings because, it was alleged, they always misrepresented speeches and proceedings. On May 17 the city's typographers gave in to Strike Committee pressure and walked out, closing down Winnipeg's three newspapers; at the same time the strikers began to issue their own daily paper. The typographers agreed to work on the labour paper without pay, and the first issue of the *Western Labor News, Special Strike Edition* appeared on the streets on May 17. This paper, edited by Rev. William Ivens, was directly controlled by the Strike Committee which set editorial policy, watched over finances and circulation, and appointed a special censorship committee.

The closing down of the daily press was not just a side effect of the general strike but was a deliberate attempt to control news fed to the public. In the second issue of the *Special Strike Edition* Ivens alleged that the daily newspapers told half-truths, misrepresented the cause of the workers, and suppressed facts. He reflected the views of the Strike Committee when he asserted that it was "a case of simple justice . . . to muzzle for a few days the enemies of freedom and truth,"[5] but this attempt to destroy press freedom in the city was ill-advised and misdirected. The *Free Press* of May 15, for example, had attacked the ironmasters for their approach to the question of collective bargaining. Their attitude, Dafoe wrote, had greatly aggravated the situation, and their decision to refuse to deal with the Metal Trades Council was "not in keeping with the times" and "directly provocative of trouble."[6] The *Free Press,* in fact, took a restrained approach to the general strike in the issues immediately preceding its shutdown on May 17. When it later reappeared on the streets produced by management staff, its tone was completely different. It had been the victim of Soviet government, it claimed, while Russell, Veitch, Ivens, Robinson, and Winning were labelled the "red five," and were accused of climbing to power in the trade union movement through the influence of Germans, Austrians, "Huns," and Russians. The strikers had made a powerful enemy without a great deal of thought as to the consequences.

The *Special Strike Edition* served the dual function of keeping its readership informed of the daily routine of the strike and explaining the philosophy of the Strike Committee. Ivens warned his readers in the May 26 edition to keep calm and do nothing that might provoke the enemies of labour: "No matter how great the provocation, do not quarrel. Do not say an angry word. Walk away from the fellow who tries to draw you. Take everything to the Central Strike Committee. If you are hungry go to them. We will share our last crust together. If one starves we will all starve. We will fight on, and on, and on. We will never surrender." Ivens continuously pounded out the theme that this strike was being fought for "principles that cannot be arbitrated." Labour's living condition in life was constant debt. The worker was affected by the high cost of living, the disparity between rich and poor, the lack of any luxuries. During the war he fought for democracy, freedom, and liberty and was told that things would be different after the fighting was over. Now, Ivens reiterated, labour's "irreducible minimum" was the right to collective bargaining, a living wage, and the reinstatement of all strikers without prejudice.[7]

The Trades and Labor Council ceased to function during the general strike and its place was taken by a Central Strike Committee which became, in effect, labour's government. After the decision to strike was made at the Trades Council meeting of May 13, a special temporary five-man committee was appointed to organize and direct labour activities until the Central Strike Committee could be elected. This group carried on until they were joined by 195 other delegates— usually three from each striking union. The Central Strike Committee was responsible for all policy matters and appointed subsidary committees to oversee various services such as food distribution, the *Western Labor News,* relief, organization of non-union workers who had joined the strike, and so on. Delegates to the Central Committee, which usually sat daily, reported to their own unions and attended sessions that sometimes stretched late into the evening.

The original Central Strike Committee was too large and cumbersome a body to act as the directing agency of the general strike. Accordingly, seven days after the strike began, the committee reorganized itself; the Central Strike Committee was transformed into the General Strike Committee and a smaller body of fifteen was appointed to act as the new Central Strike Committee. Russell, Winning, Robinson, Veitch and J. L. McBride were appointed to the latter from the original Central Committee. This new body derived its authority from the larger committee headed by W. H. C. Logan, chairman, W. Lovatt, secretary and R. Durward, assistant secretary; it was technically the final authority for all important decisions.

Strike Committee meetings usually dealt with a full agenda and could keep delegates tied up for hours. Reports on negotiation proceedings would usually be brought in by Russell or another member of the negotiating committee. Here also matters of policy were decided; mass picketing was defeated, striking yard workers were given permission to handle trains carrying returning veterans, and it was decided not to give an international officer permission to meet members of his union. The committee was also vitally interested in bringing the many thousands of non-union strikers into the fold and authorized a massive campaign which, it was estimated, brought in over five thousand new members between May 1 and 19.[8]

Two days prior to the strike the first of many requests from private business for special consideration arrived at the Labor Temple, when Crescent Creamery Company asked to be allowed to continue its daily deliveries of dairy products during the forthcoming strike. The company dealt with a necessity of life, they pointed out, and asked the strikers to consider the request from a humane point of view. The second day of the strike Canadian Northern Railways Express told secretary Robinson that they had a great deal of perishable foodstuffs on hand, including some cans of cream, and asked permission to distribute these commodities to communities outside of Winnipeg. Later the Medical Association approached the Strike Committee to complain about the lack of elevator and streetcar service and the cutting off of the supply of gasoline and milk which they claimed posed unnecessary hardship for the sick. Russell derived some small satisfaction from the process. "It is a fine spectacle," he wrote Midgley, "to see employers coming to the Labor Temple, asking permission to operate their various industries."[9]

In the period immediately following the outbreak of the strike, the Citizens' Committee of 100 was reactivated and became the nucleus around which a new Citizens' Committee of 1,000 was formed. The group, although tracing its ancestry to the previous committee, was slightly different in its membership and very different in its philosophical approach. They opposed sympathetic strikes by employees in essential services and urged that no government employee be allowed to hold membership in "unions having affiliation with outside organizations."[10] In addition, they strongly supported the principles of compulsory arbitration for workers in government or essential services. The new Citizens' Committee was called into being at a meeting of Winnipeg's "prominent business men." Their immediate aim was to create several small groups that would be responsible for the maintenance of public utilities of the duration of the walkout. General Ketchen attended this initial organizational meeting and told those present that serious trouble was about to engulf them. He asked them to assist him in getting "loyal minded citizens" to join the militia so that a sufficient force would be available to deal with possible emergencies and to "uphold constitutional authority, and law and order in the City."[11]

Who were members of the Citizens' Committee of 1,000? Although great pains were taken to keep the names of most members out of the limelight, several safe assumptions may be made about the composition of the "One Thousand." The new committee was an amalgamation of the old one and individual members of organizations such as the Board of Trade, the Manufacturers' Association, and the Bar Association. Of several names that appear frequently in newspaper accounts, for example, H. B. Lyall was an official of Manitoba Bridge and a member of the Board of Trade. A. L. Crossin was a broker with Oldfield, Kirby and Gardner, a firm dealing in insurance and loans, and also a member of the Board of Trade. A. K. Godfrey, chairman of the committee, was the 1917—18 president of the Board of Trade and an executive of the Canadian Elevator Company. J. E. Botterell was a senior partner in the grain and stock brokerage firm of Baird and Botterell and also a member of the Board of Trade.[12] Isaac Pitblado was a senior partner in the law firm of Pitblado, Hoskin and Company, which handled the personal business of Arthur Meighen.[13]

One circular letter mailed by the Citizens' Committee was given the pointed approval of the Winnipeg Board of Trade, its president, W. H. Carter, and its managing secretary, W. B. Moore.

The sources of this committee's financial support can only be discerned in an indirect and therefore imperfect manner. In August 1919 the Citizens' League of Winnipeg held its founding meeting and initiated a membership campaign among different groups who had opposed the general strike. Members of the Committee of 1,000 were asked to join, along with former militia volunteers and army officers, community clubs, and business and professional groups. This league, dedicated to carrying on "the work of the Citizens' Committee of 1,000,"[14] approached a number of business and professional associations in search of operating funds. They requested $5,000 from the Wholesale Grocers' Association, $5,000 from the Canadian Manufacturers' Association, and $2,000 each from the Winnipeg Motor Trades Association, the Manitoba Mortgage Loan Association, and the Retail Merchants' Association. Other groups approached included the Builders Exchange, Law Society, Real Estate Exchange, Medical Society, and Dental Society. Among individual business concerns approached were the Royal Alexandra and Fort Garry hotels, and Imperial Oil.[15]

The motives for supporting or joining the committee were probably as diverse as its membership. One common denominator was hysteria—fear among small businessmen and store owners that they would be economically wiped out or their establishments wrecked by riots. In the prosperous south end of the city people stood guard over their homes with rifles, expecting to be attacked by mobs of screaming radicals. Although their fears of revolution were baseless, they were the first Canadians ever to live in a city hit by a general strike called by a Trades Council which many considered more than a little "red." Others, particularly businessmen, undoubtedly lent their support cynically, to gain advantages in a bitter industrial dispute; but the support of most middle-class citizens probably reflected panic more than any other emotion.

The Citizens' Committee emerged early in the strike as one of labour's chief opponents. On Monday, May 19, the first edition of its daily newspaper appeared on the streets. The *Winnipeg Citizen*, like its opponent, the *Special Strike Edition*, carried news of the activities of its parent body and spread its ideological message to the world. The *Citizen* proclaimed on page one of its first edition that this dispute was not a strike but a revolution. There never was any dispute centred upon the question of collective bargaining, their argument ran, the real question was that of the survival of British institutions. The Citizens' Committee expended a great deal of effort to convince governments and non-aligned members of the general public that collective bargaining or union recognition was not at issue:

THE ONE BIG ISSUE is *NOT* shall Trades form Unions—it is *NOT* collective bargaining BUT—IS EVERY INDIVIDUAL DISPUTE BETWEEN EMPLOYER AND EMPLOYEE TO CONTINUE TO DISRUPT THE LIFE OF THE WHOLE COMMUNITY?[16]

Their views were echoed by the *Winnipeg Telegram,* which maintained that this was quite simply "a deliberate, criminal and fantastic attempt to make a revolution," engineered by aliens and British renegades who were a disgrace to their race.[17]

In the face of massive evidence to the contrary, the Citizens' Committee insisted that collective bargaining was not an issue. It focused on the One Big Union and equated the Metal Trades Council and its approach to bargaining with the radical new organization. The "real Trades Unionist" had a deep commitment to his city and society, they claimed, but the Bolshevik was opposed to honest labour and its every interest. When the Committee spoke of Bolsheviks, as Parnell and Hugg had in previous months, they were talking about the OBU and the Metal Trades Council which was, in their opinion, "the first step toward the One Big Union idea of Collective Bargaining." This, they explained, was bargaining by industry rather than by craft.[18]

Throughout the strike the Citizens' Committee maintained strong and usually secret ties with all three levels of government, particularly the federal. Ketchen told his superiors that the committee was giving him a great deal of assistance, supporting him fully, and had placed themselves at his disposal at all times and entirely under his orders.[19] The great value placed by federal officials on the committee's faithful service is demonstrated by the distribution to general officers commanding ten military districts in the spring of 1921 of material relating to the Citizens' Committee. A letter from General Ketchen explaining the formation and activities of the group, along with a pamphlet published by the committee after the strike, was distributed by the militia headquarters in Ottawa to districts "where disturbances of serious proportions may be expected."[20]

Other more tangible connections between the Citizens' Committee and the federal government emerged during the course of the general strike. Twelve days after the walkout began Arthur Meighen asked one of the more prominent members of the committee, A. J. Andrews, to represent the Justice Department in its efforts to ascertain if any of the actions of the strike leaders were "seditious or treasonable."[21] In addition, the federal government picked up the tab for at least one Citizens' Committee account. During the strike more than sixty employees of the Macdonald Detective Agency were brought into the city to act as "watchmen" for private firms. After the strike was over the Citizens' Committee approached the federal government with a bill from the agency for over $1,000 and Ottawa paid it in full.[22]

Alfred J. Andrews had now become a pivotal figure determining the course of events in the city and was the key link between the Citizens' Committee and the federal government throughout the strike. He had been born in the Eastern Townships of Quebec, came to Winnipeg in 1880, and served in the Northwest Rebellion of 1885. The following year he was admitted to the Manitoba Bar. Andrews was a robust man who loved golf and curling and belonged to the exclusive Manitoba Club, Carleton Club, and the St. Charles Country Club. Although his legal career always came first, Andrews had served on city council and one term as mayor of Winnipeg. He ran for the legislature under the Conservative banner in 1914 but was defeated by F. J. Dixon. Andrews was a forceful and forthright man and had taken many cases for trade unions in his career but his conservative temper, his fear of labour radicalism, and his personal identification with labour's opponents in this particular fight made him one of the strikers' most formidable opponents.

In one of the earliest official statements outlining their aims and objectives, the Citizens' Committee stated that they intended not only to keep essential services in operation but also to bring about a "just and reasonable" settlement of the original disputes from which the strike grew. They pledged to use whatever means were at their disposal to do their part in ending the walkout; but in fact the committee did just the opposite, and were responsible for standing in the way of a settlement by urging the Big Three not to negotiate. On Thursday, May 22, Mayor Gray told city council that he had met the contract shop owners and showed them a letter from Winning containing proposals for a strike settlement; but they had told him that at the request of the Citizens' Committee they had nothing to say and would not enter into negotiations.[23] J. W. Wilton also made an effort to get the two sides together, but was told by A. K. Godfrey

that established institutions had been attacked by the strike and must
be defended before any discussion of the original disputes could take
place.[24]

The Citizens' Committee of 1,000 took upon itself responsibility
for operating various public services paralysed by the strike. At its
very first formal meeting General Ketchen suggested they divide
themselves into sub-committees to look after different services. The
militia commander told them that a volunteer fire service would have
to be organized, along with a group to maintain water service, bread,
and milk depots and a transport department to include automobile
owners who could help rush troops from the barracks and drill halls
if they were needed.[25] The Board of Trade building became the headquarters of the Citizens' Committee and the place from which most
of the volunteer services, including the fire brigade, were run. The
fire-fighters were kept going around the clock, mostly by false alarms,
but managed to deal with three small conflagrations in the first six
days of the strike. The volunteers were mostly younger men, returned
soldiers, and some members of the Winnipeg Canoe Club who had,
at times, to contend with catcalls, jeers, bottles and rocks while they
were doing their work. They showed their courage, however, when
they climbed atop the roof of the old Auditorium Rink to put out a
moderate-sized blaze.

The Committee directed other volunteer efforts. An informal
patrol service was initiated in the early days of the strike, in which
young men or returned soldiers spent an hour or two in shifts each
night watching over the "better" parts of the city. The committee
was also able to gather a substitute staff to run the waterworks and
approached the city council on Tuesday, May 20, to volunteer their
services. Engineering students from the University of Manitoba were
recruited to operate powerhouses, and another group even volunteered to sweep streets and collect garbage.

The Committee of 1,000 was instrumental in pushing the issue of
alien participation in the strike to the fore, in an effort to tie Winnipeg to a world Bolshevik conspiracy and to arouse the sort of
popular prejudice which had exploded in violence in January and
February. There were probably thousands of Russians, Poles, and
Ukrainians participating in the strike, but they played almost no
role in its leadership or direction. The Winnipeg labour movement,
like that of western Canada generally, was guided almost exclusively
by Britons or Canadians. There were many vigorous and active labour
and leftist political parties and organizations operating among the

new or non-Canadians in the city, but they were either subordinate or totally independent in rallying the ethnic community to the Trades Council's cause.

In the spring of 1919 the Ukrainian Labor Temple Association was the most influential leftist foreign-language organization in Winnipeg. The association had grown out of the Ukrainian Social Democratic Party, which had become increasingly radical in the months immediately after Lenin's ascent to power, and which espoused the cause of world revolution and a Ukrainian Soviet Republic through the pages of *Robochy Narod*, the official party organ. The Labor Temple Association was initially formed as an affiliate of the party when Ukrainian leftists embarked upon the ambitious construction of a new labour centre on Pritchard Street. The federal government's order-in-council of September 1918, banning certain radical and anti-war groups, forced the party and its newspaper to fold, leaving the allegedly non-political association to carry on as the most conspicuous voice of Ukrainian radicalism.

The loss of *Robochy Narod* denied the association easy access to its own constituency and forced it to close ranks with the Trades Council and the *Western Labor News* so that the drive for building funds could be completed. In December W. N. Kolismyk, an officer of the association, published a plea for contributions in the *Labor News* and urged his followers to subscribe to the Trades Council publication in order to receive the news and information they were being denied in their own language. A copy of the paper was mailed to every name on the *Robochy Narod* subscription list with the hope that Ukrainians would subscribe to it.[26] Ukrainian radicals and their association were thus driven into the Trades Council's arms at the precise moment when it was finally emerging as an authentic voice of western labour radicalism. It is impossible to say how many Ukrainians took out subscriptions to the *Western Labor News,* but the belief that labour had a common cause regardless of ethnic origin was greatly fostered and contributed to a greater feeling of solidarity. The events of January and February notwithstanding, socialists and union men in the ethnic community undoubtedly believed the Trades Council's fight was their own and that the Anglo-Saxon union men were standing up for principles that ought to be defended regardless of cultural background. To back this up there was ample evidence that aliens were considered something less than human, and were destined to be second-class citizens in someone else's society.

The general strike was the perfect opportunity for the ethnic community to air their many complaints. They could easily recall the anti-foreign prejudices whipped up throughout the war by overly zealous patriots, the orders-in-council banning their languages and newspapers, the Wartime Elections Act which disenfranchised many thousands of them, the internments, registration and parole, and the use of these systems to suppress legitimate trade union activity. Those who were more politically active were probably closer in tune with events in Russia, Germany, and Hungary than their Canadian co-workers, and leaders such as Jacob Penner, Sam Blumenberg, John Navisivsky, and Matthew Popovitch rivalled anyone on the Trades Council in their espousal of radical ideas. Penner, Navisivsky, and Popovitch became prominent leaders of the Communist Party in later years.

Although the leaders and spokesmen of Winnipeg's foreign-language radical groups had much in common with men such as Russell, Johns, Ivens, and Armstrong, there was little intercourse between them. Ukrainians, Jews, and Russians may have been active in the union movement, believers in socialism, and ardent supporters of working class militancy, but they almost never achieved prominent positions in unions or trades councils. Speeches heard at the labour temples across western Canada were almost invariably delivered in the round tones of north England or the thick burr of the Clydeside, while names appearing in the labour press hardly ever ended with "-vitch," "-sky," "-ov," or "-berg." A. A. Heaps was Jewish, but he was also British and fitted easily into the Winnipeg scene. Language difficulty and the not unusual desire of recent immigrants to seek ties and succour amongst their own kind played the greatest part in this organizational segregation. Britons worked more easily in the Canadian context, usually had years of union experience in their background, knew the myths and methods of a British-oriented society, and were not self-conscious about expressing their beliefs in public. They seemed to assume leadership roles almost naturally and directed the trades councils, made the speeches, ran for public office, edited the newspapers, and usually made the news. Thus charges that the strike was alien-lead were completely false, and the assertions of the Citizens' Committee constituted a calculated attempt to appeal to fear and prejudice in order to mislead the public into the belief that Russians, Jews, Poles, and Ukrainians were in control and turning the labour temple into a soviet.

The Citizens' Committee's attempts to operate services abandoned by strikers pointed out the serious nature of the general strike. An entire city had been paralysed. Talk of the general strike had been heard more and more frequently since the late months of 1918, but no one took the time to think out the ramifications of a complete tie-up of all services in the city. Workers, too, had families, let alone the people who sided with neither the strikers or the employers. How were they to be fed and heated? Who was to carry away their garbage, provide them with milk and bread and, in the pre-electric refrigerator days, ice? Was there to be a complete denial of the basics of modern life? Was there to be, in the end, anarchy? The Strike Committee began to face these problems only in the first few days of the strike and soon realized that emergency maintenance facilities would have to be extended beyond the families of strikers. In a very real sense they were increasingly responsible for the welfare of a large part of a modern city, but their lack of foresight in planning for these problems led them into their first serious mistake.

The intense public reaction to the failure of bread and milk delivery wagons to make their usual rounds on the morning of Friday, May 16, stimulated a move within the Strike Committee to form a special food sub-committee to work out the problems of staples distribution. It was feared that riots and disorders might break out and troops called in if something were not done quickly. The strikers approached a city council sub-committee to work out the problem, but were insistent that depots not be used as they wished to have some way to regulate distribution.[27] The meeting between the two committees was attended by A. J. Andrews and J. E. Botterell, both of the Citizens' Committee and J. M. Carruthers, owner of the Crescent Creamery Company. Carruthers suggested that the problem of distribution could be solved by issuing special cards to delivery wagons to let the public know that the men delivering bread and milk were not "scabs."[28] The suggestion was accepted by those present, placed before the Central Strike Committee, and approved. Thereafter "Permitted by Authority of Strike Committee" placards were issued by the strikers' food committee.

As a result of this new arrangement a degree of normalcy returned. Moving-picture theatres and restaurants were allowed to reopen. Hospitals received deliveries of milk and the staff responsible for their heating, sterilizing, and laundry facilities continued to work. Gasoline filling stations reopened with police protection and baking establishments began to produce bread once again. The arrangement, however, made certain people uneasy. Mayor Gray felt it necessary to point out that there need be no fear that the necessities of life were being supplied by "the suffrage of some authority other than the constituted authority," because such reactions were an oversimplification. This explanation did not suffice to stem the criticism of those who charged that the government of the city had passed into the hands of labour. The strikers denied they were attempting to usurp authority and claimed the cards had only been issued to protect workers who might otherwise be thought of as strikebreakers. If no cards had been issued, they claimed, then the men would have refused to return to work.

Mayor Gray was now in a difficult position. He knew that the permits had been issued as a result of a compromise between the strikers, the Citizens' Committee, and the city government but the charge that it was a surrender of municipal authority implied that he had stood by, inactive, while the unions "took over." He was thus faced with the choice of defending the agreement, and appearing to some to give in to the Strike Committee, or of reversing himself and attacking the original compromise. He was incapable, by virtue of background and temperament, of making the only moral and proper decision—to stand by the original agreement.

Charles F. Gray was somewhat of an anomoly in Winnipeg politics. He was a consulting electrical engineer by profession and had no connections with any of the city's formal business or commercial organizations, such as the Board of Trade, prior to his election to the Board of Control in 1917. In 1918 he acceded to the mayoralty on a traditional honest government platform. Gray was a dapper man who desperately tried to stay friends with everyone prior to the general strike. He had thus never been identified with either capital or labour in the public mind and had never taken a strong stand on any of the issues raised by the increasing class division in his city. Gray was not a weak man, but he was rapidly becoming openly horrified at the gargantuan proportions this struggle was taking on and his middle-class instincts led him to surrender almost immediately and reverse his initial position on the permits.

When pressure began to mount for the removal of the cards, Gray and Premier Norris told the strikers' negotiating committee that they objected to the permits, even though they understood why they had originally been issued. Russell later told the Strike Committee that Gray demanded the removal of the placards prior to any consideration of the root causes of the strike.[29] The issue soon came to a head at a stormy meeting of city council on Tuesday, May 21. Gray told those present that he wanted the placards removed because they had outlived their usefulness. He realized why they had been issued but many people in all parts of the country were under the false impression that they signified the erosion of the authority of his government.[30] Aldermen Sparling, Pulford, and Fowler supported the mayor, but the labour representatives on council defended the use of the permits and asserted that they were absolutely necessary if the men operating special services were to continue to do so. A. J. Andrews said he knew beyond doubt that the Strike Committee was well-intentioned in issuing the cards and that they were undoubtedly necessary for the protection of the men, but this in itself was a strong reason to support constituted authority because, whether intended or not, the city was getting the necessities of life by permission of the strikers.[31] After the discussion the council voted seven to four to have the cards removed.

One full week after the walkout began the Strike Committee published a special notice announcing the withdrawal of the permit cards. The action was being taken to avoid any further misunderstanding on the part of the city council and other governments and henceforth men operating milk wagons, bread trucks, and other essential vehicles would carry special cards in place of the permits. The decision had been reached at a meeting of sub-committees from the city council and the Strike Committee and was announced to the city council at noon on Wednesday, May 21. Gray expressed his satisfaction with the settlement and maintained there could not now be any further misunderstanding "that the legally constituted authority has been taken out of the hands of the civic authorities."[32]

The permit episode cast a heavy shadow on the strike and the Strike Committee. The permits were not decided upon unilaterally and in fact were approved by two representatives of the Citizens' Committee and a sub-committee of city council, but their wording created the impression that the strikers alone were responsible for the maintenance of essential services in the city. This naturally led to a belief in some minds that government had passed to the Labor Temple which now appeared to have the power to operate or shut down these facilities at will. From there it was but a small step to the assumption that the Labor Temple was now the "James Street Soviet." This cry reinforced itself in the opinions, and spurred the activities, of those who claimed the strike was nothing but a revolution in the first place.

The government at Ottawa continued to keep a close watch on events in Winnipeg during the first days of the strike. Acting Prime Minister Sir Thomas White wired Borden in Europe to tell him of the news and to warn that serious rioting might occur. When Borden told White eight days later that he was coming home, he asked for the earliest possible information on the state of affairs in Winnipeg and other western cities. Upon his return he stated that his government would aim to preserve order, keep the civil service from joining the strike, and would spare no effort in bringing about an end to the walkout by conciliation. Borden's cabinet held the strong opinion that direct intervention in the strike through the use of existing federal machinery was out of the question. White, for example, wrote the secretary of the Toronto Trades and Labor Council that the ability to legislate rates of pay and hours of work remained outside federal jurisdiction, while Borden said essentially the same thing to Joseph A. Clarke, mayor of Edmonton. Hours of employment and conditions of labour had always been the subject of provincial legislation in the past, he claimed, and it was impossible for the federal government to legislate in that field. Both Borden and Meighen reiterated this stand in speeches to the House of Commons. There was no doubt in their minds that collective bargaining in the Winnipeg metal trades was a matter for provincial concern.[33] The War Measures Act might have enabled the federal government to make a momentary ad hoc intervention in the dispute, but any regulations dealing with collective bargaining would only have been temporary.

Borden claimed that his government was not subject to any outside influence or dictation in its approach to current labour difficulties and, in a strict sense, this was true; Ottawa was, however, the focal point of many direct and indirect pressures to do something about ending the strike. In the first days after May 15 the financial pages of the Toronto *Globe* made constant mention of the adverse affect the Winnipeg strike was having on the stock market, while the *Financial Post* pointed out that market activity slowed whenever important news arrived from Winnipeg. In addition, Winnipeg's troubles were receiving front page coverage in New York and Chicago. The Chicago *Daily Tribune* proclaimed that "All Winnipeg [was] Under [the] Rule of Strikers"[34] and the *New York Times* announced that the strike was "sweeping [the] West."[35] More damaging, perhaps, were the *Times's* editorials which spoke of the strike as "a beautiful demonstration of essential Bolshevism," and "an attempt at revolution and an imitation of the Soviet Autocracy." It was clear where the government of Winnipeg was now lodged, the paper stated, but what the provincial or federal authorities were going to do about it was far from clear.[36]

There was some indication that this type of hysteria was having an adverse effect on prospective American investors. A *Financial Post* reporter noted that several potential investments had been held up because of the labour trouble, while an official of the Studebaker Corporation wrote the Southern Canada Power Company that they would not consider putting money into Canada because the government was doing nothing about the Bolshevik takeover of Winnipeg.[37] One of Borden's personal friends wrote from New York that editorials such as those in the *New York Times* might "unsettle the financial community." The American press, the prime minister answered, had gone wild with exaggeration.

The federal government began to play a direct role in the strike with the arrival of Gideon Robertson and Arthur Meighen in Winnipeg. At first, the news that Robertson was once again about to intervene in a labour dispute in the city was welcomed by the strikers who thought all would be set right if he would "tell the Metal Trades employers the same story he told the city council last year." This was, however, not the summer of 1918 all over again and things would soon be very different. Robertson and Meighen were exposed to the Citizens' Committee's rather questionable interpretation of events even before they arrived in the strikebound city. At Fort William they met two members of the committee, one of whom was A. J. Andrews, and later, as their train approached the city, two more Citizens' Committee members boarded. In notes prepared for his biographer in later years, Meighen wrote that he knew most of these people personally and believed they were not the sort who would "be easily victims of fear." These Citizens' Committee representatives told the federal ministers that the strike was actually a revolution, that civil power would shortly be challenged by the unions, and that only strong and resolute action could save the day.[38]

On the night of May 21 Meighen and Robertson arrived in Winnipeg and began to meet with various officials almost immediately. They spoke with Premier Norris and General Ketchen, officials of the CPR, local postal authorities and others affected by the strike, but refused to address the Strike Committee. Almost as soon as Robertson arrived the Strike Committee sent a message asking him to come to the Labor Temple to give whatever information and counsel he could to the elected representatives of the strikers. He declined, saying it would not be consistent with the dignity of a minister to address a Strike Committee meeting but did offer to receive a deputation the next morning. Robertson was willing to talk with the strikers if they approached him; he was never this formal with members of the Citizens' Committee.

The ministers' first few days in Winnipeg were almost exclusively devoted to the strike of postal workers which was tying up all mail delivery in Winnipeg and threatening to disrupt cross-country service as well. Letter carriers and clerks claimed they had joined the strike because promises made to them by the government during the summer of 1918 had not been kept and presented the local postmaster with a list of grievances they maintained were the cause of their action.[39] This list was not taken seriously, however, because Winnipeg's postmaster Underwood was convinced that the men were merely searching for a pretext to join the sympathetic strike. Postal service inside the city was completely cut off as almost all the employees joined the strike. Clerks, sorters, railway transfer men, and letter carriers all walked out and there were indications that the railway mail clerks would soon follow. Initially postal officials attempted to send mail for other areas directly through the city, since it was a major transfer point, but the railway mail clerks refused to handle any packages forwarded through the Winnipeg office. Other arrangements were then made to put mails on non-stop trains and the backlog was gradually dealt with. Meanwhile, within the city, the only mail that moved was currency packages delivered by private messenger service to Winnipeg's banks. R. M. Coulter, deputy postmaster general, blamed this new series of postal difficulties on the government's failure to deal strongly with postal workers in the past.[40]

If the government had not applied a strong hand in 1918 it was about to rectify that "mistake." One of the solutions increasingly mentioned as the strike wore on was an ultimatum, followed by dismissal. Ottawa asked Coulter about this but he was somewhat uneasy. He believed such action too soon might set off a chain reaction of strikes in other postal departments throughout the west and that public opinion would soon become so strongly in favour of the government that an ultimatum could be successfully presented. Meighen, nevertheless, met with G. W. Allan, Conservative Unionist M.P. for Winnipeg South, and decided that the only way to deal with the situation was to give post office workers a set time to return to their jobs and then fire those who did not.[41] In a telegram to Ottawa Meighen and Robertson explained that they believed the men would probably eventually return of their own accord but that some sort of strong action was necessary to uphold the moral authority of the government.[42] Consequently on Friday, May 23, they issued an ultimatum to all striking members of the postal service that those who did not return to work by noon on Monday, May 26, would be dismissed.

The government did not wait for the expiry of the ultimatum to hire voluntary help to replace the men on strike. Approximately 150 volunteers reported for work the next morning and the Citizens' Committee promised to deliver at least one hundred more. Underwood arranged a meeting for Sunday afternoon at which Senator Robertson would address the striking postal workers but the Strike Committee would have none of this, called their own meeting and stationed pickets around the post office to direct workers to the Labor Temple. At the post office Robertson warned that the government was not bluffing about its ultimatum and would not pay any of the men for the time they had been on strike; but few of the postal workers believed him. In Underwood's opinion, they had little respect for the government and thought they could bring Ottawa to its knees.[43] At the Labor Temple they voted not to heed the ultimatum and, the next day, lost their jobs. A mere forty men returned by Monday's deadline and the post office promptly began to hire new men on a permanent basis to replace those considered dismissed.

The experience of the majority of Winnipeg's postal workers was not lost on the railway mail clerks. On Tuesday, May 27, these men notified the superintendent of the railway mail service at Winnipeg that they would leave their jobs at midnight because of the manner in which the government had issued its ultimatum to the other postal workers.[44] At midnight the strike began, but a rudimentary service was maintained because thirty men refused to join the walkout and supervisory personnel were placed on trains to help sort the mail. Robertson, however, decided to handle the crisis in the same way he had handled the previous one and gave the clerks twenty-four hours to report back to work or be dismissed. Just before the allowed time was due to expire a delegation reported at the office of superintendent Cavanagh and were told they could not see Robertson that night. The next afternoon Robertson met the strikers and told them they could return to their jobs, but that temporary workers already hired during the brief strike would be kept on. The men agreed and were allowed to return to work.[45]

By June 1, the post office situation had, in Underwood's words "passed [the] climax" and reorganization was well on its way.[46] In fact, the only thing which prevented a resumption of letter carrier service in the first week of June was the hostile attitude of citizens sympathetic to the strikers. The matter of the striking postal workers was, however, far from settled because many of them now realized that Robertson's ultimatum had been no bluff and tried to get their old jobs back. Some offered to renounce their union affiliation[47] and

Underwood himself believed they had seen the error of their ways and would not repeat their previous hasty actions. Robertson, however, held firm and urged his colleagues in Ottawa to back up his ultimatum by refusing to rehire any of the men.[48]

Shortly after they had arrived in Winnipeg Robertson and Meighen began to issue public statements containing their judgment of the causes of the dispute and its wider implications. Initially Robertson saw "merit and justification" in the grievances which touched off the wider general strike but soon changed his tune a few days later, asserting that the metal trades workers had no right at all to demand recognition for the Metal Trades Council. They were justified, in his opinion, only in asking for the recognition of individual unions which, he pointedly claimed, had already been recognized by the contract shop owners. Thus, he maintained, there was no justification for the general strike which was, in fact, "a cloak for something far deeper."[50] Robertson was simply not willing to recognize that the metal trades workers in the contract shops had any right at all to have a council bargain for them because, he claimed, the council contained members from outside the contract shops. Here he was referring to the representation and direction of the railway shop craft unions which had been so instrumental in forming the Metal Trades Council over a year ago. In other circumstances he may have had a valid point. Railway shops workers were represented on and bargained through Division 4. Thus their representation on the Metal Trades Council served only to strengthen the contract shops workers and was not necessary for the determination of their own working conditions. But Robertson also claimed that the strike was nothing but an attempted revolution, and blandly asserted that the owners of the contract shops "had no objection to their employees organizing."[51] He was making every effort within human reason to prove to anyone who would listen that collective bargaining was not a real issue in this strike but was being used to camouflage an attempt to overthrow constitutional authority. The underlying cause of the strike, Robertson maintained, was the One Big Union.

Senator Gideon Robertson was by nature a conservative man who wholeheartedly embraced the ideals and philosophies of the dean of North American labour, Samuel Gompers. Even so, he had in the summer of 1918 intervened in a British Columbia shipyard dispute and dealt with the metal trades councils of Victoria and Vancouver without any mention about their structure or constitution. In addition, he made no complaints at all when the combined shop craft unions first bargained together with the Canadian Railway War Board in the summer of 1918. The Winnipeg strikers asserted that negotiating through a metal trades council was the same as talking to management through Division 4, and they were essentially correct. The 1918 royal commission which had investigated the labour trouble in the contract shops questioned the propriety of labour's demands, but did not condemn bargaining through the Metal Trades Council. Robertson must also have been aware that there existed at least eight other such bodies across Canada in cities such as Montreal, Toronto, and Hamilton. There was, however, one factor which, in Robertson's mind, made this a very special case—the Western Labor Conference and the One Big Union.

Robertson firmly believed that the events at Calgary in March had had a definite bearing on this general strike. He claimed that the type of centrally controlled collective bargaining demanded by the metal workers in Winnipeg was the same as that which the One Big Union desired to bring about.[52] He wrote Samuel Gompers that the strike had been called to support the birth of the OBU and had as its chief aim the destruction of the internationals[53] and reiterated this to the mayors of Fort William and Port Arthur. Robertson thought this strike was inspired by the new radicalism and if defeated would seriously undermine the One Big Union movement.[54] He was not alone in this opinion, since at least one staunch supporter of the OBU held similar views. R. J. Johns, in Montreal as part of the Division 4 negotiating team, told Victor Midgley that "the western movement" ought to line up behind the strikers because if the strike was won "propaganda for the OBU [would] be easy."[55]

Robertson, supported by his colleagues in the cabinet and Prime Minister Borden, was firmly convinced of what he was fighting. Meighen, in a more cavalier moment, called the strike leaders "revolutionists of various degrees and types, from crazy idealists down to ordinary thieves,"[56] but Borden went to the heart of the matter when he told the House of Commons on May 27 that collective bargaining, when interpreted in a certain way and "carried to an extreme length" could be very damaging to the public interest. He was no doubt sincere in his belief that this strike was an attempt to oust elected constitutional authorities, but it was the spectre of a revolution in the structure and ideologies of trade unions that haunted the cabinet more than any other factor. The OBU, they feared, was the dawn of that change.

In an address to the 1920 convention of the Trades and Labor

Congress of Canada, Arthur Meighen, now prime minister, outlined his conception of the characteristics which marked responsible union-ism: "Fidelity of agreement, fulfillment of contract, the respect of public rights, the rights of the ballot, and the seeking of success through the approval of the majority of the public." The OBU and the Winnipeg strikers did not appear to hold any of these precepts dear to their hearts. Meighen claimed, during the strike, that they had destroyed the sanctity of contracts and negated the value of collective bargaining by showing that they would break their agreements with management in order to support sympathetic strikes. Meighen's most fundamental concern, however, parallelled Borden's: "If collective bargaining is to be granted as a principle . . . then there must be some unit to which the principle . . . is to apply and beyond which it cannot go." If this process of unions combining to form larger unions was not stopped, he asserted, the country would soon be at the mercy of one large conglomerate which could hold the threat of great general strikes over the head of society. That, he maintained, would be the perfection of Bolshevism and such a strike would mean "paralysis of the activities of the entire Dominion."

Does this mean, however, that Meighen agreed with the concept of collective bargaining for individual unions? Not completely; he, like the minister of labour, denied that collective bargaining had ever been an issue, claiming that the metal masters had bargained with their employees for some time and asserting that they had actually reached an agreement with their men which had been wrecked by the Metal Trades Council. Thus, he blessed the employer-operated shop committee set-up which had existed in the three plants prior to the strike with the term "collective bargaining."[57] One of his col-leagues put the matter even more bluntly in a speech at Verdun, Quebec. The minister of marine and fisheries, C. C. Ballantyne, told his audience that the Borden administration looked with favour upon trade unions as they had known them in the past.[58] That, obviously, precluded the One Big Union or anything which appeared to be connected with it.

Winnipeg was Manitoba's capital and largest city. The Liberal government of Premier Norris should have been deeply involved in the events of the strike and have taken a hand to end the dispute as quickly as possible. In fact, the premier was informed daily of events at conferences with General Ketchen, Commissioner Perry of the Royal North West Mounted Police, Mayor Gray, and his own attorney general. But Norris was anxious to appear uninvolved, and was content to let federal officials take the initiative while he followed behind. He did act to restore telephone service in the city when his government issued a warning to its telephone system employees to return to work or lose their jobs. They, like the postal workers, voted to stay out and were replaced by a new permanent staff. The provincial government, therefore, handled its employees in the same way that Meighen and Robertson were dealing with the post office staff and, in fact, issued its ultimatum the same day. This suggests prior consultations between the premier and federal ministers in an attempt to work out a joint policy. Norris was willing to work with the federal government and agreed with their ideas that strikes in the public sector could not be tolerated. When approached by Gray to attempt to bring about an end to the strike by conciliation, Norris merely insisted that no settlement could be reached until all public utilities were back in operation.[59] Norris didn't want to take the lead because he thought he had nothing to gain and everything to lose by an active intervention in the dispute. He was not willing to try Wilton's suggestion to introduce legislation to make collective bargaining compulsory because he was unsure whether he could keep the support of the legislature.[60] The strike was, in the premier's opinion, a federal responsibility and he was quite willing to let them take care of it.[61]

During the second week of the strike Norris was presented with a golden opportunity to initiate significant discussion towards bringing about a negotiated settlement. On Monday, May 26, a story appeared in the *Western Labor News* which claimed that Ed McGrath had approached the General Strike Committee on behalf of the provincial government to ask them to appoint two men to the provincial Industrial Disputes Commission established the previous March. If they would do that, McGrath was alleged to have offered, Norris would, by order-in-council, make collective bargaining compulsory. The strikers claimed that, although many among them opposed the move, they had nominated two men, notified the provincial government of this, and were then told that Norris did not know what they were talking about. The whole thing had been a double-cross.[62] Norris's story was quite different. He told the newspapers his government had never made such an offer and the notice from the Strike Committee had arrived like a bolt from the blue. Further, McGrath was prepared to back up the premier's statement that he had never made any offer to the Strike Committee.[63] On publication of this, the strikers admitted they had lied, but then made a new offer to appoint men to the commission if the government would make collective bargaining legal and compulsory and enact legislation reinstating all strikers, after which the general strike would be called off.[64] Norris would not even nibble at the bait and told Robinson in no uncertain terms that the strike had to be called off before he would even try to bring about a negotiated settlement.

The civic government was deeply involved in the events of the strike from the very beginning. Labour representatives on city council and a delegation from the running trades unions attempted to have the city take the lead in bringing the strikers and their employers together but were unsuccessful in accomplishing anything of value. In general, the city council was reluctant to do anything about collective bargaining because it believed this was the provincial government's prerogative. The mayor's initial attempts to get the two sides together had failed because of the employers' refusal to act without the approval of the Citizens' Committee. Nevertheless, on Friday morning, May 23, Gray made another try and appointed a special committee to discuss the strike and make recommendations for a possible settlement. Two representatives each from the running trades, city council, Strike Committee, and Citizens' Committee were appointed, with Gray acting as chairman. The committee did not arrive at a solution because A. J. Andrews insisted that all public utilities be restored before discussion of the initial grievances began, while James Winning maintained that the strike would be called off only after the workers were given a guarantee of collective bargaining. The Citizens' Committee was arguing, essentially, that the strike ought to end before the issues that caused it could be solved, whereas the strikers declared that the issues must be solved before the strike would end.

Any effectiveness the city government might have had as an agent of mediation was undercut by its position as an employer of workers who had joined the sympathetic walkout. At its May 20 meeting, for example, the council voted for an increase in water pressure, and those men who had been left on emergency staff by the Strike Committee promptly walked out. The issue of the right of civic employees to join the strike was raised at a council meeting on the night of May 26. Gray, now openly impatient, told reporters just before the meeting that he had tried to stay neutral as long as there was any chance of a settlement, but now realized this was hopeless. The city council was determined to end its troubles with labour once and for all. Over the repeated objections of the labour aldermen, resolutions were passed ordering the members of the fire brigade to disavow membership in any union that participated in general strikes, promise to submit all disputes and wage questions to arbitration before resorting to strikes, and prohibiting them from joining in sympathetic walkouts. The council did pass a motion calling on the provincial government to make collective bargaining compulsory but also to declare sympathetic strikes illegal. Finally they called upon the managers of all civic departments to publish a list of striking employees and authorized them to hire new workers if the strikers did not return by Thursday, May 29. All returning employees and all new personnel would now be required to sign an oath of loyalty to the city council and promise never to participate in a sympathetic strike.[65] The Civic Federation reacted to this threat by deciding to continue the walkout; by the deadline only thirty-three employees had returned to work.

By these actions the city council effectively removed itself as a possible strike mediator. Gray's statement of May 26 and the resolutions passed by the city council were directly in line with the approach being taken by the provincial and federal governments. The line was also, not coincidentally, the same as that laid down by the Citizens' Committee of 1,000. This time, the committee and the city council appeared to be telling the unions, labour had gone too far and was not playing the game by the rules any more. Labour had expected to inflict a crushing, decisive and, more important, quick defeat on the employers but the contract shop owners had found themselves powerful allies. By the end of the second week of the strike there was no early victory in sight and thus, in the midst of one of the worst heat waves in years, the city settled down to wait. But for what?

For most people life continued somehow. Burley Wallis, an apprentice employed by Vulcan Iron Works, sent home a few days after the initial walkout on May 2, was hard pressed to fill his idle hours. Sometimes he would go over to the nearest schoolyard to play baseball, or spend time tending his father's garden, but for the most part he had little to do. Others derived what entertainment they could at the movie theatres, opened with the permission of the Strike Committee, or at the almost daily open air meetings held at Victoria Park. Here they received the latest information about the strike or the state of negotiations and were continuously enjoined to keep calm and stay out of trouble. On warm sunny days or in the spring evening air they heard Russell's fiery speeches or Dixon's methodical but passionate presentations. Many simply wanted to enjoy the outside air and the contact with their fellow strikers.

This desire to keep up with the latest developments and to meet and talk with their friends proved a boon to Ivens' Labor Church which moved outside, to Victoria Park, to minister to its suddenly swollen following. On Sunday afternoons throughout the strike Ivens led services, mixing labour-oriented hymns and sermons with speeches from strike leaders or supporters such as J. S. Woodsworth, who arrived in the city on June 8 after a speaking tour of the west. Crowds sometimes numbered up to ten thousand and the proceeds of collections were used to further the strikers' cause. The silence of most traditional religious leaders and the open hostility of others left workers with little choice but to embrace Ivens' church, and they made it an integral part of their strike-bound lives. It became the workers' forum.

In the meantime there was practical work to be done on both sides. The Women's Labor League ran a meal service, first in the Strathcona Hotel, then Oxford Hall, where men and women strikers were fed and those in need were provided with the price of a room. Men were expected to pay if they were able, but the bulk of the funds were raised through the Strike Committee or at Victoria Park meetings and over 1,200 free meals were distributed daily. At the Board of Trade building, cars stood ready in the street waiting for the latest messages or errands from the offices of the Citizens' Committee inside, while on James Street the various committees and sub-committees responsible for the smooth maintenance of the strike were in almost daily session. In a desperate hope for outside intervention to end the walkout, a group of citizens met daily in the Board of Trade building to pray for a settlement which would be "to the glory of God and the welfare of man."[66]

10. ❖ Impasse: May 30-June 16

Veterans of the Canadian Expeditionary Force played an increasingly important role in the economic and political life of Winnipeg in the months preceding the general strike and continued, in the two weeks following May 15, to participate as individuals, without particular identification with the strikers or their opponents. The Citizens' Committee and the General Strike Committee recognized the vital importance of veteran support to their cause, however, and worked hard during the first days of the strike to get the returned men to stand up and be counted. It appears that the strikers were, on the whole, more successful. The first effort to swing the veterans behind the strike was made May 15 at a meeting called by the executives of the Great War Veterans. They planned a show of support for their officially adopted position of neutrality and attempted to have those present approve a resolution to that effect. Their efforts were thwarted, however, by the passage of a motion supporting the aims of the strike and expressing solidarity with the strikers, drafted in part by R. A. Rigg.[1] One official claimed that the hall had been packed and thus did not register the real feelings of all the veterans.[2]

The Strike Committee tried from the first to split the neutral executive of the GWVA away from those veterans who held pro-strike feelings, but shied away from any obvious interference in the affairs of the association. At one point the strikers published a letter purportedly from two GWVA members urging all pro-strike veterans to attend the next association meeting in an attempt to dump the executive who were "working against the will of the membership."

The next day they were forced to print an apology and denied any intention of interfering in the internal affairs of the GWVA. The strikers offered the association three seats on the Strike Committee and at a special association meeting told the veterans that the Citizens' Committee's claims that a soviet was being established were nonsense. This meeting was not as pro-strike as the earlier one, but resolutions were still passed favouring collective bargaining and advocating that it be made illegal for an employer to refuse to recognize unions. The Army and Navy Veterans and the Imperial Veterans, however, remained staunchly neutral and refused to send delegates to the Strike Committee.

It was evident that the official organizations would be difficult, if not impossible, to rally behind the strike without obvious attempts to pack meetings or intimidate individual members. Their support, however, was not necessary. Most of the veterans were former workers and were themselves affected by the same conditions which had brought on the strike. They were ready to lend their support and only needed the proper catalyst. This was provided by Roger Bray, a former Methodist lay preacher and socialist who had joined the army in 1916 because he had no work, and A. E. Moore, former CEF sergeant who was now president of the Manitoba Command of the Great War Veterans' Association, and member of Premier Norris's Alien Investigation Board. At a three-hour meeting Thursday night, May 29, these two men, together with a group of veterans sympathetic to the strike, decided it was time to take a hand in events. They planned to gather other veterans sympathetic to the workers and parade to the provincial legislature to make their demands for government action known directly to the premier.[3] The next morning a large delegation of returned soldiers crowded into the legislative chambers of the provincial capital building to confront Premier Norris. The group demanded that the provincial government guarantee the right of collective bargaining and take steps to protect the union affiliation of city policemen. They vowed to return the next morning to hear Norris's answer.

From the beginning of the walkout, the Strike Committee had urged its followers to keep calm and refrain from mass activities—they had in most instances refused to sanction peaceful picketing for fear that such demonstrations were likely to bring the militia into the streets. Now their wishes were being ignored by returned soldiers who sympathized with them but wanted to make their desires known in a loud and boisterous manner. On Saturday morning thousands of veterans followed the flag in a march through drizzling rain to the legislative buildings. Several hundred swarmed into the legislative chamber while the rest stood outside waiting for their leaders to emerge. Bray and Moore, heading the delegation, repeated their demands of the previous day and added a request that Norris withdraw his ultimatum to the telephone employees. Cheers punctuated their words as they advocated fair treatment of the city's police force (at that point under pressure to sign a loyalty oath) and demanded that they be kept on duty. Norris, continuously interrupted by jeers and catcalls, told them immediate legislation on the question of collective bargaining was impossible, and that the strike must end before his government would take action. If the veterans could get the Trades Council to nominate two men to sit on his Industrial Disputes Commission, he continued, the strike might be ended by mediation. When he finished, shouts of "resign" filled the chamber and several veterans heatedly challenged his words. Then, at Norris's suggestion, the soldiers decided to go to city hall, meet Mayor Gray personally, and present their demands to him.

The delegation moved out of the building into the now steady downpour and began to march north. In the city council chamber, Alderman John Queen had just finished attacking Gray for his opposition to the strike when shouts were heard in the halls outside. Suddenly the doors burst open, and a man with a flag marched in and stopped in front of Gray. Others crowded in behind, flowing into every corner of the chamber. Gray attempted to shout above the commotion that there were too many men in the room, but no one left until Queen suggested that everyone move outside. The soldiers then pushed to the steps in front of city hall while the mayor spoke to them. He told the group, amidst constant jeers and interruptions, that there must be no more strikes on public utilities; but the soldiers, obviously dissatisfied, promised they would parade again Monday and every day until their demands were met.[4] All three veterans organizations issued condemnations of the Saturday demonstration, but differences of opinion between the ranks and the executive continued to split the GWVA. At a meeting on Tuesday evening, June 3, two thousand veterans jammed the Manitoba Hall and passed, over the objections of their vice-president, a resolution supporting the strikers and instructing the executive to render all assistance to bring about an early settlement.[5]

Meanwhile, the parades continued. On Monday morning the pro-strike veterans again marched to the legislative building and engaged in heated argument with Premier Norris and several members of his cabinet. Before leaving they promised they would return the next day, and departed for St. Boniface where they insisted that the city council of that municipality withdraw an ultimatum to its employees. On the way they passed Citizens' Committee headquarters at the Industrial Bureau, where they booed and jeered and tore several banners off the front of the building. At the Winnipeg city hall, Gray refused to meet them and they proceeded to Victoria Park for more speeches before they dispersed.

The following morning they assembled at Market Square where Bray told them the opposition had set a trap for them and they would not be parading that day. Instead they proceeded to Victoria Park, marching along behind a flag and a drum and once there sent delegations to interview Gray, Norris, and the mayor of St. Boniface. For three hours they waited in the park, listening to speeches and singing songs; when the delegation finally returned telling them that the governments' positions had not changed, Bray promised that they would march again the next day. The parades were interspersed with meetings at Victoria Park at which the veterans were addressed by strike leaders and sympathizers. On Wednesday afternoon, James A. Duncan, secretary of the Seattle District Trades and Labor Council and a leading figure in the Seattle general strike, received a tumultuous welcome at the park.[6]

Duncan's presence posed the question of whether secret links existed between the February general strike in Seattle and the one then in progress in Winnipeg. Some strike opponents charged that his presence was definite proof that both tie-ups were the result of secret planning by revolutionary organizations, and that the failure of the Seattle strike had prompted a renewed experiment in Winnipeg. Although there were certain superficial similarities between the two events—both involved metal trades councils, both were run by large general strike committees with executive powers vested in smaller central committees of fifteen men, both sought to close down the regular daily press, and both used exemption cards or stickers—there was no connection. The Winnipeg general strike was an outgrowth of many factors. The general context of unrest in the immediate postwar period, with the Seattle strike as one of the more important events in North America, played its part in setting the stage. But Winnipeg labour leaders took very little note of events in Seattle during February; and if the *Western Labor News* can be taken as an accurate reflection of their concerns, the strike received only brief and fleeting mention. The only story on Seattle of any significance to appear was published in the *Western Labor News'* last regular issue before the Winnipeg general strike, and was actually a reprint of Duncan's speech to the San Francisco Labor Council repudiating charges made in that city by Mayor Ole Hanson a short time before.[7]

Some of the major figures leading the drive to establish the One Big Union thought at one point that Seattle might furnish fertile grounds for an OBU centre in the northwestern United States, and both Victor Midgley and William Pritchard of the Central Executive visited the city on at least one occasion. Pritchard and Midgley ran into trouble, however, because Duncan was proposing his own plan for a reorganization of the AFL and was supported by the *Seattle Union Record* in his fight to keep out the Canadian One Big Union.[8] On one of these trips in late April Midgley secured a book on the Seattle general strike and sent it to Russell.[9] It is probably safe to assume that the leaders of the Winnipeg Trades and Labor Council were familiar with the organizational forms and methods used by the Seattle strikers and conspicuously tried to avoid some of the more difficult problems facing the Seattle Committee, such as providing food for workers and their families in a totally strike-bound city.[10] They were, however, less sure of the causes of that strike and were certainly not influenced by it in their decisions of May 6 and 13. For one thing, the Seattle strike had been a failure and had put dangerous ammunition into the hands of trade union opponents. Then, too, Winnipeg workers were already enamoured with the idea of a general strike after their experiences in the spring and summer of 1918, and had discussed it as early as the spring of 1917 in connection with conscription. Further, Duncan was not in Winnipeg at the invitation of the strike committee and did not participate in the planning of the strike, although he may have offered advice on situations which were similar to those he had already experienced. He was instructed by the Seattle Central Labor Council to visit the city on his way from the coast to the AFL convention and once there was asked to speak at Victoria Park. The charge that Winnipeg was either a model or an extension of the Seattle general strike was thus simply another example of the growing tendency to believe that conspiratorial men were working in secret on an intercontinental scale to bring western society crashing down.

On the day of Duncan's speech a confrontation was narrowly averted when parades of pro-strike and anti-strike veterans nearly met at the legislature and city hall. Bray's followers, singing and cheering, had proceeded south from the park, crossed the Maryland Bridge over the Assiniboine River, paraded through the fashionable Crescentwood section, and then re-crossed to the north side of the river over the Osborne Street Bridge. At the parliament buildings and then again at city hall the two groups almost met before the pro-strike veterans returned to Victoria Park. The anti-strike group, carrying Union Jacks and banners denouncing revolution and "alien enemies," had decided to stage a parade of their own to show Norris and Gray that there was also a substantial degree of anti-strike feeling among the returned men.[11] If the two groups had met the outcome would undoubtedly have been a disaster.

The parade of the anti-strike veterans had been organized largely through the efforts of Frederick G. Thompson. Thompson was a native of Winnipeg and had begun to practise law in the city before his enlistment in the Winnipeg Grenadiers. In August 1918 he was wounded in action during the Amiens campaign and returned to Winnipeg to recuperate and to take up his practice shortly after the armistice. Thompson joined the Great War Veterans' Association and was elected to the executive of the Manitoba branch. When the strike began he proposed that the association send a delegate to the Citizens' Committee and was chosen for the job. He was a rather hard-nosed individual who was greatly disturbed by the rise of labour radicalism and the prospects of revolution. In order to rally support against the strike he organized a meeting of anti-strike veterans for the morning of June 4 in a vacant lot on the corner of Main and Broadway. Thompson told the gathering that something must be done to aid those in authority to re-establish law and order and end the strike. He was, he said, not judging the event itself, but was opposed to extremist agitators and alien enemies. At the conclusion of the meeting, it was decided to march to meet the premier and Mayor Gray. From the vacant lot the group paraded to the legislative buildings, where Norris spoke, then to city hall, where Gray told them he was glad to see them because their presence testified to the fact that there would not be many "reds or anarchists" left in his city within a short time.[12] After the parade, the marchers decided to meet again on Friday, June 6, at the Auditorium Rink, where they founded the Returned Soldier's Loyalist Association.

Thursday, June 5, witnessed the most impressive display yet by the pro-strike veterans when they assembled in the morning at Victoria Park to hear addresses by James Winning and Bob Russell. Thousands of men then paraded to the tune of pipes and drums as they proceeded south along Main Street to Portage Avenue, then swung west for eight blocks to Kennedy and south to Broadway. From there they marched east to Main and north to the city hall and Victoria Park. It was a colourful procession led by a slowly moving car with a man on the hood waving a large Canadian flag. Inside the car sat soldiers with blue armlets and behind it were three pipers and two drummers. The men marched in separate lines in parade formation and carried banners reading "We stand for 35,000 against 1000," "Britons shall never be slaves," and "Deport all undesirables."[13]

Again a clash between pro- and anti-strike veterans was narrowly averted and it seemed apparent to General Ketchen that these daily parades would have to be stopped if serious rioting was to be avoided. Thus he advised Mayor Gray to issue a public proclamation forbidding any further street demonstrations.[14] On Friday morning, June 6, a proclamation banning street parades appeared in the morning papers. But the pro-strike veterans meeting in Victoria Park gave no indication that they were about to bow to Gray's wishes and prepared to march as they had done all week, this time joined by a brass band from Transcona. The leaders of these men, unsure of their position, attempted to meet Gray to ask why he was outlawing public demonstrations and what the ban included; but when they were unsuccessful in locating him, it was suggested that perhaps orderly parades were legal after all. The procession began, the men marching up Rupert Street to Main and then south to city hall. They were met by a group of city police, led by Deputy Chief Newton, who persuaded them to return to Victoria Park and told them he would listen to their complaints and urge the mayor to allow the parades to continue. Thus ended the last veterans' parade until Saturday, June 21.

On Saturday morning, June 7, thousands of returned men crowded into Victoria Park to hear Gray's explanation for the ban on parades. There were essentially three questions the men wanted answered: would further parades be permitted? Would the city government end its attempts to split the police from the rest of organized labour? Why did the mayor not ask pro-strike veterans to join the unofficial corps of special police that was being formed? Gray demanded that there be no further parades and maintained that he could not answer for the actions of the Police Commission. He asked the men to send a delegation to the person in charge of the special police, Major Lyle, if they thought they could keep the peace in an unbiased manner. Keeping calm throughout his speech, he denounced the connection between the police, firemen, and Trades Council. When he finished, the men cheered him and resolved that they would no longer parade unless given official approval.

Just prior to this meeting Canon F. G. Scott, former first chaplain of the CEF's First Division in France, arrived in Winnipeg. He went to the strike-bound city to "see some of the thousands of friends" he had made in France and to attempt to discover what had caused such grave splits in the Great War Veterans' Association.[15] He took advantage of the almost daily meetings in Victoria Park to address the returned men and once shared the platform with General Ketchen. There he told the throng to loud cheers that there had been misunderstandings on both sides, but that the initial error had been the employers' refusal to recognize unions. He also tried to heal the split in the veterans' ranks at two meetings with five representatives of the Returned Soldiers' Loyalist Association and four delegates from the strikers.[16] One of the men who sat in on these meetings as a strikers' delegate had just arrived in Winnipeg, W. A. Pritchard of British Columbia. Pritchard was cast in the same rough mould as so many other western union leaders of the time. He had come to Canada from England in 1911 to settle in Vancouver and was soon caught up in the turmoil of British Columbia unionism and socialist politics. He was physically tough and mentally agile. Pritchard was a member of the Socialist Party of Canada and the Vancouver Trades and Labor Council and first came to know Russell and other Winnipeg radicals at the Western Labor Conference, where he had been elected to the Central Committee set up to organize the OBU.

Pritchard had been sent to Winnipeg as an observer by the Central Committee, and initially attended meetings of the Strike Committee and addressed a number of gatherings at Victoria Park. He was urged to attend Scott's meeting accompanied by Russell, Tipping and Alfred Scoble, president of the Street Railwaymen's Union. Here there was little dialogue. The leader of the Returned Soldier's Loyalist Association's delegation, F. G. Thompson, fired a series of questions at the strikers in an attempt to get them to admit connections with the One Big Union and to find out the names of those men on the Strike Committee who had been in Calgary the previous March. The strikers answered that they could not repudiate a connection with the OBU since there was none, and furnished the names of thirteen strike committee delegates who had attended the Western Labor Conference.[17] Nothing came of these meetings and Scott returned to the east soon afterwards. Although the reasons for his departure remain shrouded in mystery, he himself had little doubt that the government had arranged to have him recalled and had handled his case by "Prussian methods."[18]

The police had remained on duty after the general strike began at the specific request of the Strike Committee, but they warned they would not be partial to strikers breaking the law and would enforce order regardless of who conspired to disrupt it.[19] Even so, there was some question in the minds of government officials as to whom the police owed their loyalty and, more fundamentally, for whom they were in fact working. In any case, a force of police officers relatively sympathetic to the aims of the strike was not exactly the type of law and order the strikers' opponents were willing to live with. Ketchen, for example, was firmly convinced that the police, though remaining on duty were working "hand in hand with the strikers,"[20] and towards the end of the second week of the strike he and his allies set out to rectify that situation.

On Tuesday, May 27, the Winnipeg Police Commission called in two representatives of the policemen's union to find out if they intended to leave work should they be asked to do so by the Strike Committee. The representatives would not commit themselves and could not say for certain what their members would do if asked to join the strike, but after this meeting the Police Commission announced that they believed the police to be loyal and would remain so for the duration of the strike. Two days later they did a complete turnabout and asked each officer to sign a pledge of loyalty to the city and promise not to join any union affiliated with "outside" organizations. Notice was officially given to the members of the force on Thursday morning, May 29, that they must comply by 1:00 P.M. the next day or be dismissed.[21] The oath the officers were being asked to sign made them acknowledge the Police Commission as their supreme governing authority, pledge they would not join unions connected with outside councils or congresses, or participate in sympathetic strikes.

By 10:00 A.M. the next morning only three officers had signed the pledge, even though they had been addressed by Mayor Gray and Alderman Sparling, chairman of the Police Commission, at a meeting in the police court Thursday night. There they were told the strike was a Bolshevik attempt to overturn constituted authority and that they had violated their agreements with the city by taking the strike vote.[22] After Gray and Sparling had finished speaking, however, the men refused to take the oaths. They claimed they were not being given enough time to fully consider the ultimatum and that the Police

Commission was itself violating signed agreements by insisting on the pledge. The men also vowed to stand behind constituted authority and continue to uphold law and order.

The deadline passed with only twenty-five members having signed the oath. The city was clearly in a bind, because if it now dismissed the force en masse it would be doing what the Strike Committee itself had not dared to do, leaving an entire city without civil police protection. On the other hand, if the ultimatum remained ignored and unenforced, what authority could the city council's rulings carry in future?

Gray's immediate problems was solved by G. K. Wark, vice-president of the Brotherhood of Locomotive Firemen and Enginemen, and A. McAndrews, assistant general chairman of the CPR section of the Brotherhood of Maintenance of Way Employees. These two men offered their services as mediators and urged city council to extend the ultimatum an additional twenty-four hours to Saturday, May 31. Sparling complied and made the announcement. Late on the night of May 30, McAndrews and Wark met the members of the policemen's union and persuaded them to accept their services as mediators. The atmosphere in the city was now very tense, because many believed the police would react to the ultimatum by walking out. Senator Robertson postponed his return to Ottawa, at the urging of the Citizens' Committee and the provincial government, to see what the outcome of these negotiations would be.

The results of the Brotherhood officials' quiet efforts at diplomacy became known at a night meeting of the Police Commission held at city hall on Saturday, May 31. The members of the policemen's union agreed not to join the present sympathetic strike and promised they would remain at work even if extra men were added to the force.[23] This position was reiterated the following Tuesday, when union members told Sparling there was "absolutely no chance of a sympathetic strike taking place during the present crisis."[24] These assurances were not enough, however, because no promises and no pledges could wipe out the strike vote taken prior to May 15. In the eyes of civic authorities and the Citizens' Committee, the police remained sympathetic to the strike and that, in itself, would not do.

On May 29 General Ketchen had urged Gray to employ a force of special police before trying to put streetcars back into operation.[25] Six days later, at a meeting convened by Premier Norris attended by Gray, A. J. Andrews, and a representative of the RNWMP, he again put forward his suggestion. He urged the city to immediately engage special constables to supplement the regular police in protecting those businesses still in operation, and convinced those present that at least one thousand men ought to be employed as quickly as possible.[26] Almost immediately, fifty men were sworn in and placed on the streets alongside the regular police, ostensibly under the direct control of the Police Commission.

The move to employ special police as quickly as possible was given greater urgency by a Strike Committee decision to pull out those men who had been allowed to return to work soon after the beginning of the strike. On Thursday night, June 3, the strike leaders decided to put extra pressure on the Norris government because of its refusal to budge on the question of legalizing collective bargaining. They maintained that it was the government's business to feed and care for the people, not the strikers', and therefore they would no longer assume this responsibility.

The next day all deliveries of ice, bread, and milk ended once again. This time, however, the Citizens' Committee and the city were ready. Citizens' Committee volunteers with cars aided the municipal government in the establishment of a city-wide staples distribution system with depots set up in schools and, in a short time, were even able to restore partial house-to-house delivery.[27] There can be little doubt that Ketchen and the others present at the meeting of June 4 intended to use the temporary special police to protect the distribution system then being set up. In addition some members of the press were claiming that the regular police could not control the situation and provide the law and order to which the city was entitled. To counter the Strike Committee's claims that everything was quite peaceful, the *Free Press* asserted that the courts would actually be overflowing if the police were doing a truly effective job.[28]

The campaign to recruit a force of auxiliary police began in earnest on June 5, when the city decided to aim for an initial enrolment of two thousand men and pay each of them $6 per day. Mayor Gray personally chose the man who would lead the new force, and the decision was also made to add a mounted detachment. Major Hillyard Lyle was put in charge of the operation while Captain J. Dunwoody was responsible for the mounted men. Lyle was to be the senior of the two and make decisions in consultation with Mayor Gray and Alderman Sparling.

Ketchen took a hand with the organization right from the start and urged veterans to sign on at the first meeting of the Returned Soldiers' Loyalist Association in the Auditorium Rink on June 6.[29]

The mayor also urged members of the association to join the force; both their efforts succeeded in attracting approximately three hundred volunteers who proceeded directly to city hall where they were sworn in.[30] Not all of the men who joined were hard-core anti-strikers. Some, such as Graham Spry, were not fully aware of the close connection between this new force and the Loyalist Association and signed up simply because they believed they should contribute their share towards the maintenance of law and order. Spry, a returned soldier attending classes at the University of Manitoba, joined when word was circulated that "specials" were being signed up at $6 per day.[31] By the end of the third week of the strike Winnipeg had, in effect, two police forces and it was quite clear to certain high officials that there was only room for one.

On Thursday, June 5, an incident occurred which cast a shadow over the impartiality and competence of the regular police. It was a comedy of errors, but it helped provide a background for the dismissal of most of the official force. On that afternoon, city police emerged from the Royal Alexandra Hotel with a man they had just arrested for possession of a revolver. This man, unknown to the police, was a special agent of Senator Robertson and fully authorized to carry a gun. When Mayor Gray found out about the arrest he sped to the scene by car and attempted to have the man released. In the midst of the argument a surly crowd of strikers surrounded the mayor and began to jostle him. Then, according to the *Western Labor News,* a policeman put his arms around the mayor to protect him and was told to take his hands off. The *Winnipeg Citizen* claimed that the mayor had been assaulted by a crowd of strikers as two members of the city police force stood and watched.[32]

The following weekend the Police Commission, emboldened by its new force of specials, exhumed its ultimatum to the regular officers and demanded they sign the original oaths by Monday, June 9, or face dismissal. The Police Commission threw away the compromise suggestions of Wark and McAndrews and ordered the police to withdraw their original strike notice, pledge never to join any sympathetic strikes, and pull their delegates out of the General Strike Committee.[33] One member of the commission, Alderman Wiginton, counselled moderation and suggested that the ultimatum be withdrawn until after the strike was over, but his pleas were ignored. This time there was no need for the city or the Citizens' Committee to worry about dismissing the regular police; A. J. Andrews did not much care whether they remained at work or not. Whatever they did now, he wrote Meighen, would not really affect the situation.[34] He was correct insofar as the Citizens' Committee and the government were concerned, but the dismissal of the regular force would have a very great affect on the fortunes of the strikers. It would replace a sympathetic or neutral civil authority with one that was, without pretence, hostile. Consequently, on Monday afternoon, June 9, the Police Commission fired those 240 members of the regular city police who had refused to sign the loyalty oaths.

The next day approximately 1,800 special police, under the command of Deputy Chief Newton, took to the streets to enforce law and order in Winnipeg; at the same time the regular head of the police force, Chief Macpherson was given an enforced three months' leave of absence by the Police Commission and Newton became Acting Chief. The specials, mounted and on foot, had been preparing for their task for days and were thought to be fully ready to assume responsibility for the protection of the city. In fact, the very first day they were on duty the worst incident of violence thus far took place, and they were right in the middle.

The mounted specials were organized under the command of Captain J. Dunwoody, formerly of the Fort Garry Horse. Dunwoody believed such a force would be of great value should trouble break out, because mounted men would be effective in riot control and could cover more territory. When he found out about the organization of the special police he approached Gray with a suggestion to put together a mounted unit manned by veterans of the Fort Garry Horse, Strathcona Horse, and Royal Canadian Horse Artillery. Gray accepted and Dunwoody set about contacting the necessary personnel and approaching various businesses in the city, including Eatons and the dairy companies, to secure the necessary horses. About three or four days after the group was formed, Dunwoody was told by Acting Chief Newton that he could begin regular mounted patrols.

On the afternoon of Tuesday, June 10, the mounted specials rode down Main Street to a point near the junction with Portage where a crowd had gathered to hear a man speaking from a parked car. The specials, armed with clubs, attempted to disperse this group and rode up on the sidewalk. As they began to walk horses slowly into the crowd, swinging their batons where necessary to force the group to disperse, one of their number was thrown from his horse and badly beaten. Sergeant Major F. G. Coppins, V.C., was guiding his mount slowly along the sidewalk when someone cupped his hands under Coppins's stirrup and heaved upward, unseating him. As this happened several men grabbed Coppins, helped pull him off the horse, and began to beat him. The special, already injured, jumped to his feet swinging his club but had to be rescued from the crowd by fellow officers,[35] who then took him suffering from severe bruises to Tuxedo Military Hospital.

This first attempt at crowd control was a complete failure. Ketchen criticized Dunwoody in a report to Ottawa and asserted that the mounted men had been thrown into the fray without any plan of action and could have handled the crowd tactfully in the first place.[36] The following day the mayor issued his second proclamation against public demonstrations in the city streets, and warned that he would resort to whatever measures were necessary to maintain the peace. That afternoon a delegation of pro-strike veterans exacted a promise from Major Lyle that the mounted specials would be withdrawn and that foot patrols would be issued regulation billies instead of the large clubs they were carrying.[37]

The specials, nevertheless, were not trained policemen, and continued to show their incompetence in a Keystone Cops—style shooting incident. A patrolling constable was jostled at the corner of Main and Higgins, just south of the CPR subway, and after a short argument hit the offender with his baton. Almost immediately a crowd gathered and a great deal of jostling and shoving began. Within minutes a car pulled up carrying two specials, one of which fired a shot into the crowd which ricochetted and hit his colleague in the leg. Several men in the crowd tried to help the wounded man into the car and force the gun-toting auxiliary to show his authority to carry a weapon, but were not successful.[38]

While the police crisis deepened, the general strike was having far-reaching effects upon organized labour across Canada. Other strikes, called to support the campaign in Winnipeg, broke out in Calgary, Lethbridge, Edmonton, Regina, Saskatoon, Prince Albert, Brandon, Fort William, Port Arthur, and Toronto. Most of these were limited in scope and did not last very long. At one point it was feared that Toronto might be completely paralysed, but the decision of the street railwaymen's union to keep working defused the situation. The most serious of these echoes of the Winnipeg crisis was the general strike which broke out in Vancouver.

On May 22 the Vancouver Trades Council voted to call a general sympathetic strike should the federal government use military force to break the walkout in Winnipeg. Jack Kavanagh warned Prime Minister Borden five days later that action would be taken if the government did not end its "opposition to collective bargaining through joint councils" and call back its ultimatum to Winnipeg's striking postal workers.[39] Shortly afterwards the Trades Council issued five demands to be fulfilled if a general strike on the coast was to be avoided, including the reinstatement of the Winnipeg postal workers, a guarantee of collective bargaining rights, and the six-hour day in all industries suffering from unemployment. At the same time arrangements were made for a strike vote to be completed by Sunday, June 1, and a deadline was set for June 3. In Vancouver the vote in favour of strike action was not as one-sided as it had been in Winnipeg, 3,305 workers voting in favour and 2,499 against.

Almost ten thousand workers walked off their jobs on Tuesday, June 3, and the strike soon settled into the type of pattern already established in Winnipeg. In Vancouver, however, the strikers were much more lenient in allowing essential services to continue, while a group of people opposed to the strike set up a Citizens' League, patterning themselves after the Winnipeg Citizens' Committee. The strike in Vancouver lasted longer than the one in Winnipeg, but was not nearly as effective.[40]

In the midst of these events, the Central Committee set up at the Calgary Western Labor Conference under the direction of Victor Midgley prepared to hold the founding convention of the OBU. The voting which had been initiated at the Western Labor Conference was now completed for most points west of Port Arthur with 258 locals reporting results: 24,239 union members favoured formation of the new union, 5,975 objected, and a further 11,151 declined to vote. Winnipeg workers had been too involved in the events of the strike to cast ballots and had, therefore, not officially decided whether to secede or not.[41] Midgley nevertheless urged the Winnipeg strikers to send delegates to the forthcoming convention in Calgary, especially in view of the strikes which were then taking place or about to take place throughout the west.[42] Ernie Robinson, however, told Midgley a scant four days before the meeting that it would be impossible to send any delegates until the general strike was over, and urged him to cancel the convention because he did not want to "fizzle it."[43] Midgley would not entertain any idea of cancelling the convention; he reminded Robinson that other Trades Councils would be fully represented and told him that Winnipeg could surely spare three delegates from its ranks. They could not, however, and the founding convention of the OBU took place without the presence of a single Winnipeg delegate.[44] A RNWMP undercover agent who attended the Calgary convention asserted that the delegates were unsure of themselves because of the apparent weakening of the sympathetic strike movement and, in his opinion, "A firm and consistent attitude, coupled with an announcement of the government's policy," would probably nip the movement in the bud.[45]

Even though the federal government was indeed preparing to take strong action to end the strike, they first put their faith in one last attempt by outside parties to bring about a negotiated settlement through mediation. In the last few days of May, H. E. Barker, chairman of the Train Service Employees Committee and representing six railway brotherhoods, approached Norris, Gray, the employers, and the strikers with an offer to mediate the dispute. Both the employers and the strikers accepted and the mediation committee began its efforts to work out a settlement. On Wednesday, June 4, after considering the positions of both sides, the mediation committee drafted a memo containing what it believed to be a fair solution to the impasse. The committee agreed with the strikers on most disputed points and approved their desire to bargain through a metal trades council. The draft agreement stipulated:

> The members of the various Trades Organizations employed in the Metal Trades Shops, shall have the right, through the Metal Trades Council, to present and negotiate schedules covering wages, hours and working conditions, with individual employers, or collectively with the employers of the Metal Trades.[46]

This proposal was accepted by the strikers and rejected by the metal trades employers.

There was no reason why the mediation committee should see anything strange about several unions bargaining through a single council. Although they themselves were members of the highly individualistic running trades, they must have been well aware of the formation of Division 4 in 1918, and obviously believed that the Winnipeg Metal Trades Council was asking for the same type of bargaining. The General Adjustment Committee of the Brotherhood of Locomotive Engineers, represented on the mediation committee by assistant grand chief, Ash Kennedy, adopted a resolution in early June endorsing the strikers' demands for the same type of "committee representation" enjoyed by railway employees. In addition, the executive of Division 4 expressed amazement that so much trouble could develop over an attempt to institute a type of collective bargaining which they had been enjoying for over a year. Thus on June

7, after receiving a rejection of this proposed settlement, Barker wrote the metal trades employers that he was not surprised that a strike had occurred because his committee also believed that proper recognition of collective bargaining "would carry with it recognition of the Metal Trades Council."[47]

The contract shop employers' official reply to the mediation committee demanded that the sympathetic strike be called off before any further negotiations were conducted. It also contained a draft proposal devoid of any mention of the recognition of either individual craft unions or the Metal Trades Council. The following morning Barker announced to the public that the employers had refused to accept the compromise offered to them by the mediators and would not recognize the Metal Trades Council even if the sympathetic strike were called off.[48]

On Friday, June 6, General Ketchen sent a rather cryptic message to Ottawa, relaying the information that the running trades mediation board claimed they were close to a settlement. The matter had not been finally disposed of, Ketchen warned, but the whole thing looked like a "frame up."[49] Three days later Meighen received a note from A. J. Andrews, who had received word that Senator Robertson was about to come to Winnipeg for the second time and was elated because he greatly feared that the running trades mediators were about to issue a final report condemning the metal trades employers. He told Meighen that Robertson could persuade the mediators to support the contract shops or, at the least, dissuade them from issuing any report at all. In the meantime, he told Meighen, the employers were stalling for time.[50] Andrews, however, misread Robertson's intentions, because the minister apparently had no initial desire to rig the proceedings.[51]

Robertson arrived in Winnipeg late Tuesday night, June 10, and in the early hours of June 11 conferred with the Citizens' Committee, the running trades mediators, and representatives of the provincial government. He believed the situation was now more serious than it had been at any time since the strike started, and was aware that the Strike Committee was bending every effort to widen the dispute. During his first visit to the city in May he had expressed fears that train service would eventually be curtailed if the strike lasted long enough; now he was no doubt aware that the Strike Committee was trying to get members of the running trades to join the walkout. Any spread of the strike to the running trades unions would, in Robertson's words, be "a matter of national importance,"[52] because Canada's key rail junction, repair depot and marshalling yard system, and the heart of the transcontinental railroad network would be closed to all rail traffic.

On Wednesday evening, June 11, Robertson began his efforts to convince the mediation committee to come up with some sort of a solution. He met Barker and convinced him to issue a public statement announcing that mediation efforts would continue, in spite of the prior announcement to the press that a deadlock had been reached.[53] Robertson was working against a background of growing tension and dissatisfaction amongst the running trades. That night he spoke not only to Barker but to a meeting of running trades union members at which four delegates from the Strike Committee urged the men to join the sympathetic strike.

On Thursday Robertson attended a joint conference between the mediation committee and the employers and said he would like to bring about a settlement without his influence appearing. That very day the majority of switchmen in the CNR yards in and around the city walked off their jobs. At noon the next day two locals of the Brotherhood of Locomotive Firemen and Enginemen presented an ultimatum to city council threatening that they, too, would walk out at 6:00 P.M. if the regular police and other civic employees were not reinstated. In addition, they demanded the right to collective bargaining and what they called a living wage. Mayor Gray tried to convince them that the police were fools who had been misled by agitators, and Alderman Fowler told them the strikers would not be reinstated. That evening the firemen, along with members of the Brotherhood of Railroad Trainmen, joined the strike against orders of their international officers. Robertson reported to Ottawa that the situation was rapidly deteriorating and that Canadian Pacific and the other railways were having difficulty getting crews together to man passenger trains.[54]

On Saturday, June 14, the *Western Labor News* announced that Canadian Pacific trainmen were conducting a strike vote and that Grand Trunk Pacific trainmen and firemen were expected to join the walkout within hours. Robertson reported to Ottawa that no yard service was being performed on the Canadian National system and that services at Union Station were being kept going only by the efforts of management officials. Canadian Pacific was faring somewhat better, he reported, but neither railway was able to maintain adequate passenger service and there was every chance the situation could get worse. He confirmed that firemen, switchmen, and trainmen were leaving work in increasing numbers and added ominously that some locomotive engineers were also joining the strike, "professedly in sympathy with the cause of the Metal Trades."[55] On Sunday evening at 6 o'clock, the situation was further complicated by the strike of switchmen and trainmen on the Canadian Pacific system; at the same time further meetings were being held at other western points in an effort to get all the running trades to join the spreading strike.[56]

While railway service was in the process of falling apart, Robertson worked frantically throughout the weekend to force the contract shop employers to agree to a limited form of collective bargaining. On Saturday he met Barker's committee together with the managers of the Canadian Pacific, Canadian National and Grand Trunk Pacific railways. Robertson was in no mood to delay—he believed the adoption by the employers of a policy of union recognition would remove the justification for the sympathetic walkout of the railway employees. After talking to the managers of the railroads and the members of the mediation committee, the contract shop employers were asked to the meeting and Robertson dropped his bombshell. He demanded that they approve collective bargaining by individual unions without equivocation[57] and gave them twenty-four hours to accept his proposals. The next evening, the employers consented and promised to recognize craft unions and bargain collectively with them.[58]

The following morning the *Free Press* hit the streets with a front-page statement signed by the metal trades employers containing their acceptance of Robertson's terms. There was, however, not a single word about the Metal Trades Council and not a hint that anything other than traditional craft unions would be dealt with. The employers were indeed conceding the right of collective bargaining, but only as Robertson and the government conceived of it. This statement was accompanied by affidavits signed, in turn, by Robertson, the three managers of the railways, and the mediation committee. Robertson and the managers maintained that the employers' offer was a full recognition of collective bargaining as practised on Canada's railroads. The mediation committee agreed:

> The undersigned representatives of the train service organizations, being familiar with collective bargaining as practised by the organizations we represent, endorse the policy of collective bargaining as outlined by the metal trades employers . . . being in principle and effect the same as that enjoyed by these organizations.[59]

The same as the running trades, perhaps, but certainly not the same as the shop crafts unions. This statement was designed to have a direct effect on the strikers, especially those members of the running trades who were in the process of joining the spreading walkout. The declaration published on June 16 did not tally with Barker's letter of June 7, with the position of the General Adjustment Committee of the Brotherhood of Locomotive Engineers, or with the statements of the executive of Division 4. The collective bargaining arrangements outlined in the June 16 statement only partially coincided with the practices of Canadian railway unions. What accounted for the change in position?

The six members of the mediation committee, all leaders of craft unions, had much to fear from the rising popularity of the One Big Union. They were, to say the least, worried about the spreading sympathetic strike movement that appeared to be luring away so many running trades union members. In early June, for example, two of the members of the mediation committee, Ash Kennedy and G. K. Wark, declared against sympathetic strikes and warned their followers not to join any walkouts which had not been sanctioned by the international offices.[60] Wark was, in the words of Timothy Shea, president of the Brotherhood of Locomotive Firemen, in Winnipeg "looking after the interests" of his union, and one of these interests was to prevent members from joining what Shea called "an illegal strike."[61] James Murdock, vice-president of the Brotherhood of Railroad Trainmen, had been specifically asked to join the mediation proceedings by the minister of labour. Robertson had anticipated trouble amongst the railroad employees before he left Ottawa; so he had got in touch with Murdock in Toronto to ask him to join his train at North Bay and go with him to Winnipeg.[62] Robertson himself, of course, came from the ranks of the railroad telegraphers and probably had little trouble convincing these men, whom he undoubtedly knew well, that their approval of a limited form of collective bargaining might damage the OBU beyond repair. In fact, when firemen and trainmen walked out on Friday evening, several members of the mediation committee told him that this strike "emanated from the Red element" and asked the government to "remove this menace and prevent further injury."[63]

There was another, more tangible, ground for the growing panic among craft union leaders. In the early days of the strike Winnipeg members of the Brotherhood of Railway Carmen of America seceded from their parent union and formed an autonomous Carmen's Council. Several international organizers arrived in Winnipeg to attempt to end the secession, but their efforts were successfully resisted by the strikers. C. P. Cooper, secretary-treasurer of the renegade council, published a notice in the *Western Labor News* that his organization had been officially recognized by the Winnipeg Trades and Labor Council. If the carmen's organization in Winnipeg was falling apart and if union members were willing to defy the orders of their international officers and join the sympathetic strike, how long might it be before the entire craft union structure came tumbling down? And who but the One Big Union would give it the final push? These thoughts must have run through the heads of the members of the mediation committee and were given added stimulus by Robertson, who believed all along that the OBU was behind the strike and was able to pressure the already wavering committee to help him out. In addition, the prime minister had authorized him to use drastic measures "as a last resort" to keep the trains running[64] should mediation fail. These measures were never made public but they must have had a powerful effect on the swaying committee.

The *Western Labor News* of Tuesday, June 17, issued a warning to its readers that rumours of a settlement in the metal trades were not true and that the employers' latest offer was not satisfactory. Later they claimed that as of Friday, June 20, they never received an official copy of Monday's declaration. It would have been almost impossible for Robertson to have submitted the proposals to the Strike Committee between the time the employers signed them Sunday night and the time they were published Monday morning. This was, to say the least, a strange way to submit a proposal. Robertson, however, had no intention of discussing the statement, since he planned to place the declaration of June 16 before the strikers on a take-it or leave-it basis; when they decided not to take it he told Borden that it was clearer than ever that the OBU was the real issue in the dispute. Since this was the case, he believed, there was little more the government could do but take direct action while "the strikers were divided among themselves as to the advisability of returning to work."[65] Thus, in the early morning hours of Tuesday, June 17, less than twenty-four hours after the publication of the Robertson proposals, the government moved to arrest several of the more radical strike leaders.

11. ❖ Defeat

The decision to imprison the strike leaders was not made without a good deal of planning and was timed to coincide with the climax of the mediation proceedings. As early as May 26, General Ketchen told his superiors in Ottawa that he thought the bottom could be knocked out of the strike by taking the leadership into custody.[1] A. J. Andrews agreed with him, and was particularly angered at the apparent impotence of federal immigration laws when James Duncan arrived in the city. He tried to get immigration authorities to stop Duncan, but was told they could do nothing under existing law.

Andrews was not able to get immediate satisfaction but the federal government was working to arm itself with new legislation as quickly as possible. On June 6 they introduced an "Act to Amend the Immigration Act," which was one of the least debated and most hurriedly passed pieces of legislation in the history of Canada. In a mere forty-five minutes this bill was given three readings in the House, three readings in the Senate, and the approval of the governor general. The legislation amended an immigration bill that had already been given final approval of both Houses and gave the government the added power to deport any person who "by word or act" sought the violent overthrow of constituted authority in Canada. This meant, in essence, that any person deemed to be a revolutionary who was born outside of Canada, whether a British subject or naturalized Canadian, could now be summarily shipped back to the land of his birth.

The federal government actually consulted the executive of the

Trades and Labor Congress before introducing the new amendment into the Commons. P. M. Draper told Senator Robertson that he thought the move was "positively in the best interest of organized labour as well as the State itself."[2] After the change was put into force, congress president Tom Moore asked for and received assurances that it would not be used to interfere with the normal activities of international officers entering Canada on union business.[3]

Senator Robertson began to make contingency plans for the arrests almost as soon as he arrived in Winnipeg on the night of June 10. After consulting with General Ketchen, he decided his only possible course, if arrests and immediate deportation were to be carried out, was to use the provisions of the new Immigration Act amendment.[4] Borden placed Robertson in complete charge of the operation with A. J. Andrews, who was doing the actual planning aided by Immigration Department officials, under his direction. Robertson, senior government official on the spot, was the final authority and completely responsible for the decision of whether or not to proceed with the arrests.[5]

In the days after Robertson's arrival and while the mediation proceedings were being pushed to a conclusion, plans were laid for the arrests. Robertson's initial impulse was to seize the radical strike leaders, place them aboard trains bound for internment camps at Kapuskasing, and then have boards of inquiry deal with them.[6] This idea was soon abandoned, probably at Andrews's instigation, in favour of a policy designed to make a better impact on public opinion. By Monday, June 16, all was ready. When the Strike Committee rejected the collective bargaining proposals published in the morning newspapers, Robertson put the carefully laid plans into operation.

Tuesday, June 17, was barely two hours old when eight automobiles sped through the darkened streets of Winnipeg's north end. Each car carried three men armed with search and arrest warrants, and all were on their way to visit the houses of specified strikers. Soon sleepy men were being rousted out of bed and taken to the nearest police station in preparation for the drive to Stony Mountain Federal Penitentiary. On Burrows Avenue, Alderman Abraham A. Heaps was arrested on the spot when he opened his door to two government officials. His friend and colleague, Alderman John Queen, staying with the Heaps family while his own wife and children spent a short vacation at Winnipeg Beach, was also arrested.

Heaps, Queen, and the other prisoners were taken briefly to the north end police station, where a battery of government legal advisors took care of the immediate technicalities before sending the arrested men directly to prison. Warden W. R. Graham was not used to receiving men who had not been convicted of any crime, but put the delivered prisoners directly into confinement at the explicit orders of Senator Robertson and A. J. Andrews.[7] While Heaps, Queen, Armstrong, Russell, Ivens, and Bray were being incarcerated with a token handful of "alien enemies," government agents carried out a thorough search for evidence of sedition and revolution as the Labor Temple was broken into, office doors were smashed, files scattered about, and desks thrown over in the quest. The offices of the *Western Labor News* and the Ukrainian Labor Temple were also visited.

The arrests were carried out under the auspices of the new Immigration Act amendments as Robertson had planned it, but what he failed to realize was that the action should first have been approved by the minister of immigration, J. A. Calder. Calder was not informed of the arrests, though he was aware that they were being planned, until mid-afternoon on June 17. Thus, to make things legal, Calder sent his official authorization to "take into custody and detain for examination for purposes of deportation" all those persons who had been arrested the previous night![8] For this half-bungled and probably illegal operation Prime Minister Borden sent Robertson his "warmest congratulations."

The arrests stimulated immediate protest and indignation in pro-strike circles. Ketchen told Ottawa that the Strike Committee was thrown into confusion by the action, though he could not say whether or not the walkout would be prolonged. The pro-strike veterans held large protest meetings in Victoria Park on Tuesday and Wednesday nights to condemn Roger Bray's arrest and demand the release of the prisoners. Emotions ran high, causing one speaker to warn the men to calm down and keep their pledge not to take part in street parades. The Strike Committee also vigorously condemned the arrests and demanded the release of the prisoners as one more condition for a settlement.

The government now had its prisoners, but what was to be done with them? In the next few days many messages passed between Ottawa and Winnipeg as Robertson, Meighen, Andrews, and Ketchen debated the fate of the arrested men. Meighen doubted the legality of the arrests but wished to proceed with deportation anyway as rapidly as possible,[9] while Robertson warned that public opinion would not stand for the expulsion of British-born individuals.[10] Andrews also wanted the men out of the way quickly, but thought nothing ought to be done until the prisoners had been given a trial. In fact, he wanted to allow the men out on bail on condition that they take no further part in the conduct of the strike—a suggestion that raised Ketchen's ire. He told his superiors that bail would be received most unfavourably by the militia. By early Friday morning a decision had been reached. The six most prominent prisoners charged with seditious conspiracy were given their freedom on bail, in return for a pledge that they would stay out of the strike for its duration. A small convoy of friends and relatives, led by T. J. Murray and a group of bail bondsmen, drove to the prison in the pre-dawn hours to greet the prisoners, post bond, and take them back to Winnipeg. Andrews explained that the men were to be afforded the full protection of the law and would be given trials by jury before facing deportation. Five other men, all with non-Anglo-Saxon names, were not so fortunate and were forced to remain in custody.

At about the time Russell and his colleagues were being given their freedom, W. A. Pritchard was losing his. Pritchard had left Winnipeg bound for Vancouver before the arrests were carried out and did not learn of them until he reached Brandon. He was advised by a friend that a warrant had been issued in his name but decided to try to make his way to Vancouver before giving himself up. On Thursday evening, June 19, RNWMP officers boarded his train at Calgary, took him into custody, and lodged him in the city jail. Shortly afterwards he was sent back to Winnipeg to share the fate of the other men.

With one bold stroke the radicals among the strike leadership were cut off from the direction of strike policy. Those men considered the most dangerous and the most intransigent were isolated from their followers, at a time when many workers were beginning to waver in their determination to keep the strike alive. Moderate leaders, even those who had participated in the planning and direction of the strike to as great a degree as Russell, Ivens, and Bray, were not touched. J. L. McBride, Ernie Robertson and James Winning was deliberately passed over and left in control of events. The publication of the mediation committee's report on June 16 planted firm seeds of doubt in the minds of many strikers,[11] and the arrests were designed to silence the persuasive power of the radicals. Henceforth the lack of firm leadership in the Strike Committee became more evident because, dedicated as they may have been, the leaders now holding the reins of decision lacked the driving power of religious-like conviction.

The arrests of the radical strike leaders and the final report of the mediation committee coincided with the completion of a military buildup which had been going on, largely at the direction of General Ketchen, since the first days of the strike. Seven years after the event, Arthur Meighen told the House of Commons that "No troops whatever were ordered into Winnipeg . . . none went in and none had anything to do with the labour trouble."[12] This statement was technically correct because no units of the regular army were sent into the strike-bound city other than the 27th Battalion which was in the process of demobilizing. No regulars were used since there was no need for them. Ketchen and the RNWMP authorities built a force of Mounties and militia that was quite capable of dealing with almost anything. The federal government was trying, throughout the six weeks of the strike, to undermine wild stories such as those being published in the *New York Times,* and it would have defeated its own purposes by appearing to admit that the situation was so completely out of control as to require the presence of regular troops.

On May 15 there were only small numbers of infantry, mostly conscripts, and two troops of the Depot Squadron, Fort Garry Horse, in Winnipeg. They composed the usual local garrison, carried on with their regular duties irrespective of the strike, and were not demobilized until one or two months after the walkout was over. Shortly after the strike began these men were reinforced, when General Ketchen, at the request of Mayor Gray, began to call out the active militia. Gray feared disturbances might arise which the civic authorities would not be able to handle and asked Ketchen for military assistance. Ketchen planned to call up about five hundred men each day, have them spend a night in barracks brushing up their training, then send them home; in this way he hoped to amass a large force in a reasonably short time.[13]

Ketchen planned to build up the ranks of the militia with the active help of the Citizens' Committee and issued a call for volunteers through their auspices. In a short time he had several thousand men "from amongst the best business class in the City," and assigned officers from overseas service to each of the volunteer units.[14] Ketchen modified his plans with so many volunteers on his hands and began, instead, to call approximately three thousand men at a time into barracks for a period of ten days, after which they were allowed to go home. This enabled him to count upon six thousand men after every three weeks of the strike. In addition, special signals were arranged for summoning those men living at home on short notice, using a system of sirens and steam whistles on the "large Manufacturing

Concerns" and other buildings such as the *Manitoba Free Press* and the T. Eaton Company.

While Ketchen was busily engaged in building up the volunteer forces, Ottawa turned its attention to the returning 27th Battalion. Brigadier General Hill met them at Montreal early Saturday morning, May 24, to inform them of the situation in Winnipeg and told them that the government wished to maintain a certain force for the protection of the city. He tried to ascertain if some of the men might voluntarily remain on duty for the duration of the strike and took pains to point out that the government had no intention of using the troops as strikebreakers.[15]

Ketchen had requested Ottawa to forward a consignment of machine guns to Winnipeg, and secret arrangements were drawn up by which the weapons would be delivered via the 27th Battalion. An officer met General Hill at the Turcot Yards in Montreal on Saturday morning and delivered a small number of ordinary-looking packing crates marked "Regimental Baggage, 27th Battalion." The crates were placed on the unit's first train and were joined by other, similarly marked, boxes at Smith Falls, Ontario. These crates contained a total of twenty Lewis machine guns destined for Ketchen's command. The operation was carried out in complete secrecy because it was desired "that these guns reach Winnipeg without anyone being the wiser."[16] Ketchen took delivery of the weapons but saw little need for keeping the 27th active and ordered the unit demobilized the same day it arrived.

The Royal North West Mounted Police, involved in protection and intelligence work in Winnipeg from May 15 on, was also heavily reinforced during the strike. At first the RNWMP detachment in the city consisted of 8 non-commissioned officers and 19 men. But on May 16 they were joined by Inspector Mead and 20 additional men sent to Winnipeg under the express order of Commissioner Perry. Soon after, a further group of 172 men and one officer, who had served in Europe, were ordered directly from Halifax to Winnipeg under the command of Inspector Jennings. On May 23 the RNWMP shored up its mounted strength by sending 62 horses from headquarters at Regina, and on June 17 a final group of 52 men arrived in the strike-bound city.[17] Thus approximately 245 men were added to the force's original complement of 27.

By Tuesday, June 17, Ketchen had a formidable group of Mounties, militia and civilian auxiliary volunteers at his disposal. At Fort Osborne Barracks an armoured car equipped with three machine guns and manned by three officers, two drivers, and six riflemen was kept in readiness. The Citizens' Committee had formed an auxiliary motor transport service for the rapid movement of troops and placed it under Ketchen's command. The Mounties, in addition to their reinforced complement of officers and men, had been issued four machine guns mounted on motor trucks and could put sixty men on horses into the streets in a matter of minutes. In addition, Ketchen organized two mobile militia units, one stationed at Minto Barracks and the other at Fort Osborne Barracks. Each consisted of a troop of Fort Garry Horse, one motor machine gun section with two guns apiece, infantry escorts in motor trucks, and one company of motorized infantry. The total force immediately available in an emergency numbered eight hundred, and Ketchen had worked out special arrangements to call the rest of the militia into action at a moment's notice.[18]

The absence of streetcars was perhaps the most visible and, to the city administration, most disturbing sign of the general strike. Without the usual public transit system businesses suffered, cheap and easy transportation was denied to those not able to afford automobiles, and an essential civic service was still beyond the control of city hall. By the fifth week of the strike, all other essential public services were back in operation on a regular or emergency basis; only the streetcars were not running and this irked the anti-strike members of the city council.

Initial efforts to get the street railway into operation began as early as May 27 when the city council asked city solicitor T. A. Hunt if they could force the Winnipeg Electric Railway Company to provide its regular services. Hunt told the aldermen they could formally ask for a resumption of operations and cancel the Electric Railway's franchise if it did not comply, but he did not advise them to do so because this might cause serious riots. On the basis of his advice, nothing further was done about the streetcar service at that time. On June 9, however, the city council's special transportation committee, under the chairmanship of Alderman John K. Sparling, recommended that the Electric Railway Company be notified to begin immediate services in the city. Over the next few days the management of the company tried to convince its employees to return to work, while Strike Committee representatives urged them to stay on strike. On the afternoon of Thursday, June 11, street railway employees voted overwhelmingly to stay out and sent a letter to manager A. W. McLimont informing him they would not return to work because the strike situation was still too complicated and streetcar operation would be "a serious mistake."[19] The next day McLimont told city council that there was no hope of resuming service because he could not secure enough men to run the cars.

The long strike, the metal trades employers' apparent willingness to give in on the question of collective bargaining, and the arrests of the strike leaders, however, eroded the opposition of some street railwaymen, who began to drift back to work. These men, aided by management officials, provided a work force large enough to allow the streetcars to be taken out of their barns. On Tuesday, June 17, the Winnipeg Electric Railway Company finally informed the city council that it would begin operations the next morning and would offer the greatest possible service under the circumstances. They expected protection for their own cars and employees, and when the cars rolled out the next day special police were placed on street point duty to watch over the operations.

The resumption of streetcar service helped push the general strike to a climax. On Wednesday morning, June 18, reports that the cars were back in operation spread like wildfire through the pro-strike veterans' meeting in Victoria Park. Some men urged violent confrontation, but the speakers on the platform told the veterans to stay away from the streetcars and their occupants. "To win," the men were told, "the strikers must be calm and do nothing." This was good advice, but becoming harder for the pro-strike forces to follow. On all sides the walkout appeared to be collapsing and the return of the streetcars was only the latest and most visible sign.

While tension mounted among the ranks of the pro-strike veterans, the now truncated leadership of the Strike Committee was desperately attempting to salvage some kind of arrangement which could be sold as a victory. Robertson believed he was making progress towards a final settlement after meeting with strikers' representatives on Thursday and Friday.[20] The absence of the arrested leaders was having a telling effect on the morale of the strikers, and the *Western Labor News* went so far as to declare that "the principle of collective bargaining [had been] conceded."[21] Winning, chief negotiator in Russell's absence, told Robertson at the Friday meeting that he was trying hard to get the metal trades employees to accept the terms offered by the contract shop owners. Robertson then planned a further meeting for Saturday morning and hoped that a final agreement between employers and employees might be concluded.[22]

That meeting was never held. On Friday morning the pro-strike veterans, now in an ugly mood, gathered at Victoria Park and decided they would not be hidden away any longer. That evening, they assembled in Market Square, across from city hall, passed resolutions seeking access to the Industrial Bureau in order to hold meetings, and demanded that streetcar service be ended within forty-eight hours. In conclusion, they announced that they would gather the next afternoon to parade to the Royal Alexandra Hotel in order to have Senator Robertson address them.

At his meeting with Strike Committee negotiators that afternoon, Robertson pointed out that public demonstrations might be seen as one result of the release of the arrested strike leaders and asked Winning to try to keep people off the streets. Winning wholeheartedly agreed and said he would do his best to help maintain peace and order in the city. He now believed it was possible to end the strike but knew public demonstrations would ruin all chance of compromise. The unions, Ketchen told his superiors in Ottawa, were now anxious for a settlement; the only disturbing element was the conduct of the pro-strike veterans.[23]

On Friday night, while the veterans met in Market Square, Mayor Gray reissued his proclamation which, for the third time, forbade parades or public demonstrations in the streets. Robertson sent word to the men offering to address them in Victoria Park the next afternoon, thereby avoiding the necessity for a procession, and then prepared to prolong his stay another few days. At 10:00 P.M. Ketchen wired Ottawa that the meeting in Market Square, though orderly, had passed resolutions in favour of a parade the next day. He did not know what the civic authorities were doing but hoped that the Mounties and militia were ready.

At approximately 10:30 A.M. the next morning Robertson, Gray, Andrews, and Perry met three pro-strike veterans' delegates at Robertson's suite in the Royal Alexandra Hotel. The soldiers told Gray they were going to hold a parade from city hall to the Royal Alexandra Hotel where, they hoped, Robertson would address them. They would then go to the Industrial Bureau and take possession of it. They offered to call off the parade if the strike were settled by 2:00 P.M., the streetcars taken off their routes, and Robertson would speak to them in the Industrial Bureau. Gray told them it was impossible to settle the strike in such a short time and that he had no intention of ending streetcar service, but that an effort would be made to secure the Industrial Bureau.[24] Andrews thereupon left the room, went immediately to the building, and was able to arrange a meeting hall for the afternoon. By the time he reported back to the hotel, however, events had already passed him by.

The argument in the room continued after Andrews had left. The veterans continued to insist on the right to hold a parade, while Gray told them this was in direct violation of three proclamations he had issued and could not be countenanced. He would stop the demonstration, "peacefully if possible," but if not, "other measures would have to be taken."[25] While this argument raged events were already beginning to move out of control as crowds began to gather in the street across from the city hall in anticipation of the parade's 2:30 starting time. At 1:45, Chief Newton telephoned Gray at the hotel and told him about the crowds. Gray hurriedly went to city hall by way of back streets and was told that the specials could not handle the situation. Gray suggested they call on the Mounted Police; Newton concurred and the mayor drove to RNWMP headquarters and formally requested Perry to send his force out to patrol the streets.[26] Perry complied and dispatched fifty-four men on horses and thirty-six in trucks.

By 2:30 the crowds were gathering in larger numbers, mostly on the east side of Main Street between William and Rupert. A streetcar moving slowly north along Main was surrounded by several hundred people who tried unsuccessfully to stop it. When it got through they turned their attention to a south-bound car, pulled its trolley off the wires, and began to smash several windows. The crowd, now almost completely out of control, rocked the car back and forth, trying to tip it on its side; when the task proved too great, the remainder of the windows were broken, the seats inside slashed, and the interior set ablaze.[27] While this attack on the streetcar was in progress the Mounted Police made their first appearance. They swung north along Main from Portage Avenue, half in khaki coats and half in the traditional scarlet, batons in hand. As they rode north the crowd parted to let them through, booing and jeering as they went. One man jumped in front of a horse waving his hat in an attempt to frighten the animal and a few scattered missiles were thrown. The Mounties proceeded up to James Street, turned around, and again rode through the crowd. This time they were hit with bricks, stones, and bottles but sustained few injuries. They went as far south as McDermot and then turned north again.

On their return from this second charge north, one Mountie's horse caught its leg in a fender which had been torn from the streetcar and stumbled and fell. The rider was thrown off but his foot caught in the stirrup and he was dragged along the street until stopped by a large man who began to beat him. When the other Mounties saw this they quickly turned north for the third time but now rode with "revolvers cocked in their hands."[28] Mayor Gray, watching these events from the parapet of the city hall building, decided to take further action and read the Riot Act. The time was now 2:35,[29] and the crowd was given thirty minutes to get off the streets or be liable to arrest. As Gray turned to go inside the building, he heard gunshots.[30]

The officer commanding the Mounted Police detachment, inspector Mead, judged that his small corps of mounted men could not handle the large and excited group without extraordinary measures and decided "to fire a volley into the crowd."[31] The order to use firearms was issued only moments after Gray had read the Riot Act, and firing continued intermittently for several minutes afterwards. One man was killed instantly and many others were wounded. It was claimed afterwards by Mayor Gray, the *Free Press,* and the Mounties, that the order to fire was given only after the Mounties had themselves been shot at by individuals in the crowd. They were certainly under attack from bricks, stones, and bottles, but the only shots fired that day came from police revolvers. Monday's issue of the *Free Press* listed all serious wounds sustained during Saturday's riot including those suffered by four RNWMP officers, and not one of them had been hit by a bullet. Gray told the newspapers he heard no shots fired until shortly after he read the Riot Act and "presumed" they came from the crowd; but, in fact, this was almost exactly the time when Mead was giving the order to use pistols. In addition, Mead later reported that he had given the orders to shoot after he realized how hard-pressed his force was and made no mention of being fired upon.[32]

Panic swept the crowd when the bullets started to spatter against the streets and walls and people fell where they stood. Hundreds trying to escape police bullets swept down back alleys and ran up the streets where they met cordons of special police, armed with clubs and revolvers, thrown across Main Street and other streets and alleys in the vicinity of city hall. Now fights broke out and many were arrested, while the Mounties and specials proceeded to clear the downtown area. Meanwhile, Gray decided on one last measure when he heard the first gunshots and drove immediately to Fort Osborne Barracks to formally ask Ketchen to turn out the militia. The general complied, dispatched the emergency force at hand, and within minutes a mixed group of cavalry and the motor machine gun section began to move into the downtown area in the auxiliary transport provided by the Citizens' Committee.[33]

By this time most of the crowd was trying in every way possible to escape the scene. Over eighty who were not successful were arrested in the specials' dragnet. The specials and the army, aided by the Mounted Police, threw up cordons to block access to Portage and Main from Garry in the south to the CPR station in the north and remained on duty until midnight.[34] "Bloody Saturday" was over.

The last act, however, had not yet been played. When William Ivens was arrested during the night of May 16–17, James S. Woodsworth and Fred Dixon continued publishing the *Western Labor News,* Woodsworth acting as editor and Dixon reporter. The Monday following the riot, A. J. Andrews decided to move against the paper, stop its publication and convince the provincial government to arrest Woodsworth.[35] He justified his actions by pointing to Monday's issue of the paper as an example of seditious libel and likely to incite further riots. Andrews sent a letter to the Winnipeg Printing and Engraving Company in his official capacity as agent for the Department of Justice, ordering them to stop printing or distributing the publication. Woodsworth, on his way to notify the Strike Committee of the forced shut down, was picked up and arrested on charges of seditious libel shortly afterwards.[36] Dixon went into hiding and managed to keep the paper going, first as the *Western Star,* then as the *Enlightener,* until he, too, was arrested three days later.

It had become impossible for the strike to continue much longer. The Mounties, military, and specials were masters of the streets. When rumours of another parade began circulating on Monday, police and soldiers with rifles, accompanied by machine gun—bearing trucks, turned out in the early afternoon and began to patrol the downtown area.[37] Many individual strikers were drifting back to work, streetcar service was increased, and all outdoor meetings of any kind were forbidden by the mayor's proclamation. Hopes of a quick victory had faded long ago and now after six weeks pocketbooks were empty, cupboards were bare, and men were emotionally drained.

On Tuesday morning a delegation from the Central Strike Committee visited Premier Norris and promised to call the strike off if the provincial government would appoint a royal commission to study general labour conditions as well as the causes of the strike.[38] The Citizens' Committee objected strongly to this proposal, but Norris accepted and Wednesday's edition of the *Enlightener* notified its readers that the strike would be called off as of 11:00 A.M. the next morning, six weeks to the day after it had begun.

Thursday morning most strikers returned to work with the exception of small groups who insisted that the walkout continue. Railroad and civic teamsters and several classes of railway storemen, who refused to return to work, were the exception, however, rather than the rule. There was a great deal of confusion in certain quarters, with charges made that no votes had been taken and that the decision to end the strike was arbitrary. But there could be little doubt now that the great strike was over at last. The workers' battle was lost. In defeat the unions girded themselves for the next struggle: ". . . get ready for the next fight. Labor must speak in no uncertain tones at the next municipal elections. Now is the time to select candidates. Now is the time to begin the campaign. . . . Don't slink to the rear and be slaves. Keep in the forefront of battle. Labor must fight on until she wins the long war for freedom. Never quit. Never say die. Carry on."[39]

So ended the greatest industrial battle in Canada's history. The Winnipeg general strike had finally revealed the futility and tragedy of massive confrontation combined with hysteria and intransigence.

12. ❖ Confrontation in Retrospect

The Winnipeg general strike was one of the most complete withdrawals of labour power ever to occur in North America and dealt a mighty blow at one of trade unionism's strongest bastions. The strike, from the labour viewpoint, was a complete failure in the short run and no amount of post-strike rhetoric could cover up this fact. As international organizer Fred Varley observed in early June 1919: "There never was in history a strike in which the workers answered the call so spontaneously, and there never was a strike in which the workers were so badly trimmed."[1]

After eight weeks of struggle with the owners and operators of the contract shops, the metal workers won nothing more than a reduction in the work week from fifty-five to fifty hours at the same rate of pay. Deacon, the Barretts, and Warren had signed a declaration, published on June 16, undertaking to recognize individual craft unions in their plants; but they never lived up to the pronouncement. They knew they had beaten the union and the withering away of both machinists Lodge 457 and the Metal Trades Council[2] in the months following the strike was mute evidence of their total victory. They fought the metal unions for thirteen years and in the end smashed their power. In November 1919, T. R. Deacon capped this success by introducing a works council plan into his shop which closely followed a scheme in use by the International Harvester Company. These councils had power to make recommendations concerning matters of interest to employees but no power to take effective action —they were glorified advisory boards, nothing more.[3]

Building trades workers were more fortunate; their dispute was never as bitter as the struggles in the contract shops and their past relations with employers had been much more amiable. In large measure, wages paid in this industry reflected the state of construction in the city and the summer of 1919 was no exception. After the general strike was over the Builders Exchange entered into negotiations with individual unions and by the end of August signed agreements with a number of them which, in every case but one, set new rates retroactive to July 1 higher than those offered prior to the strike. The same builders who had claimed vehemently in May that they would like to meet the demands of their workers but could not pay a penny more than they were offering, paid more than a few additional pennies. In May the construction industry was in the same depressed condition it had been in throughout the war years, but by the end of August construction was booming in Winnipeg and the demand for skilled tradesmen was high. The building trades unions went on strike on May 1 because they could not wrest substantial wage increases from their employers and the demand for a living wage, based on this dispute, turned into a major rallying point. But in late summer they were given increases that in most cases amounted to 15 cents per hour. The state of the economy was responsible—the general strike itself played no role in their good fortune.

The building trades was the only bright spot in an otherwise gloomy picture. Varley commented that the only thing to do was "kneel in reverence before the employers"[4] and that was precisely what many did. Prospective applicants for positions in the city's civil service were forced to sign an oath promising not to join a union connected with other labour bodies and not to participate in sympathetic strikes.[5] General Ketchen noted on the last day of the strike that approximately three thousand veterans had found jobs while the walkout was in progress and there was no reason to believe any would be dismissed so that strikers could be re-hired.[6] The way was eventually cleared for the re-employment of postal workers though the process was not completed for over a year and even then the men were forced to re-apply and start at the bottom.[7] Railway workers who had answered the general strike call were almost all taken back but lost their seniority and as late as 1945 were engaged in a fight to regain their pension rights.

The general strike drained much of the vigour from the city's unions. Winnipeg was almost completely free of work stoppages in the eighteen months following the general strike and there were only two walkouts of any significance.[8] This was the least in many years and shows graphically that workers had had their fill of strikes. A labour force that had expended every possible effort to win a six-week general strike but had been totally defeated was certain to be more docile in the months and years ahead; the workers were simply too exhausted mentally and economically to offer much industrial resistance. The unions' vitality was also sapped as a result of the OBU secessionist movement. Efforts to line up organized labour in the city behind the OBU reached a climax when the Trades Council voted to affiliate with the new union on July 29.[9]

Thus the battle which many had pinned their hopes on, the struggle which would culminate in better wages, union recognition, and management's acknowledgment that workers were a power to be dealt with, had ended in total failure. The union leaders who led the Trades Council to the brink in early May, many believing there would be no need for a strike because the employers would surely back down, were proven wrong. They made several grave miscalculations and in many cases were so convinced of the righteousness of their cause that logical and concise thinking and planning were notably absent. Many workers knew only that the hour for confrontation had finally come and religiously believed in their own ultimate victory.

The strikers were not revolutionaries and did not seek the violent overthrow of the existing social and political order. The leaders of the city's labour movement did not attempt to solve their problems by wiping out the opposing class, but they did want to assert a comparable authority. What they did not see in their enthusiasm, however, was that a general strike must create great social chaos and by itself brings society crashing down unless special measures are taken. It is an admirable weapon for revolutionaries but those who do not want social collapse must work to undermine its effectiveness. This is what the Citizens' Committee tried to do but were not nearly as effective as the General and Central Strike committees. The workers themselves became the chief strikebreakers when they accepted a responsibility to keep society functioning at the very beginning of the walkout. They undermined the effectiveness of the strike, prolonged it, and contributed immeasurably to their own defeat. All this was done because they were not revolutionaries and had made the grave mistake of assuming that the general strike was a viable and effective industrial weapon. It was not an industrial weapon but a political one because workers' families needed milk as much as the sons and daughters of the employers.

Once the workers began to assume a partial administrative responsibility for the maintenance of water, heat, light, power, and food distribution, their position in society was radically altered and their power greatly enhanced. They were now as important to the everyday directing of society as was capital and they began to rival capital's power to exert leverage on the government. They became directly involved in the operation of essential services, though their authority was exercised in co-operation with civic officials and, in certain cases, owners and managers. They never intended to create a revolutionary situation but were trapped into appearing to be doing so by their own inexperience and lack of planning. Permit cards read "by authority of strike committee" but should also have mentioned the municipal administration and the managers. This would have been more accurate and would have undermined charges that the strike committee had taken control of municipal government.

By carrying on in the manner that they did, labour appeared to be assuming governmental authority and was not equipped or prepared to cope with the political or military implications of this new situation. By launching a general strike the workers had embarked on a radical course but were not radical enough to escape the consequences of their action. They were providing governments with an obvious excuse to intervene and were unable or unwilling to meet the challenges of the intervention. Once the unions had decided to shut down the entire city and keep it shut until they had won, they ran directly into the power of all three levels of government and had to choose to either "get guns" or give in. All their life experiences would not allow them to take the former course; thus the latter was forced on them. When the federal government decided to involve itself in countering a revolution which never existed the workers were lost. Their only choice was between unacceptable compromise, complete defeat, or direct, perhaps armed, resistance.

The Winnipeg general strike was not a revolution and was never planned to be one. It did, however, raise basic questions concerning the nature and composition of "constituted authority" as well as what qualifies as a *bona fide* challenge to that authority. There can be no doubt that the strikers intended to enhance their own position at the expense of the normal political and economic power of capital. In using as blunt an instrument as a general strike, however, they also ran the risk of challenging the *de facto* power of at least one level of government. General strikes are intended to bring the normal functions and activities of society to a standstill and they therefore transfer to the workers part of the option of what will continue to operate and what will not—this is inevitable if anarchy is to be avoided. To this degree the existing order is undermined, whether by accident or design and whether on a purely local level or a more national one. The rapid increase of labour's power in Winnipeg was a shock to the cosy arrangements and alliances that had existed for at least four decades. This threat to the status quo was compounded by the belief in some quarters that the workers were embarked on a campaign to supplant the municipal and even the provincial and national governments. The charge was not true but reflected the unions' rapid rise to new positions of power. Thus, the political implications of a general strike were far more widespread and potentially serious than those of more ordinary industrial disputes, a fact the workers failed to realize.

The roots of the general strike are intricately intertwined with the social and industrial development of the city and bitter animosities between labour and management can easily be discerned as early as 1906. The disputes of that year which wracked the contract shops and street railway were marked by the use of professional strikebreakers, military aid to the civil power, and the injunction. In both episodes labour and management were willing, possibly eager, to test out the limits of their own power; industrial development was still at an early stage in the city and both sides were probably attempting to set precedents for the future. The street railway dispute was a standoff and the antagonists fought each other constantly through the succeeding years. This was probably beneficial, since each learned to respect the strength of the other. But the contract shops dispute was a disaster for the union and the experience created hatred and enmity for years to come. Here there was no respect, only scorn and fear.

The contract shop employers were of that special breed of self-made men who tended to be intolerant towards the members of the classes from which they themselves had risen. To a man like Deacon the union was merely another obstacle to overcome in any way possible if success was to be achieved. Such a man was loath to accept what he would have called "dictation by his employees" and the Barrett brothers, who had built upon the early successes of their father, were of the same stripe. They had, after all, declared at one point that they would never allow a union to tell them what to do.

These men were not apt to forget that they had been strong enough to defeat the union in 1906 and would not give way easily in the future.

The unions also did not forget, but their memories were bitter ones, of defeat aided by court injunction and long legal battles. These workers were also strong-minded men, many experienced in the socialist politics and industrial struggles of their native Great Britain and they came back again and again to challenge the power of their employers. Each time they did so defeat became less acceptable and the stakes were raised on both sides. When the machinists realized they could not win on their own in 1917, they combined with other metal workers in the Metal Trades Council and when that failed in 1918 they called upon all the unions in the city to back them. They successfully convinced the majority of Winnipeg's trade union members and many non-union workers as well that general principles were involved and that the strike was a crusade for collective bargaining in all industries.

Winnipeg was Canada's largest and most important rail centre. Key to three transcontinental railroad systems, the city was home to sprawling marshalling yards and repair shops. By the beginning of the First World War the men who worked in these yards and shops were highly organized and their unions were among the most powerful in Canada. These same unions, however, could not make a dent in the city's independent contract shops—a situation they found unacceptable. They were powerful against the largest railroads in Canada but impotent when challenging three relatively small establishments. This pushed them in their unceasing efforts to organize the contract shops and to obtain the same wages and working conditions enjoyed in the railway shops. Power and prestige were just as important as economic gain.

The situation in the building trades was different because relations in this industry were never marked by the rancour and bitterness evident in the metal trades. The dispute in the spring of 1919 was almost solely an economic one, even though in the context of a general unrest both sides attempted to make of it a holy crusade. The Builders Exchange were parroting the contract shop owners when they declared in late April that they would have nothing more to do with the Building Trades Council. This was a tactic that further clouded the main issue but was only to a small degree motivated by ideological considerations. Though complicated by an atmosphere of mistrust, the dispute was initially caused by the rising cost of living, the small pay increases earned by construction workers during the war, and the inability of the employers to grant wages as high as those demanded by the unions. Building trades workers were not given substantial wage increases during the war largely because their employers were starving for business. At first there was a great number of tradesmen unemployed and the unions were unable to press their demands for higher pay. Later, when many construction workers had joined the army and the unions were in a better position to put pressure on their employers, the Norris government stepped in to stabilize conditions in the trade and the industry was upset by only one strike of any real consequence in the entire wartime period. When the unions approached the Builders Exchange in the spring of 1919 they were impatient. There was no war now to blame the situation on and they were determined to improve their position in relation to prices. Their employers, however, who were probably unable to pay the new wage scales set by the unions, refused to meet the demands, thus creating militancy in an industry noted for the lack of it.

When the call for a general strike was issued every union but one willingly answered and, more significantly, many thousands of non-union workers responded as well. The war placed great strains on the social fabric by aggravating old problems, creating new ones, and setting the stage for the five months of uncertainty and unrest which immediately preceded the general strike. Wartime inflation, scandals, the government's treatment of large numbers of new Canadians, and its tight controls on the use of foreign languages were compounded by the conscription crisis and the government's attempt to ban the use of strikes and lockouts. The war created conditions favourable to the rapid growth of the trade union movement and that expansion itself created militancy as a by-product.

The government of Prime Minister Robert Laird Borden did almost nothing to aid the growth of Canadian unions during the war. The most significant and openly favourable action, its informal sanction of the creation of Division 4 and the extension of the McAdoo Award to Canada, came late in the war. For the most part unions in Canada grew through immense organizing efforts conducted among workers growing more and more dissatisfied with their lot. In order to attract new members the unions had to demonstrate they could offer tangible gains in return for union dues, and they had to show prospective members as well as workers already in the fold that they were respected by bosses and governments. To make tangible gains they had to demand more and be unwilling to settle for less. These conditions create militancy. Those who are more militant are less willing to compromise because in many cases they deeply believe in the virtue and justice of their own cause. Thus power and prestige became interrelated with a crusading, evangelistic spirit.

The events of the summer and fall of 1918 played a significant role in the creation of an atmosphere conducive to a general strike. The success of the sympathetic strike in May, combined with the victory of the western postal workers in August and the failure of the contract shops' strike, gave radical union leaders a powerful and convincing argument. Though moderates such as McBride, Robinson, and Winning were always in the majority on the Trades Council it was radicals such as Russell and Johns who called the shots. They could and did point to the 1918 disputes to prove their contention that militancy paid off and the lack of it was bound to be disastrous. They impressed the moderate majority with the argument that extraordinary times demanded extraordinary actions, including the organization of "industrial" unions and the use of the general strike. Russell and his followers challenged the moderates to accept their responsibility as union leaders and sanction more radical action. The power and persuasiveness of the radicals grew in direct proportion to the growth of war-related problems and the demonstrated inability or unwillingness of governments to cope with them. The radicals tended to present their arguments in black and white terms and combined deep and thoughtful analysis with simplistic solutions. One was either for them or against them. They carried the fight to the moderates and forced them to choose.

These radical leaders were well known, respected, and liked. So they successfully convinced the moderate majority that the One Big Union type of organization and the general strike were logical and necessary answers to the workers' problems. Many moderates were swept up in the growing enthusiasm for radical solutions with little or no thought to the consequences of such action. They began to look upon the general strike as merely another tool to be used in industrial disputes, a larger strike, nothing more. In the year prior to May 1919 the call for a general strike was heard with increasing frequency, but not a single page of the *Western Labor News* or *The Voice* was devoted to a discussion of its social and political ramifications. Some leaders may have believed they would never have to resort to the use of the general strike, that the very threat would suffice, while others thought the power of the workers combined with the righteousness of their cause would assure quick, easy, and relatively painless victory. Why should one trade have to endure a long, costly struggle when the massive, combined power of every union member in the city could quickly win a dispute with little risk to the workers? The victory of the 1918 sympathetic strike was, in reality, disastrous in the long run.

There was much on the line during the 1919 general strike—the high stakes help account for the length of the affair and the tactics used on both sides. In downing their tools on the morning of May 15, the unions in Winnipeg laid their power and prestige on the line—this was the long-awaited confrontation. There was now no higher level of escalation, all the bets were on the table, nothing held in reserve. The idea that the continuous application of greater power was bound to result in success was to receive its greatest test. Once they had gambled everything they must win or lose all. The thought that compromise on the main issues might still be a viable alternative was no more acceptable to them than to their employers. It no longer really mattered whether the aims were justifiable, the cause righteous; it was a matter of total victory or total defeat.

The employers and their allies were fully cognizant of this—they had never been willing to compromise and were always determined to smash the union. In the past they had used every weapon at their disposal and knew that if they were defeated by the general strike they would lose the last and most important battle. The contract shop owners were the leaders in this but others, members of the Citizens' Committee, closed ranks behind them in a show of solidarity calculated to match that of the unions. If the strike could be defeated the power of the unions would suffer a heavy and perhaps mortal blow. For some the fear of revolution and the spirit of crusade was undoubtedly genuine, but for the most part the belief that a union victory would set society on its head and place workers in a position where they would sit as equals with management at the bargaining table spurred them on. This thought was intolerable to the leaders of the business community.

Governments also had a great deal at stake in the general strike. Some public officials, panicked by the fear of Bolshevism and the Russian revolution, genuinely believed they were meeting a challenge to constitutional authority. The prime minister was content to listen to the explanations and follow the advice of Meighen and Robertson, but appears to have had little to do with their conduct. The minister of the interior and the minister of labour were at least as interested in preserving the status quo in labour-management relations as they were in countering a revolution. They wanted to nip the One Big Union movement in the bud, shore up the position of the international unions, and ensure the survival of craft unionism. They were willing to see the strike ended peacefully as long as there was no recognition of the Metal Trades Council, but if this could not be accomplished then the strike must be decisively crushed.

The advocates of the One Big Union took up the government's challenge and adopted the position that once the strike had been identified with the OBU it must be won. Johns was perfectly aware of what he was writing when he told Midgley that they could not afford to let the strike be lost. There was precious little reason for W. A. Pritchard's presence in the city other than as an observer for the Central Committee appointed by the Western Labor Conference. The strike was certainly not an OBU effort. The OBU was not founded until after the strike had started and the various provincial committees responsible for organization which were struck in March 1919 took no part in any of the decisions to call the strike. There can be no doubt, however, that the OBU loomed in the minds of many men—strikers and their opponents—and was made an issue before the strike was over.

Two groups played key roles in events leading to the strike and were of crucial importance after May 15. The returned soldiers, pro-strike and loyalist, were determined to collect what they thought was due them from society, and the new Canadians undoubtedly believed they would gain a new human dignity through victory. The impact of the veterans is relatively easy to determine, for they were loud in proclaiming their sympathies and the reasons for them. But the eastern Europeans stuck to their traditional silence and, though blamed as the driving force behind the strike, played a relatively passive role.

There were probably two basic desires burning inside most veterans when they returned to Canada in late 1918 and 1919—the wish for peace in their own lives and the determination to avoid further wars. Veterans voiced their aspirations by demanding that society make good on its promises of a better postwar world and some made ready to do battle with those individuals they believed were threatening the civilization just saved from the Kaiser. A returned soldier, therefore, decided to join the strikers or the Citizens' Committee, depending on which desire was strongest and how he wished to see it fulfilled. Those who tended to sympathize with the

Citizens' Committee were probably of more well-to-do families, while those who supported the strikers were former workers or trade union members. They were all men of action—they had just finished proving this—and saw little sense in "sitting tight and doing nothing."

The part played by new Canadians remains a matter of some mystery. At the time of the strike and for a short period afterwards every event that smacked of radicalism was blamed on enemy aliens, who were usually described as anarchists and Bolsheviks capable of the most sinister deeds. Both anti- and pro-strike veterans paraded under banners damning the alien enemy. Nevertheless, a careful study of the key names in the Winnipeg Trades Council from 1913 to 1920 reveals only three men with non-British or Canadian names —Harry Veitch, Abraham Heaps, and Sam Blumenberg. The last man was a figure of minor importance, whereas both Veitch and Heaps were born in Britain. One may also look in vain for articles or letters submitted to Anglo-Saxon trade union newspapers by eastern Europeans; they simply did not get involved in the political or trade union activities of British and Canadian workers, though they often supported groups of their own.

Before August 1914, new Canadians suffered the trials and tribulations undergone by most immigrants in a new land; but after the outbreak of war many also became "illegal" and were forced to register and carry cards proclaiming them to be "enemy aliens." Some were wrenched from their houses and sent to detention camps in northern Ontario. With the passage of the Wartime Elections Act in the summer of 1917 they lost their political rights, and when veterans began to return to Canada in increasing numbers many were physically assaulted and dismissed from their jobs. By the spring of 1919 they, too, were ready to participate in the crusade to build a new society, and many of the approximately 30,000 to 35,000 workers who joined the strike must have come from this group.

The opponents of the strike had compelling reasons to smash it with all the powers at their command. The co-operation of all three levels of government with the Citizens' Committee was the key factor determining the strike's outcome. When Meighen and Robertson laid the prestige of the federal government on the line, the outcome could no longer be doubted; the strikers' cause was lost. They worked closely with Norris, Gray, and the Citizens' Committee to put every obstacle in the path of the strikers and force them into impossible situations. It is hard to judge the degree of collusion but its presence is undeniable; the governments identified their interests with those of the employers and sided with them almost from the start.

There were five key steps which led to the final defeat of the general strike and the federal government was deeply involved in all of them. The dismissal of the regular police and their replacement by the specials put a large anti-strike, pro-Citizens' Committee force into the hands of municipal authorities. At the same time as this was taking place the federal government was quietly but quickly building up the militia and RNWMP forces at its disposal so that by June 16 Winnipeg was virtually an occupied city. This set the stage for Robertson's intervention in the proceedings of the mediation committee and the arrest of the radical strike leaders—two closely connected events. The minister of labour was anxious to have contract shop employers make concessions and probably thought their June 16 declaration was reasonable, but the Strike Committee was not given a chance to discuss these proposals because the arrests were carried out less than twenty-four hours after their publication. Robertson probably hoped a strike committee devoid of Russell, Johns, and their colleagues would be more pliable.

It is impossible to determine whether or not Russell or any other of the arrested men could have dissuaded the veterans from organizing a march on June 21. What is clear, is that Winning could not. After the arrests the Strike Committee drifted, stunned and leaderless, incapable of decisive action. Once the march had been broken on the day known to history as Bloody Saturday, the strike could no longer continue. It had become more than apparent that victory was an illusion and this loss of faith made the other discomforts of the six-week strike intolerable. The decision to return to work was an anticlimax.

The Winnipeg general strike was not an attempted revolution. There has never been a shred of evidence to prove that claim—the issue was manufactured from the start. Was it, however, fought for the purposes so often repeated by the Strike Committee and historians sympathetic to it: collective bargaining and the right to organize industrial unions? The evidence suggests that these issues may have been oversimplified.

One of the most persuasive arguments used by general strike advocates was that such action was necessary to win collective bargaining as a universal principle and put an end to attacks on the system by employers such as those who owned the contract shops. Many of the approximately 12,000 trade unions members who struck on May

15 were already bargaining with their employers, and any man who worked in one of the city's railway repair shops was represented in negotiations with management by Division 4 (where collective bargaining had reached a highly sophisticated level of practice). Therefore, the strike was actually fought to win a particular type of collective bargaining in one particular industry and this very specific demand was turned into a call for legislation of collective bargaining on a province-wide basis. The strike leaders converted the walkout into a campaign to give union recognition and collective bargaining a status in law so that employees would no longer have to depend on the whims of their employers for decent wages and job security.

Industrial unionism had little or nothing to do with the strike. The bargaining system demanded by the contract shop workers was actually committee representation of the type used by the railway shop craft unions; the Metal Trades Council did not seek to form an industrial union. It is possible that industrial unionism in the contract shops was something to try for after the achievement of committee representation, but this was not emphasized by the strikers. Many historians have attempted to use the issue both ways but they cannot; either the Metal Trades Council was patterned after the OBU's proposed form of organization, as Robertson and Meighen charged, and was a type of nascent industrial union, or it was not—and the evidence points to the latter.

The Winnipeg general strike was not, however, fought merely to win collective bargaining. To the contrary, everything suggests it was a modern version of the Children's Crusade and was marked by the same lack of planning, religious zeal, and plethora of causes that characterized the original. The presence of religious figures such as Rev. William Ivens and J. S. Woodsworth, and the popularity of the Labor Church are only the most obvious manifestations of this. The whole manner in which workers answered the call, the unshakable belief in ultimate victory, the lack of thorough planning, the pacifism which marked the appeals of the strike leaders are also evidence of the strike's character. Russell, Johns and other dedicated socialists probably had no religious convictions at all but replaced Christianity with Marxism. But a crusade it was, and, like the originals, one with a distinct purpose.

The one element which united moderates and radicals in their thinking and planning was the desire to achieve control over their industrial lives. For too long the labour movement in Winnipeg had lived in a vacuum divorced from the centres of decision-making.

Workers were in the majority in the city but could not capture city council. Their representation in the provincial legislature was small and attempts to elect a federal member to Parliament in 1917 were singularly unsuccessful. Workers felt themselves cut off and treated like social outcasts. They meant to gain dignity and respect and were determined to break through the barriers that separated them from those who governed. The general strike was one battle in a long campaign to achieve that measure of power necessary to sit and be recognized as equals with employers and government. In some manner never fully defined victory would give them that power, at one stroke, in a way that would never be challenged.

The Winnipeg general strike was a manifestation of the continuing class division that has marked the history of the city for over half a century. The events of May and June, 1919, were preceded and followed by growing splits in society and were largely products of those divisions. The strike was the most traumatic of events which contributed to class memory and polarization, but it did not initiate these psychological attitudes. Class consciousness was a strong factor in Winnipeg prior to the strike, laid the foundation for labour's political successes of the 1920s, and was largely responsible for the continuing division of Winnipeg into those whose parents or grandparents were strikers, and those whose forebearers were members of the Citizens' Committee.

Early polarization developed in Winnipeg, stimulated by the same conditions which created division elsewhere—workers were those who received a wage, employers were those who paid it. Industrial workers in Winnipeg, however, felt a particularly close community of interest. They were the vanguard of the industrial working class on the prairies and often the vanguard of trade unionism as well. They lived in a closely defined geographic area and were isolated from the great centres of working-class power in Ontario and the United States. From the very beginning of the emergence of trade unionism in Winnipeg there were articulate critics who pointed out the horrors of the new industrial society and continually harped on the precariousness of life for workers. The worker could be killed on a job, displaced by unskilled immigrants who were willing to work for less, lose his job in winter, or see his small savings wiped out in one of the periodic economic fluctuations.

To combat these conditions workers turned increasingly to trade unionism. In the days before the closed or union shop and automatic checkoff this very process further increased his awareness of himself as a member of a group with a special interest in society and very particular desires and ambitions. Union members began to believe that they were a special group, should be recognized and accepted as such and should be given a share of power and responsibility with other groups.

These aspirations clashed with the interests of Winnipeg's owner-managerial class which was supported, before 1915, by civic and provincial governments. The tightly knit elite of brokers, merchants, lawyers, and manufacturers who ruled the business world refused to concede anything to labour because they refused to recognize that industrial workers or trade unions were entitled to any special considerations in the plants or halls of government. They saw labour as a resource, a commodity, and had no intention of relinquishing any of their power in the community to it. When labour threw out its first tentative challenges early in the century they were met by intransigent employers who used every weapon at their disposal to crush the budding power of trade unions. This process tended to increase class polarization and undermined the influence of any labour leader who dared assert, in the face of injunctions, strike-breakers, yellow dog contracts and hostile or apathetic governments, that capital and labour shared a basic community of interest.

Immigration, depression, and war further stimulated the development of class polarization in Winnipeg. The influx of large numbers of new settlers tended to underline the wide gulf that separated workers from employers, rich from poor, while the decision of many middle- and upper-class citizens to settle in the southern part of the city added the factor of geographic identification to the process. In the years prior to the First World War the north end and Wellington Crescent became attitudes as well as places; the rich grew richer but the poor remained mired in poverty.

When the depression struck in 1913 the skilled British and Canadian workers were hit harder perhaps than any other group. Machinists waited outside factory gates for long hours and construction workers looked in vain for new building sites, but wherever they turned for help they were rebuffed. All Trades Council suggestions to the civic and provincial administrations for dealing with depression and unemployment were ignored, except for pious pleas to the federal government to end immigration. Workers were forced to dig ditches where they could or listened to government officials discussing resettlement of urban wage earners on empty lands. Workers, therefore, came face to face with their helplessness and powerlessness in the community and this strengthened the feelings of class separateness.

War put the finishing touches to a process already well under way. Workers believed they were being forced to suffer low wages and rising prices while the wealthy raked in fat war profits. They saw that without men to fire the guns or run the lathes there would be no war effort. They heard stirring pronouncements from their national leaders and flowery statements from local, "part-time" patriots; but when they asked government for concessions in the form of fair wage clauses in war-supply contracts they were turned back. Once again it appeared as though those in power would not recognize the special desires or necessities of workers and they became more convinced than ever that they had little or nothing in common with employers or governments composed of and supported by the wealthy.

These processes were evident throughout Canada in the first decades of the twentieth century but were particularly pronounced in Winnipeg. Here the owner-managerial class was newer, fewer in number and more tightly knit than in many other industrial centres. All frequented the same clubs and associations and lived in the same areas. Some, such as A. M. Nanton, T. R. Deacon, and the Barretts were *nouveaux riches,* recently arrived at the pinnacle of power and not yet mellowed by the passage of time or the self-assuredness that generations of wealth sometimes brings. This class deeply believed they would be the elite of a new industrial centre that might, with luck, ambition, and intelligence, soon rival Chicago as the western capital of the continent. Winnipeg had the raw manpower, the large pool of immigrants, the railways, the geographic location at the entrance to the prairies and, by the First World War, the financial and industrial strength, to enable it to fulfill its great promise. There was no room here for a powerful trade union movement, especially one that contained so many socialists among its leadership and held so many radical ideas. It was imperative, therefore, to challenge the rising power of the unions and sap the strength of the industrial working class. There might be room for paternalistic regulation, but not for recognition of an equal status for trade unions. When labour resisted these impulses class polarization was strengthened further.

Winnipeg's entrepreneurs were constantly trying to lower the costs of their operations by holding down wages. Almost every business engaged in manufacturing or distribution of consumer or capital goods was at a certain disadvantage in comparison with companies in eastern Canada or the United States because of the great distances to sources of raw materials or wholesale distributors. Deacon frequently complained that he had great difficulty trying to compete with eastern or American companies, and the unimportance of Winnipeg to national war production is ample evidence of the truth of his assertions. The Shell Committee and the Imperial Munitions Board had to make special provision for western shell manufacturers because greater shipping distances and, consequently, higher freight costs would have made the granting of contracts unfeasible. There was, thus, little difference in the approaches of local corporations to their labour problems. Vulcan and Manitoba Bridge, owned in Winnipeg, were allied to and supported by Dominion Bridge, a branch operation. All attempted to keep the one great variable, labour costs, as low as possible.

The war increased cost pressures on local businessmen and at the same time put workers under an additional strain. Manufacturers and suppliers were under even greater pressure to keep labour costs as low as possible because they were forced to pay more for raw materials while workers were pressured by rising retail prices to demand higher wages. The squeeze was particularly felt by workers in industries not essential to the war effort who had little bargaining leverage; those who were essential to war industry—machinists, for example—were more able to keep ahead of the inflationary trend. Winnipeg did not have many war workers because it was awarded so few contracts. Thus, a large number of workers hardly improved their position at all during the war or else saw their wages eaten away by inflation. They were determined to make up for lost time with peace and the normalization of economic conditions and industrial production.

The main exception to the cost-squeeze situation was the transportation industry. The railways had built their yards and repair shops at Winnipeg and it was precisely here that their costs were lowest. They did not need to compete with eastern or American corporations and did not have to import capital or consumer goods for wholesale or retail distribution. The need for their services was constant and the pressure of competition on them was less than on other corporations in the city. In this industry management and ownership had been divorced early, unions in the running trades had been accepted by the turn of the century, and those men responsible for the operation of the systems saw that unions were essential to the stabilization of the daily relationship between an employer and his men. Railway shop craft unions were therefore the most fortunate of organizations, with the exception of the running trades. Here, however, militancy and radicalism—class consciousness —was particularly strong, even though it did not develop from intense pressures placed on the unions. In fact, the opposite was the case: workers here turned increasingly to radicalism because they had tasted power and influence in this one industry, but were denied it elsewhere. The shop craft unions were determined to rectify this situation, raise the standard of living of workers in general, and enhance their own positions in the process.

Class polarization can be seen at work in Winnipeg in the street railway and contract shop disputes of 1906, in the Great West Saddlery lockout of 1911, and the debates over unemployment and depression in the months preceding the war. As time passed without any change in the existing social order or alterations in the thought patterns of the business and governing classes, the effectiveness of moderate thinking waned; attitudes began to gel into dogmas and doctrines. Many workers began to believe in the idea that there were only two classes of consequence in society, those who produced and those who lived off the producers. The eventual acceptance of this philosophy allowed workers to think in terms of general strikes or the creation of a single union of all wage earners. The belief, expressed in the actions of the Strike Committee, that they could allow just so much water pressure in the pipes, enough to service single-story dwellings, and thus easily separate owners from workers, followed naturally. This same mode of thought had contributed to the intense industrial struggles of 1917, 1918, and 1919 and the feverish labour political activity before and after the general strike. It led to the refusal to believe in the good will of a provincial government that had passed much favourable labour legislation, enforced measures on the books, introduced a comprehensive compensation scheme, regulated working conditions in the construction industry, and fixed minimum wages for women.

By the spring of 1919 the process of class polarization had gone so far that Winnipeg had been divided into two camps with little communication between them. Along the way moderates were discarded, as the most radical on one side and the most intransigent on the other emerged as ideological leaders. This is why labour spurned Norris's Industrial Conditions Act and ridiculed Parnell's belief that labour and capital had much in common. It also explains why the Builders Exchange reversed their earlier position and declared that they would not deal with the Building Trades Council. Labour's frame of mind allowed a general strike because workers had arrived at the conclusion that there was no such thing as a neutral citizenry. The middle class had aided the wealthy in their campaign against unions by their silence, and were thus almost as guilty. Under these circumstances the defeat of the strike did not reverse class polarization but rather aided it further.

It has often been observed that workers in Winnipeg turned to politics after the strike; but in fact they were engaged in steadily increasing political activity for over a decade before the war. Political activity had always been looked upon as complementary to industrial action, and the working class in the city had been more successful in electing its own candidates with each successive year. By the spring of 1919 they had representation in the halls of civic government and had elected MLAs to the provincial legislature. After the general strike they continued their political activity but were more successful because of the increased class consciousness which the strike and the methods used to defeat it generated. The great success of labour candidates in the 1920 provincial voting and the election of J. S. Woodsworth to the House of Commons in 1921 were actually manifestations of the same class polarization which had enabled so complete a general strike to take place and has been so strong a factor in the fortunes of the city for at least five decades. Fifty years after the general strike there were still bitter debates over its causes and meaning, and there continued to be a north end in attitude as well as geographic fact.

The Winnipeg general strike has been the key event in the collective memories of both groups who fought it. The strike provided the original mythology and martyrology that strengthened division within the community. The CPR tracks separated north from south physically, but the strike has separated them socially and historically. In both areas generations grew to maturity who continued to re-fight the battle of 1919 in almost every arena of social conflict, from school sports to the street battles of excitement-seeking juveniles to civic and provincial politics. In time, the class division symbolized by the strike was joined by ethnic and religious differences which further polarized society in the city. The lethargy which began to affect the community in the 1920s, holding development back and forcing some of Winnipeg's talented and ambitious sons and daughters to seek greener fields elsewhere was, at least in part, a result of these chronic divisions. The south end became the bastion of the English Establishment and those sons of immigrants who achieved financial and social success rarely moved there.

The victory of the New Democratic Party in the Manitoba election of 1969, fifty years after the defeat of the general strike, was in large measure a victory for attitudes and beliefs rooted in the old north end. Finally, seventy years after Sifton's immigrants began to arrive in Canada and labour began its long and frustrating campaign for political power, a government came to office which represented the sons and daughters of both groups.

13. ❖ A Longer View

Both the Winnipeg general strike and *Confrontation at Winnipeg* continue to generate controversy among Canadian historians. Since the publication of this book, that controversy has formed the backdrop for a number of publications which have attempted either to add to the scope of *Confrontation* or to point out its ideological "errors." Articles of the first variety have covered the reaction of the farming community to the general strike, the role of aliens and women in the strike, and the impact of the strike on Winnipeg municipal politics. Works in the second category have been largely historiographical with the exception of an article on the general strike in Amherst, Nova Scotia, that took place between May 20 and June 12, 1919. It was designed to show that workers all across Canada, and not just in the west, were fired by the ideal of class warfare in the period immediately following World War I.

One of the earliest post-*Confrontation* works to appear was an essay by Donald Avery which purported to answer two important questions that had not, he claimed, been explored: "Why . . . was there such a tragic breakdown in communication between the . . . Central Strike Committee and the Citizens' Committee of One Thousand? And why were Dominion officials prepared to accept the allegation that the Strike was a prelude to revolution . . . when there was ample evidence that it was a legitimate industrial conflict?"[1] The answers to both questions are the same, according to Avery: the presence in Winnipeg of alien radicals.

In expanding on his answer, Avery surveys the history of the ethnic labour movement in Winnipeg, thus adding some detail to what was already well known. He adds little else of importance. The fact is that no one who has written on the strike ignored the important role of immigrant workers in it. But it is clear from the evidence of the press, government documents, strikers and Citizens Committee records, and eye witnesses not only that no non-Anglo Saxon (i.e., British or Canadian-born) leader played a role of any significance in the strike but that everyone at the time knew this to be true. Avery's article actually confirms this.

In fact the article is an artificial construct from start to finish. It is perfectly clear that the trouble between strikers and the Citizens' Committee of One Thousand stemmed from their radically different ways of looking at the world. It was far from being the mere "breakdown in communication" that Avery says it was. And it is equally clear that Meighen saw the strike as a "prelude to revolution" because the Strike Committee had assumed statutory authority (unwittingly or not) that it had no business exercising, and not because there were radical aliens in Winnipeg.

The same *festschrift* which contained Avery's essay included an article by J.E. Rea on the impact of the general strike on municipal politics in Winnipeg between 1919 and 1945.[2] The work was apparently done as part of a study commissioned by the government of Manitoba on political parties in the Winnipeg City Council and was an expansion of an earlier piece entitled "The Politics of Conscience: Winnipeg After the Strike." There he had argued that the strike had been "the fundamental determinant in the modern, political history of Winnipeg."[3]

Rea's second article advanced the notion that the general strike had institutionalized Winnipeg's class division to such an extent that city politics in the decades afterwards was marked by "class polarization." He claimed that "at every election and on major economic and ideological issues [the political descendants of the strikers and the Citizens Committee] confronted each other directly and consistently."[4] Switching from historical to statistical analysis, Rea attempted to prove his case by constructing "a socioeconomic profile" of each side's representatives in the city council, followed by an analysis of the roll-call voting behaviour of these groups. He concluded that in the period under study there was a high degree of background similarity within each group and that their votes were almost always cast in the same fashion (and against each other) on six basic issues: social welfare measures, working conditions and wage rates, taxation levels, public service measures, committee appointments, and electoral reform.

When an event as cataclysmic as a six-week general strike is being analysed, it is all too easy to over-emphasize its impact on an urban community and Rea's argument is a classic case of this. There are two basic problems with it. First, the strike reflected the more than a decade and a half of growing class polarization that had preceded it. Although it clearly marked a new and higher level of class conflict, it was also one of a long series of events that began before it and continued long after it. Indeed, the politics of the City of Winnipeg before the strike was clearly marked by intensified assaults by labour on the Chamber of Commerce's control of City government. It was not easy, given the property qualification laws in effect in the city and the multi-voting allowed those who owned property in different wards, but labour was more successful with each passing year. Thus the polarization in city politics predated the strike. And although the strike undoubtedly played a role in civic politics afterwards (and in other areas as well), other factors were also important.

This leads to the second flaw in Rea's hypothesis—his contention that the polarization was so all-pervasive and that it lasted so long. In a 1983 article in *Urban History Review*, P.H. Wichern took him to task by pointing out that Rea's use of roll-call votes was full of pitfalls because these were taken only when called for, as when one side or the other was posturing for its supporters. Since the majority of the votes were not of this variety, Wichern submits, it is impossible to trace the true voting patterns in the City Council in these years. Wichern points to the founding of Winnipeg's first "Citizens" group in 1884 as evidence that civic boosterism played a major role among Winnipeg's elites and that this boosterism was itself the major determinant of Winnipeg politics. Indeed, Wichern claims, there was little difference between "left" and "right" on boosterism even after 1919: anyone not supporting local economic growth and development was "beyond the pale." He calls boosterism the "third face of power" and considers it "a much better candidate than the 1919 strike as 'the fundamental determinant in the modern political history of Winnipeg.' "[5]

In 1989 David P. Yeo shed light on a little known side-effect of the strike in his article "Rural Manitoba Views the 1919 Winnipeg General Strike." In it he took issue with views expressed by D.C. Masters, W.L. Morton, and Martin Robin that the rural community was hostile to the strike and that the strike undermined the chances of farmer-labour cooperation in the years that followed. While admitting that there is little direct evidence of what farmers themselves thought of the strike, Yeo asserts that information from the rural press suggests that the picture was more complex than has hitherto been recognized. Some country newspapers, such as the *Weekly Manitoba Liberal*, were indeed hostile to the strike, but others— the *Neepawa Press*, for example—"talked in glowing terms of the strikers' actions and of the worthy principles involved in their fight."[6]

With the upsurge in the writing of women's history, it is not surprising that several articles have chronicled the role of women in the general strike. The earliest was that by Mary Horodyski, who showed that thousands of women were active on both sides—as strikers and strikebreakers—which was a logical consequence of their high participation in the workforce. According to Horodyski these women have been ignored by "male-dominated historians" because of the "patriarchal ideology that has dominated history."[7] This sort of *ex cathedra* pronouncement ruins what is otherwise a fine survey which outlines the many different ways that women were involved in the events of May 15 to June 26. But Horodyski leaves unanswered the question of why women played almost no role in the strike leadership—indeed in the Winnipeg labour movement—when almost one in four workers in the city was female. The only leader of any sort to emerge from the women's ranks in the strike, as she points out, was Helen Armstrong, who attempted throughout the strike to use the walkout to bring unorganized female workers into the labour movement and was, at one point, arrested for her efforts.

Two more recent articles include a short piece by Pam Tranfield for *Newest Review* and a longer study by Linda Kealey of women in the 1919 labour revolt, which contains a short section on the Winnipeg general strike. Both are surveys which add little to the work done by Horodyski, although Tranfield does attempt to explain why women were virtually absent from the strike leadership and why Helen Armstrong was not supported by the male strike leaders: "The labour and popular presses marginalized women and disconnected their roles as wage workers, strikers and militants" she says.[8] Given the prevailing notion among male Anglo-Saxon workers that a working wife was a sign of failure both as a bread-winner and as a man, little else could have been expected of them.

Tranfield and Horodyski focus on women as particular players in the events of 1919; Kealey does not. Although she highlights the activities of the few women who were prominent in the labour revolt of 1919 in Winnipeg and elsewhere, she is much more concerned to show that female workers participated in the revolt for the same reasons as men and that the revolt was national in character: "The surge of organization and unrest which culminated in 1919 built upon the more general unrest and momentum stemming from wartime conditions and opportunities which women also shared in. The general strike phenomenon, then, for women as for men, demonstrated class conflict and considerable unrest, heightened by a boom and bust cycle associated with war."[9] Kealey's aim is not so much to write about women, but about women-as-part-of-the-proletariat in a further effort to counter non-Marxist historians who have claimed that western labour was especially radical and, therefore, more prone to revolt. Thus her failure to add anything to the work on women qua women already done by Horodyski.

While much written about the strike since the first appearance of *Confrontation at Winnipeg* has tried to add new knowledge to what is known about the events of May and June, 1919, much more has attempted to re-interpret *Confrontation*. Marxist historians raised three basic objections to the book. They attacked it for (1) ignoring "the structural basis of the permanent industrial conflict characteristic of all capitalist societies,"[10] (2) concluding that the strike was a crushing defeat for the labour movement,[11] and (3) characterizing the strike (and the parallel rise of the One Big Union) as the result of *western* labour radicalism, rather than as part of a general class-based uprising of Canadian labour generally.[12]

Confrontation does not, in fact, explicitly advance the argument that Marxists refer to as "western exceptionalism"—the notion that a variety of unique conditions made western workers more politically radical (as opposed to more militant) than their counterparts in central Canada or the Atlantic provinces. It does reflect the view, strongly held by many western workers themselves, that they were more radical, more "advanced," and thus in a unique position to serve as the Canadian vanguard of the postwar workers' revolt that seemed to be sweeping the globe. As such *Confrontation* forms part of a larger body of work which advances the notion that western workers were more radical. Such writings include Gerald Friesen's article " 'Yours in Revolt': The Socialist Party of Canada and the Western Canadian Labour Movement," A.R. McCormack's book *Reformers, Rebels and Revolutionaries: The Western Canadian Radical Movement, 1899–1919*,[13] my article "Labour Radicalism and the Western Industrial Frontier, 1897–1919,"[14] and my book *Fools and Wise Men: The Rise and Fall of the One Big Union*.

The most noteworthy attack on this view came from Gregory S. Kealey, long-time editor of *Labour/Le Travail*, author of the Macdonald Prize–winning *Toronto Workers Respond to Industrial Capitalism, 1867–1892*,[15] and acknowledged leader of the "new" labour historians in Canada. It came at the Winnipeg General Strike Symposium held at the University of Winnipeg in March, 1983.

Kealey's contribution to the symposium—"1919; The Canadian Labour Revolt"—presents a simple message: "that the revolt [of 1919] was national in character and that its seeds were not rooted in any unique regional fermentation. The 'radical' west and the conservative east have become sorry shibboleths of Canadian historiography. The foundations of our understanding of 1919 must be built on national and international conjunctures."[16] In comparing the testimony of Canadian workers before the 1919 Royal Commission on Industrial Relations headed by Justice T.G. Mathers—a source Kealey relies on heavily in this piece—with the opinions expressed by workers during the 1886 Royal Commission into the Relations between Capital and Labour, he finds a major difference. The worker testimony of 1886 was, he claimed, marked by "cautious . . . respectability and . . . near deference"; that of 1919 was thoroughly defiant and revolutionary. From this he concludes that the "message the Commission received was the same across the country. The capitalist system could not be reformed, it must be transformed."[17] The remainder of his essay consists of a statistically based chronicle of the many 1919 strikes, combined with the by-now conventional attacks on western exceptionalism pioneered by Bryan Palmer and others.[18]

It is important to Kealey to try to prove that 1919 was a national, class-based revolt against capitalism which was connected ideologically and economically to worker revolts in Europe, the United States, and elsewhere if he is to slay the dragon of Western exceptionalism and preserve a Marxist view of events. If the Winnipeg general strike and the One Big Union were largely the result of localized disputes and conditions largely specific to western Canada, then the Marxist argument that the relationship between workers and employers is always basically the same and produces (or will sooner or later produce) the same results fails. Kealey does a great deal of asserting in this piece; he even presents a welter of strike statistics and anecdotal evidence from the labour press to demonstrate the already well known fact that there were a lot of strikes in Canada in 1919. He buttresses this with proclamations from workers who took the witness chair before the Mathers Commission. But his claim that all this amounted to a working class revolt is just that—an unsubstantiated claim.

There are several major problems with Kealey's evidence. First, his use of Mathers Commission testimony to show the revolutionary nature of Canadian workers is faulty. Such testimony is self-selected, prone to overblown exclamations on the part of the witnesses, and simply not verifiable as to whether or not it truly reflected the views of Canadian workers. Second, no one doubts that there were very many strikes in 1919, but very few were politically motivated and those that were—the Vancouver general strike, for example—were dismal failures. Does the obvious fact that Canadian workers were fed up with inflation, rising unemployment, government heavy handedness, employer intransigence, and so on mean that they were consciously trying to overthrow capitalism? That is a far-fetched conclusion. Finally, Kealey ignores the overwhelming evidence that SPC-led efforts to launch sympathetic strikes in Calgary, Edmonton, and Vancouver were total failures because the workers refused to follow the radicals. He claims that "the strike wave . . . gained SPC leadership only begrudgingly."[19] He offers not a word of evidence to support this preposterous assertion because there is none. In fact, the evidence shows the exact opposite to be true. The best example is the Vancouver general strike which dragged on from June 3 to June 30. In that city only 5,804 workers out of 16,000 union members voted in the general strike referendum; 3,305 voted to strike, 2,499 voted against. The trades council, dominated by SPC members such as Jack Kavanagh, called a general strike anyway.[20] The workers were thoroughly defeated.[21] Does Kealey think of this as an irresistible flood tide of revolt? Apparently yes. Thus Kealey's essay, for all the footnotes, amounts to little more than pamphleteering. He is rallying the revolutionary troops; he is certainly not advancing scholarship.

Even Kealey's piece, however, is not the most absurd example of this tendency of some Marxist labour historians to romanticize the events of 1919 and try to shoe-horn them into a revolutionary mold. The worst example is Nolan Reilly's introduction to the volume of *Labour/Le Travail* which contains the Kealey essay. Reilly was the author of a fine article on the 1919 general strike in Amherst, Nova Scotia which, although cast as an attack on "western exceptionalism" —i.e., it proved that workers in one Atlantic community had been radicalized enough to launch a general strike—added important new information to our picture of Nova Scotia labour history.[22] Unlike that article, Reilly's introduction to the special issue of *Labour/ Le Travail* was not based on primary source work and was not designed to add to our knowledge of the events of 1919. Nevertheless, he took it upon himself to impose a historiographical interpretation by consensus! His effort is worth quoting at length: "During the sessions of the conference . . . a consensus emerged that the Winnipeg confrontation was only the tip of an iceberg of class conflict that stretched from Nova Scotia to British Columbia . . . Workers in no one region were found to be exceptionally radical or conservative . . . This line of reasoning marked a significant revision of the historiography and popular thinking on the 1919 General Strike."[23] It did? Did this happen because the participants (all the major paper givers were apparently selected by Reilly) took a poll of some sort and decided to establish (or, in this case, reaffirm) a particular party line? Does Reilly really look at the process of historical interpretation that way? Does Kealey, who edits the journal this bit of nonsense appeared in?

Perhaps the final word on Kealey, Reilly, et al. should be left to Lyle Dick of Parks Canada who reviewed a booklet entitled "1919: The Winnipeg General Strike, A Driving and Walking Tour," prepared for the Manitoba Department of Culture, Heritage and Recreation by Nolan Reilly and Gerry Berkowski. Dick points out that the booklet—admittedly designed to be read by non-experts— is not so much a history as a romance. The strike story as told in this booklet shares common characteristics with the romance form: there is the struggle of good (the strikers) with evil (the employers); there is the struggle of the hero (the working class is the collective hero, R.B. Russell the individual one) against the villain (prominent industrialists and military leaders).

This approach solves one mystery—why leftist historians are determined to assert, in the face of all the evidence, that the strike was a triumph after all, even though it was smashed and many of the unions participating in it subsequently withered away. Since Reilly et al. view the strike as a romance, Dick asserts, their claim that the strike was ultimately successful must follow: "the presentation of a heroic conflict . . . demands a conclusion consistent with this structure. . . . Inasmuch as the actual events of the Strike do not provide sufficient hope for labour's transcendence, so the authors must look forward to a subsequent resolution. This is provided in the epilogue's reference to the fruition of industrial unionism in the 1940s." Dick concludes that this booklet too is not a serious effort to relate the story of the strike; rather, it is a rallying cry for radicalism: "Gerry Berkowski and Nolan Reilly seem . . . intent on recapturing the energy and vitality of Winnipeg's strikers as a source of inspiration to present-day workers."[24]

The workers were the major participant in the general strike—there would have been no such event without them—but the impact of the strike on labour in Winnipeg and elsewhere in Canada is still an obvious source of controversy. As Dick points out, the argument has been removed from the realm of historical debate. It has, instead, become part of the mythology and martyrology of the Canadian left. The fairy tale goes something like this: evil, corrupt, and decadent employers undermined the independence, self-respect, and economic well-being of an otherwise vigorous and energetic working class until the workers revolted in self-righteous fury. They fought a clean fight against a secret conspiracy of business and government, but they were defeated by trickery, chicanery, and, ultimately, brute force. But the defeat was only momentary because their cause was too righteous to be truly defeated. In the end, phoenix-like, they rose again, in other forms (i.e., industrial unionism, the CCF), and triumphed.

There is a thread of truth to this, as there is to most legends, but the hard realities were very different. For example, take the skilled craft unionists who led the labour movement in Winnipeg and who called the strike. In the two decades prior to the strike they made virtually no effort to organize the truly downtrodden of Winnipeg—unskilled labour, immigrants, and women workers. In fact, they generally spurned them. Most tried to keep their union locals as lily white as they could. They were class conscious only to the extent that they were conscious of themselves as a labour elite, even as a social elite within the labour movement, and they were determined to keep it that way.

When these men (for they would never let a woman among them, for all their socialist bleatings) leaped into the 1919 general strike, they betrayed the trust of their followers with an ill-conceived, poorly executed action that was bound to be defeated in the way that the Seattle General Strike (an event they were well aware of) had been defeated several months earlier. Did they not pause for one moment to take the measure of what they were doing? There was certainly justice in their demands to have the metal trades council recognized, but there was no truth whatever to their claim to be fighting for collective bargaining in Winnipeg. They were fighting a propaganda war just as intense as the propaganda war fought against them. They gave the federal government the excuse it wanted to crush the strike, instead of working carefully toward their objectives.

Their defeat was as complete a defeat as ever was. There is no connection whatever between the Winnipeg general strike and the rise of industrial unionism in the 1940s. There is only the most slender thread connecting the strike to the rise of the CCF (or the Communist Party of Canada, for that matter). The strike brought only defeat and the sapping of the strength of the Winnipeg labour movement for years to come so that it could offer little or no resistance to the employer counter-offensives of the 1920s.

It is harder to measure the impact of the strike on the employers of Winnipeg. H.C. Pentland was the original purveyor of the notion that the strike sapped their strength as well.[25] Certainly the strike seemed to mark the end of the decades-long Winnipeg boom, but did it actually mark the end or only coincide with it? Surely the most important factors for the decline of Winnipeg's economic vitality in the post-1919 period were the end of large-scale immigration to the west, the end of homesteading on the prairies, and the rapid post-war growth of Vancouver as the major entrepot of the Canadian west. These factors, far more than the docility of the post-strike Winnipeg labour force, were responsible for miring Winnipeg in stagnation. Perhaps Pentland was trying to produce a theory that demonstrates that those who sowed despair (the Winnipeg employers) reaped it in return. That would fit the concept of the strike as a romance. In any case, his theory is not based on any evidence at all.

The Winnipeg general strike was an important event in Canadian history. It affected tens, even hundreds, of thousands of Canadians, embroiled three levels of government, and attracted the attention of observers all over the world. It had an important, lasting impact on all who participated in it. This would be true of any event of such magnitude. But to seek hidden inner meanings to this event, rather than to study it for what it was, is to impart to it more than anyone has a right to do. The Winnipeg general strike, like every other event in human history, was a unique occurrence that took place for particular reasons and which had specific consequences. It is no less important for that.

❖Notes

CHAPTER 1: The Early Years

1. Grant MacEwan, *Between the Red and the Rockies,* p. 106.
2. W. L. Morton, *Manitoba: A History,* p. 172.
3. Ibid., p. 194
4. R. G. MacBeth, *Sir Augustus Nanton: A Biography, p.* 21.
5. Canada, *Fifth Census of Canada, 1911,* II, p. 447 (henceforth cited as *1911 Census*).
6. *1891 Census,* III, p. 382.
7. *1901 Census,* III, p. 161.
8. *Industrial Canada* (Toronto), April 1913, p. 1214.
9. A. R. Allen, "The Social Gospel in Canada, 1890—1928," *Canadian Historical Review,* December 1968, p. 381.
10. K. W. McNaught, *A Prophet in Politics,* p. 41.
11. Victoria University Archives (VUA), Bland Papers, Box I, No. 56. Speech of October 29, 1909.
12. Ibid., Box I, No. 28. Speech of February 13, 1905.
13. Ibid., Box I, No. 68. Speech of December 15, 1912.
14. Ibid., Box I, No. 66. Speech of November 25, 1912.
15. M. Norell, "Labor in Winnipeg: The Rise of Trade Unionism," p. 10.
16. D. R. Kennedy, *The Knights of Labor in Canada,* p. 38.
17. Norell, "Labor in Winnipeg," p. 10.

18. Kennedy, *Knights of Labor,* p. 39.

19. Ibid., H. A. Logan, *Trade Unions in Canada,* pp. 52, 55-56. The name *The Peoples' Voice* was later shortened to *The Voice.*

20. Norell, "Labor in Winnipeg," p. 11.

21. Manitoba, *First Annual Report of the Bureau of Labor: 1915— 1916,* p. 9 (henceforth cited as *Manitoba Bureau of Labor, 1916*).

22. C. Lipton, *The Trade Union Movement of Canada, 1827—1959,* pp. 99-100.

23. Ibid.

24. P. Phillips, *No Power Greater,* pp. 37-39.

25. Lipton, *Trade Union Movement,* pp. 100-101.

26. *The Voice* (Winnipeg), March 23, 1906, p. 1.

27. *Manitoba Free Press* (Winnipeg), March 26, 1906, p. 8.

28. Ibid., March 28, 1906, p. 15,

29. *The Voice,* March 30, 1906, p. 1.

30. *Manitoba Free Press,* March 30, 1906, p. 1.

31. Ibid., March 31, 1906, p. 3.

32. Bland Papers, Box I, No. 35. Speech of April 1, 1906.

33. *Manitoba Free Press,* April 2, 1906, p. 7.

34. Ibid.

35. Ibid., March 31, 1906, p. 1; *The Voice,* April 6, 1906, p. 1.

36. Canada, *Labour Gazette,* May 1906, pp. 1265-1266.

37. *Manitoba Free Press,* May 22, 1906, p. 1.

38. *The Voice,* May 25, 1906, p. 1.

39. Ibid.

40. Ibid.

41. Ibid., July 20, 1906, p. 1.

42. M. Robin, *Radical Politics and Canadian Labour,* p. 37.

43. Ibid., pp. 62-64.

44. Ibid., October 17, 1911, p. 24; *Labour Gazette,* November 1911, p. 477.

45. *Manitoba Free Press,* October 17, 1911, p. 24.

46. McNaught, *Prophet in Politics,* p. 53; *The Voice,* October 27, 1911, p. 1.

47. Canada, *Annual Report on Labour Organization in Canada,* 1913, p. 64 (henceforth cited as *Labour Organization in Canada*).

CHAPTER 2: The Depths of Depression

1. *The Voice,* November 7, 1913, p. 4.
2. Ibid., January 30, 1914, p. 1.
3. Ibid., September 11, 1914, p. 3.
4. Ibid., October 9, 1914, p. 4.
5. Ibid., February 20, 1914, p. 1.
6. Ibid., August 7, 1914, p. 1.
7. Ibid., July 4, 1913, p. 1.
8. *Trades and Labor Congress, Report of the Thirtieth Annual Convention of the Trades and Labor Congress of Canada,* 1914, pp. 35-36 (henceforth cited as TLC Proceedings).
9. *The Voice,* September 13, 1913, p. 4.
10. Based on figures in M. C. Urquhart and K. A. M. Buckley, eds., *Historical Statistics of Canada,* p. 515.
11. Construction permit figures may be examined in the monthly listings of the *Labour Gazette.*
12. *TLC Proceedings,* 1915, p. 25.
13. *The Voice,* June 2, 1916, p. 8.
14. Ibid., October 3, 1913, p. 1; January 16, 1914, p. 5.
15. Ibid.
16. Ibid., December 5, 1913, p. 1.
17. Ibid., May 29, 1914, p. 8.
18. Ibid., July 3, 1914, p. 7.
19. *TLC Proceedings,* 1915, p. 25.
20. *The Voice,* December 18, 1914, p. 4.
21. Ibid., January 8, 1915, p. 1.
22. Ibid., March 5, 1915, p. 8.
23. Ibid., April 2, 1915, p. 5.
24. Ibid., June 11, 1915, p. 8.
25. Ibid., October 30, 1914, p. 1.

CHAPTER 3: The Trials of War

1. *The Voice,* July 20, 1917, p. 1.
2. Cost of living figures are compiled from monthly statistics in *Labour Gazette.*

3. Wage for 1915 from PAC, Borden Papers, RLB 1419, R. S. Ward to War Office, London, June 28, 1915; Wage for 1918 from Department of Labour Papers, File 1. Wage Scale Compilations, n.d.

4. Canada, *Wages and Hours of Labour in Canada:* 1901—1920.

5. *The Voice,* June 18, 1915, p. 1.

6. Cost of living figures are compiled from monthly statistics in *Labour Gazette.*

7. *The Voice,* July 20, 1917, p. 1.

8. PAC, Flavelle Papers, File 96, report of total business placed in Canadian cities and towns, January 24, 1919.

9. *Industrial Canada,* July 1915, pp. 310-312.

10. Author's interview with F. G. Tipping and L. Paulley, May 9, 1969.

11. Author's interview with Alex Shepherd, May 6, 1969.

12. Flavelle Papers, File 11, E. Barrett to Flavelle, September 15, 1916.

13. Borden Papers, OC 235, R. A. Rigg to Director of Army Contracts, London, July 10, 1915.

14. *TLC Proceedings,* 1916, p. 170.

15. *The Voice,* February 5, 1915, p. 4.

16. Ibid., March 12, 1915, p. 4.

17. Borden Papers, RLB 1419, The Duke of Connaught to A. Bonar Law, December 17, 1915.

18. Ibid., Lloyd George to Borden, August 8, 1917.

19. Ibid., Crothers to Borden, June 9, 1917.

20. Ibid., Governor General to A. Bonar Law, December 17, 1915.

21. J. M. Bliss, "A Canadian Businessman and War: The Case of Joseph Flavelle," in J. L. Granatstein and R. D. Cuff, eds., *War and Society in North America,* pp. 20-36.

22. *TLC Proceedings,* 1917, pp. 32-34.

23. Flavelle Papers, File 11, Flavelle to Barrett, September 12, 1916.

24. M. Robin, "Registration, Conscription and Independent Labour Politics, 1916-1917," *Canadian Historical Review,* June 1966, p. 111.

25. L. Heaps, "A Rebel in the House," p. 23.

26. Ibid., p. 26.

27. *TLC Proceedings,* 1917, p. 142; author's interview with R. Durward, May 13, 1969.

28. *Labour Organization in Canada*, pp. 40-41.

29. *The Voice*, June 22, 1917, p. 1.

30. *Bulletin*, (Winnipeg), September 1917, p. 1.

31. PAM, Winnipeg Board of Trade, Executive Minutes, January 16, 1917, p. 277.

32. *Manitoba Free Press*, August 1, 1917, p. 9.

33. DND Papers, File 3686, Vol. I, General Officer Commanding Military District 10 to Ottawa, July 7, 1917.

34. Ibid., File 2115, G.O.C. M.D. 10 to Ottawa, August 13, 1917.

35. Ibid., File 2102, District Intelligence Officer to Assistant Director, Military Intelligence, Ottawa, March 27, 1918.

CHAPTER 4: Injunction City

1. *The Voice*, June 8, 1917, p. 4.

2. *Bulletin*, May 1917, p. 2.

3. See L. Orlikow, "The Reform Movement in Manitoba, 1910—1915," in D. Swainson, ed., *Historical Essays on the Prairie Provinces*, pp. 215-229.

4. *Manitoba Bureau of Labor*, 1916, pp. 9-10.

5. Ibid., pp. 28-29.

6. Manitoba, "An Act to Establish and Protect the Wages of Workmen Employed on Public Works," 1916, C.121.

7. PAM, Manitoba Department of Public Works, File "Fair Wages 1915—1919," Minutes of Fair Wages Board Hearing, October 1, 1917 (henceforth cited as Manitoba Fair Wages File).

8. Ibid., Oxton to H. B. Lyall, August 19, 1916.

9. *Labour Gazette*, September 1916, p. 1588.

10. J. W. Wilton, "Any Man," p. 235.

11. *Labour Gazette*, May 1916, pp. 1163-1164; *Industrial Canada*, March 1916, p. 1183.

12. *Industrial Canada*, March 1916, p. 1183.

13. *Manitoba Bureau of Labor*, 1917, pp. 29-31.

14. *Industrial Canada*, February 1920, p. 59.

15. *Labour Gazette*, August 1918, pp. 681-682.

16. *TLC Proceedings*, 1917, p. 59.

17. *The Voice*, June 8, 1917, p. 8; *Labour Gazette*, August 1917, p. 612.

18. D. C. Masters, *The Winnipeg General Strike*, p. 15.

19. F. G. Tipping to author, January 5, 1969.

20. Canada, "Evidence Presented to the Royal Commission on Industrial Relations," (henceforth cited as Mathers Commission Evidence), testimony of T. R. Deacon, pp. 150, 156.

21. Ibid., p. 152.

22. *Industrial Canada*, February 1917, p. 1159.

23. A. Shepherd to author, February 3, 1969.

24. *Industrial Canada*, July 1915, p. 303.

25. *Bulletin*, November 1915, p. 3; Thwaites, "The International Association of Machinists in Canada: To 1919," p. 68.

26. Author's interview with Alex Shepherd, May 6, 1969.

27. Flavelle Papers, File 11, report of August 28, 1916 in E. Barrett to Flavelle, September 15, 1916.

28. PAM, interviews conducted by Lionel Orlikow for the Manitoba Historical Society, 1961; interview with R. B. Russell.

29. *Bulletin*, October 1914, p. 3.

30. Ibid., May 1914, p. 8.

31. Ibid., April 1918, p. 2.

32. Ibid., April 1917, p. 3.

33. Ibid., June 1917, p. 1.

34. *The Voice*, June 22, 1917, p. 8.

35. *Labour Gazette*, August 1917, p. 609.

36. *Manitoba Free Press*, June 2, 1917, p. 1.

CHAPTER 5: The Triumph of Radicalism

1. *Manitoba Free Press*, May 4, 1918, p. 13.

2. *The Voice*, May 10, 1918, p. 1.

3. Ibid.

4. *Manitoba Free Press*, May 13, 1918, p. 1.

5. Winnipeg, *City Council Minutes*, May 13, 1918, pp. 258-259.

6. *Manitoba Free Press*, May 14, 1918, p. 1.

7. *The Voice*, May 17, 1918, p. 1.

8. *Manitoba Free Press*, May 15, 1918, p. 1.

9. Ibid., May 16, 1918, p. 11.

10. Ibid., p. 1.

11. Ibid., May 20, 1918, p. 11.
12. See *Labour Gazette,* June and July, 1918, for information on strikes.
13. *The Voice,* May 24, 1918, p. 1.
14. Borden Papers, OC 505, G. W. Allan to Borden, May 20, 1918.
15. Ibid., A. L. Crossin to Allan, May 17, 1918.
16. Rigg/Rees Papers, Murray to Rigg, May 28, 1918.
17. Borden Papers, OC 505, Borden to Crossin, May 18, 1918.
18. Dixon Papers, M. McBride to Dixon, March 8, 1920, contains portion of a letter from Robertson to McBride, June 15, 1918.
19. *Manitoba Free Press,* May 25, 1918, p. 1; Rigg/Rees Papers, Murray to Rigg, May 28, 1918.
20. *Manitoba Free Press,* May 28, 1918, p. 8.
21. Ibid., May 25, 1918, p. 9.
22. *The Voice,* May 17, 1918, p. 1.
23. Ibid.
24. Ibid., May 24, 1918, p. 1.
25. *Labour Organization in Canada,* 1918, p. 62.
26. Rigg/Rees Papers, Murray to Rigg, May 28, 1918.
27. *Manitoba Free Press,* May 25, 1918, p. 9.
28. *Bulletin,* June 1918, p. 1.
29. Rigg/Rees Papers, Murray to Rigg, May 28, 1918.
30. *Bulletin,* June 1918, p. 3.
31. Board of Trade Executive Minutes, July 24, 1918, p. 317.
32. *Manitoba Free Press,* July 27, 1918, p. 9.
33. *Western Labor News* (Winnipeg), August 2, 1918, p. 1.
34. *The Voice,* May 24, 1918, p. 2.
35. *Manitoba Free Press,* July 4, 1918, p. 1.
36. *Bulletin,* October 1918, p. 1; *Manitoba Free Press,* July 20, 1918, p. 4.
37. H. A. Logan, *Trade Unions in Canada,* p. 148.
38. *Bulletin,* October 1918, p. 1; *Manitoba Free Press,* July 20, 1918, p. 4.
39. *Manitoba Free Press,* July 23, 1918, p. 14.
40. *Labour Gazette,* August 1918, pp. 604-606; *Western Labor News,* August 2, 1918, p. 1.

41. *Manitoba Free Press,* June 22, 1918, p. 1.

42. Author's interview with F. G. Tipping and L. Paulley, May 9, 1969.

43. *Manitoba Free Press,* July 4, 1918, p. 9.

44. *Labour Gazette,* August 1918, p. 607.

45. Author's interview with F. G. Tipping and L. Paulley, May 9, 1969.

46. *Labour Gazette,* August 1918, pp. 604-610.

47. Author's interview with F. G. Tipping and L. Paulley, May 9, 1969.

48. *Western Labor News,* October 4, 1918, p. 1.

49. Ibid., October 4, 1918, p. 1.

50. Ibid.

CHAPTER 6: Socialists and Soldiers

1. *Western Labor News,* August 30, 1918, p. 1.

2. *TLC Proceedings,* 1918, pp. 138-139.

3. *Western Labor News,* October 4, 1918, p. 1.

4. Borden Papers, OC 505, Privy Council report of July 11, 1918.

5. Flavelle Papers, File 1918—1919, 1924, Irish to Crothers, June 28, 1918.

6. *Labour Gazette,* August 1918, pp. 616-618.

7. Ibid., November 1918, pp. 983-984.

8. Ibid., December 1918, p. 1101.

9. *Western Labor News,* October 18, 1918, p. 1.

10. Ibid.

11. DND Papers, File 2102, Chief Commissioner of Dominion Police to General Gwatkin, August 27, 1918.

12. *Labour Organization in Canada,* 1918, pp. 36-37.

13. *Western Labor News,* December 13, 1918, p. 1.

14. Ibid., December 20, 1918, p. 1.

15. Author's interview with Alex Shepherd, May 6, 1969.

16. Robin, *Radical Politics and Canadian Labour,* pp. 168-169.

17. *Western Labor News,* December 27, 1918, p. 1.

18. Ibid., p. 4.

19. Russell Papers, Exhibit No. 15-100A, W. Breeze to Anon., February 1, 1919; *Western Labor News,* January 24, 1919, p. 1.

20. PAC, Millar Collection, D. Millar interview with Alex Shepherd, July 1969; *Manitoba Free Press,* January 27, 1919, p. 1.

21. *Western Labor News,* January 31, 1919, p. 1.

22. *Manitoba Free Press,* February 7, 1919, p. 2; February 8, 1919, p. 1.

23. *Western Labor News,* February 7, 1919, p. 1.

24. Wilton, "Any Man," pp. 335-336.

25. *Ontario Labor News* (Toronto), May 15, 1919, p. 3.

26. DND Papers, File C2051, Superintendent F. J. Horrigan to A. B. Perry, January 30, 1919.

27. Ibid., File C3686, Vol. I., intelligence report of March 22, 1919.

CHAPTER 7: The One Big Union

1. See John Reed, *Ten Days That Shook the World,* pp. 68-155, and Alan Moorehead, *The Russian Revolution,* pp. 234-250.

2. See J. R. P. McKenzie, *Weimer Germany,* pp. 25-43.

3. R. K. Murray, *Red Scare: A Study of National Hysteria, 1919-1920,* pp. 3-17.

4. M. Dubofsky, *We Shall Be All, A History of the Industrial Workers of the World,* pp. 385-392, 406, 422.

5. Murray, *Red Scare,* p. 68.

6. Ibid., pp. 58-60; R. L. Friedheim, *The Seattle General Strike,* pp. 123-145.

7. See *The Voice,* from October 1917 to the last issue. The first small article dealing with the Bolshevik Revolution was published on January 18, 1918.

8. *Western Labor News,* February 14, 1919, p. 2, and other issues published during these months.

9. Ibid., April 25, 1919, p. 1; Russell Papers, Russell to Midgley, April 17, 1919.

10. Ibid., May 16, 1919, p. 2.

11. Interviews conducted by Lionel Orlikow for the Manitoba Historical Society, 1961. Interview with R. B. Russell.

12. *Western Labor News,* September 13, 1918, p. 8.

13. Ibid., November 22, 1918, p. 6.

14. Russell Papers, "Revolutionary Industrial Unionism: Tactics and Plan of the Workers International Industrial Union," pamphlet published in South Melbourne, Australia, September 1918.
15. *Western Labor News*, March 7, 1919, p. 4.
16. Ibid., March 14, 1919, p. 1.
17. Ibid.
18. Robin, *Radical Politics and Canadian Labour*, pp. 170-173.
19. Ibid., p. 177.
20. *Labour Organization in Canada*, 1919, pp. 22-27.
21. Masters, *Winnipeg General Strike*, p. 38.
22. Russell Papers, Russell to Midgley, March 28, 1919.
23. Ibid., April 11, 1919.

CHAPTER 8: Towards the Brink

1. *Western Labor News*, February 21, 1919, p. 1.
2. Dixon's address to the jury, p. 15.
3. Manitoba, "An Act Respecting Industrial Conditions," 1919, c. 43.
4. *Western Labor News*, April 18, 1919, p. 1.
5. *Industrial Canada*, April 1919, pp. 55-56.
6. Ibid., April 1919, p. 55.
7. Ibid., February 1919, pp. 67-68.
8. *Western Labor News*, February 14, 1919, p. 1.
9. Ibid., May 9, 1919, p. 1.
10. Mathers Commission evidence, testimony of J. B. Hugg, pp. 7-32.
11. PAC, Meighen Papers, File 31, J. McDougald to Manitoba Bridge, January 23, 1919, No. 2617-8.
12. Ibid., Meighen to Deacon, February 14, 1919, No. 2628.
13. Author's interview with F. G. Tipping and L. Paulley, May 9, 1969.
14. *Western Labor News*, May 16, 1919, p. 1.
15. Ibid.
16. Ibid., April 25, 1919, p. 1.
17. Mathers Commission evidence, testimony of J. B. Hugg, p. 14.
18. *Western Labor News*, May 16, 1919, p. 1.
19. Ibid., May 9, 1919, p. 1.

20. Ibid.

21. *Bulletin,* March 1919, p. 5.

22. *Western Labor News,* May 16, 1919, p. 8.

23. Ibid.

24. Ibid., June 4, 1919, p. 3; *Winnipeg Citizen* (Winnipeg), May 20, 1919, p. 1.

25. PAC, White Papers, Gray to White, May 15, 1919, No. 14030.

CHAPTER 9: Battling for the Lord: May 15-29   (pages 115-141)

1. *Western Labor News,* May 15, 1919, p. 1.

2. DND Papers, File 5678, Ketchen to Ottawa, May 19, 1919.

3. PAC, Secretary of State Papers, File 170, E. J. Chambers to Gwatkin, May 19, 1919.

4. Ibid., Minutes of meeting of western division Canadian Press, June 9, 1919.

5. Anon., *"Saving the World from Democracy": The Winnipeg General Sympathetic Strike, May–June 1919,* pp. 49-50 (henceforth cited as *Winnipeg Sympathetic Strike*).

6. *Manitoba Free Press,* May 15, 1919, p. 11.

7. *Western Labor News,* various articles in editions of May 26, 28, 29, and June 2, 1919.

8. Ibid., May 19, 1919, p. 2.

9. Russell Papers, Russell to Midgley, May 19, 1919.

10. *Winnipeg Citizen,* May 23, 1919, p. 3.

11. DND Papers, File C3576, Ketchen to Elmsley, May 13, 1921.

12. Board of Trade, *Annual Report, 1918.*

13. Meighen Papers, File 30; Dickson to Meighen, July 16, 1918, No. 2737; Pugh to Meighen, August 31, 1919, No. 2697.

14. PAM, Manning Papers, File 47, Citizens' League recruitment leaflet.

15. PAM, Citizens' League account book.

16. Typed leaflet under head of *Winnipeg Citizen,* issued May 22, 1919.

17. *Winnipeg Telegram,* May 28, 1919, p. 1.

18. Anon., *An Address on the Subject of the Winnipeg Strike, May–June 1919,* p. 11.

19. DND Papers, File C3576, Ketchen to Elmsley, May 13, 1921.
20. Ibid., Col. W. Gibson to Gen. W. King, *et al*, June 20, 1921.
21. PAC, Woodsworth Papers, File 61, Vol. 14, "Sidelights on the Winnipeg Trials," pp. 4-5 quotes Meighen to Andrews, May 26, 1919.
22. PAC, Royal Canadian Mounted Police Papers, File 5, N. W. Rowell to A. A. Maclean, August 19, 1919.
23. *Western Labor News*, May 23, 1919, p. 2; *Winnipeg Citizen*, May 22, 1919, p. 2.
24. Wilton, "Any Man," p. 351.
25. DND Papers, File C3576, Ketchen to Elmsley, May 13, 1921.
26. *Western Labor News*, December 6, 1918, p. 1.
27. Ibid., May 17, 1919, p. 2.
28. *Winnipeg Sympathetic Strike*, p. 51.
29. *Western Labor News*, May 21, 1919, p. 1.
30. *Winnipeg Citizen*, May 21, 1919, p. 2.
31. Ibid., p. 2.
32. Ibid., p. 3.
33. Canada, *House of Commons Debates*, June 2, 1919, p. 3042 (henceforth cited as *Hansard*); Borden Papers, OC 557, Borden's speech notes of June 2, 1919.
34. *Chicago Daily Tribune* (Chicago), May 21, 1919, p. 1.
35. *New York Times* (New York), May 28, 1919, p. 1.
36. Ibid., May 22, 1919, p. 14.
37. Borden Papers, OC 564, Studebaker Corporation to Southern Canada Power Company, May 23, 1919.
38. R. Graham, *Arthur Meighen*, Vol. I: *The Door of Opportunity*, pp. 236-237.
39. PAC, Post Office Subject Files Vol. 122 (henceforth cited as Underwood-Bower Correspondence), memo of May 20, 1919.
40. PAC, White Papers, Coulter to White, May 22, 1919, No. 14065-71.
41. Ibid., Underwood to Coulter, May 22, 1919, No. 14078.
42. Ibid., Meighen and Robertson to White, May 23, 1919, No. 14082.
43. Underwood-Bower Correspondence, Underwood to Cooligan, May 26, 1919.

44. Ibid., May 28, 1919.
45. Ibid., May 29, 1919.
46. Ibid., June 1, 1919.
47. Ibid., Coulter to Underwood, May 29, 1919.
48. Borden Diary, entry of June 3, 1919, p. 425.
49. White Papers, Robertson to White, May 22, 1919, No. 14057.
50. *Winnipeg Citizen*, May 24, 1919, p. 1.
51. Borden Papers, OC 564, Robertson to R. C. Marshall, May 26, 1919.
52. *Toronto Star*, May 26, 1919, p. 1.
53. *Hansard*, June 2, 1919, p. 3014. Lapointe quotes Robertson to Gompers, May 29, 1919.
54. Ibid., June 2, 1926, p. 4005. Heenan quotes Robertson to Borden, May 25, 1919.
55. Russell Papers, Johns to Midgley, May 19, 1919.
56. *Western Labor News*, June 23, 1919, p. 4, reprints interview published in *Literary Digest*.
57. *Hansard*, June 2, 1919, pp. 3035-3043.
58. Ibid., June 9, 1919, p. 3241.
59. *Winnipeg Citizen*, May 22, 1919, p. 2.
60. Wilton, "Any Man," pp. 355-357.
61. Millar Collection, D. Millar interview with Col. Macpherson, August 1969.
62. *Western Labor News*, May 26, 1919, p. 1.
63. *Winnipeg Telegram*, May 29, 1919, p. 2; *Manitoba Free Press*, May 27, 1919, p. 1.
64. *Winnipeg Telegram*, May 29, 1919, p. 2.
65. City Council Minutes, May 21, 1919, p. 4.
66. *Manitoba Free Press*, June 5, 1919, p. 4.

CHAPTER 10: Impasse: May 30—June 16

1. *Western Labor News*, May 17, 1919, p. 1.
2. Borden Papers, OC 564, Biggar memo, May 20, 1919.
3. *Winnipeg Sympathetic Strike*, p. 83.
4. *Western Labor News*, June 2, 1919, p. 1.
5. Ibid., June 5, 1919, p. 1.

6. Ibid., p. 1.
7. Ibid., May 16, 1919, p. 2.
8. Russell Papers, Midgley to Russell, April 21, 1919.
9. Ibid., Midgley to Russell, April 21, 1919.
10. Ibid., Evidence Book, Russell to Tallon, May 15, 1919.
11. *Western Labor News,* June 5, 1919, p. 4.
12. *Manitoba Free Press,* June 5, 1919, p. 2.
13. *Western Labor News,* June 6, 1919, p. 1; *Manitoba Free Press,* June 6, 1919, p. 3.
14. Borden Papers, OC 564, Ketchen to Maj. Gen. J. H. Elmsley, Ottawa, June 5, 1919.
15. McCord Museum, Scott Papers, Scott to (?), June 21, 1919.
16. F. G. Thompson, "OBU General Sympathetic Strike, 1919: Intervention of Returned Soldiers."
17. Scott Papers, minutes of meeting of June 13, 1919.
18. Ibid., Scott to C. G. Power, September 7, 1919.
19. *Winnipeg Sympathetic Strike,* pp. 124-216.
20. DND Papers, File C3576, Ketchen to Elmsley, May 13, 1921.
21. *Winnipeg Telegram,* May 29, 1919, p. 1.
22. Ibid., May 30, 1919, p. 1.
23. *Manitoba Free Press,* June 4, 1919, p. 7.
24. *Winnipeg Citizen,* June 4, 1919, p. 2.
25. Borden Papers, OC 564, Ketchen to Elmsley, May 29, 1919.
26. Ibid., June 4, 1919.
27. *Winnipeg Citizen,* June 18, 1919, p. 1.
28. *Manitoba Free Press,* June 5, 1919, p. 1.
29. Ibid., June 7, 1919, p. 3.
30. Millar Collection, H. J. Riley to D. Millar, January 31, 1966.
31. Author's interview with G. Spry, May 1, 1969.
32. *Winnipeg Citizen,* June 6, 1919, p. 2; *Western Labor News,* June 6, 1919, p. 1.
33. *Toronto Star,* June 10, 1919, p. 2.
34. Borden Papers, OC 564, Andrews to Meighen, June 9, 1919.
35. Millar Collection, D. Millar interview with J. Dunwoody, August 1969.

36. DND Papers, File 5678, Ketchen to Elmsley, June 20, 1919.
37. *Western Labor News,* June 12, 1919, p. 1.
38. Borden Papers, OC 564, Ketchen to Elmsley, June 12, 1919; *Western Labor News,* June 13, 1919, p. 4.
39. Borden Papers, OC 564, Kavanagh to Borden, May 27, 1919.
40. Phillips, *No Power Greater,* p. 81; Masters, *Winnipeg General Strike,* pp. 91-92.
41. *Labour Organization in Canada,* 1919, pp. 24-25.
42. Russell Papers, Exhibit Book, exhibit No. 263, Midgley to Robinson, May 20, 1919.
43. Ibid., Robinson to Midgley, May 31, 1919.
44. *Western Labor News,* June 16, 1919, p. 1.
45. Borden Papers, OC 559, report of RNWMP operative, June 7, 1919.
46. *Western Labor News,* June 20, 1919, p. 2; Scott Papers, Mediation Committee memo, n.d.
47. Scott Papers, H. E. Barker to L. R. Barrett *et al,* June 7, 1919.
48. *Western Labor News,* June 12, 1919, p. 1.
49. Borden Papers, OC 564, Ketchen to Elmsley, June 6, 1919.
50. Ibid., Andrews to Meighen, June 9, 1919.
51. Ibid., Borden's copy of this message contains the following note written by Meighen: "This letter shows clearly the purpose Andrews had in suggesting the Minister go West—the opposite purpose than that for which he is going."
52. Ibid., Robertson to Borden, June 15, 1919.
53. *The Globe,* June 14, 1919, p. 11.
54. Borden Papers, OC 564, Robertson to Borden, June 13, 1919.
55. Ibid., June 14, 1919.
56. Ibid., June 15, 1919.
57. Ibid., June 14, 1919.
58. Ibid., June 17, 1919.
59. *Manitoba Free Press,* June 16, 1919, p. 1.
60. *Toronto Star,* June 2, 1919, p. 1.
61. Borden Papers, OC 564, T. Shea to G. B. Nicholson, May 28, 1919.
62. Ibid., Robertson to Borden, June 13, 1919.
63. Ibid.

64. Ibid., June 14, 1919.
65. Ibid., June 17, 1919.

CHAPTER 11: Defeat

1. Borden Papers, OC 564, Ketchen to Elmsley, May 26, 1919.
2. Ibid., Robertson to Borden, June 14, 1919.
3. Ibid., Calder to Moore, June 16, 1919.
4. Ibid., Ketchen to Elmsley, June 12, 1919.
5. Ibid., Meighen to Andrews, June 13, 1919.
6. Ibid., Robertson to Borden, June 13, 1919.
7. *Manitoba Free Press,* December 5, 1919, p. 3.
8. Borden Papers, OC 564, Calder to Starnes, June 17, 1919.
9. Ibid., Meighen to Andrews, June 17, 1919.
10. Ibid., Robertson to Borden, June 17, 1919.
11. *Winnipeg Sympathetic Strike,* p. 200.
12. *Hansard,* June 2, 1926, p. 4009.
13. DND Papers, File 5678, Ketchen to Elmsley, May 19, 1919.
14. Ibid., File C3576, Ketchen to Elmsley, May 13, 1921.
15. Ibid., File 5678, Adj. Gen., Ottawa, to Brig. Gen. Hill, May 23, 1919.
16. Ibid.
17. Royal Canadian Mounted Police, Annual Report 72-5, 1919, p. 4.
18. DND Papers, File 5678, Ketchen to Elmsley, June 17, 1919.
19. *Western Labor News,* June 14, 1919, p. 2.
20. Borden Papers, OC 564, Robertson to Borden, June 20, 1919.
21. *Western Labor News,* June 20, 1919, p. 1.
22. Borden Papers, OC 564, Robertson to Borden, June 20, 1919
23. Ibid., Ketchen to Elmsley, June 20, 1919.
24. Ibid., Robertson to Borden, June 21, 1919.
25. *Manitoba Free Press,* June 23, 1919, p. 1.
26. Ibid.
27. Ibid., p. 2.
28. Ibid., p. 4.
29. City Council Minutes, June 23, 1919, pp. 438-439.
30. *Manitoba Free Press,* June 23, 1919, p. 1.

31. Ibid.
32. Ibid.
33. Borden Papers, OC 564, Ketchen to Elmsley, 11:00 P.M., June 21, 1919.
34. *Manitoba Free Press,* June 23, 1919, p. 4.
35. Borden Papers, OC 564, Andrews to Meighen, June 24, 1919.
36. *Western Star,* June 24, 1919, p. 1.
37. *Enlightener,* June 25, 1919, p. 2.
38. Borden Papers, OC 564, Ketchen to Elmsley, June 24, 1919.
39. *Enlightener,* June 26, 1919, p. 2.

CHAPTER 12: Confrontation in Retrospect

1. Rigg/Rees Papers, Varley to ? (T. Moore or P. M. Draper), July 12, 1919.
2. Author's interview with Alex Shepherd, May 6, 1969.
3. *Labour Gazette,* May 1919, pp. 577-581.
4. Rigg/Rees Papers, Varley to ? (T. Moore or P. M. Draper), July 12, 1919.
5. See City of Winnipeg employment application form in Manning Papers, File 47.
6. Borden Papers, OC 564, Ketchen to Elmsley, June 26, 1919.
7. See Borden Papers, OC 564, and Post Office Records Vol. 124, for correspondence and documents relating to the efforts of postal employees to regain employment.
8. *Labour Gazette,* February 1921, pp. 165-189.
9. Rigg/Rees Papers, Rigg to Moore, August 9, 1919.

CHAPTER 13: A Longer View

1. Donald Avery, "The Radical Alien and the Winnipeg General Strike of 1919," p. 209.
2. J.E. Rea, "The Politics of Class."
3. J.E. Rea, "The Politics of Conscience: Winnipeg after the Strike," *Historical Papers, Communications Historique* 1971, pp. 276–288.
4. Rea, "The Politics of Class," p. 233.

5. P.H. Wichern, "Historical Influences on Contemporary Local Politics," p. 42.
6. David P. Yeo, "Rural Manitoba Views the 1919 Winnipeg General Strike," p. 30.
7. Mary Horodyski, "Women and the Winnipeg General Strike of 1919," p. 37.
8. Pam Tranfield, "Girl Strikers," p. 35.
9. Linda Kealey, "No Special Protection—No Sympathy," p. 135.
10. Review of *Confrontation* by Reginald Whitaker in *Canadian Journal of Political Science*, March 1976, pp. 133-134.
11. Review of *Confrontation* by Norman Penner in *This Magazine*, May–June 1975, pp. 28-31.
12. Bryan Palmer, "Working-Class Canada: Recent Historical Writing," *Queen's Quarterly*, winter 1979-80, pp. 598-599.
13. A.R. McCormack, *Reformers, Rebels, and Revolutionaries: The Western Canadian Radical Movement, 1899-1919.* (Toronto, University of Toronto Press, 1977).
14. David J. Bercuson, "Labour Radicalism and the Western Industrial Frontier, 1897-1919, *Canadian Historical Review*, June 1977, pp. 154-175.
15. G.S. Kealey, *Toronto Workers Respond to Industrial Capitalism, 1867-1892* (Toronto: University of Toronto Press, 1980).
16. G.S. Kealey, "1919," p. 15.
17. Ibid., p. 12.
18. Palmer, "Working-class Canada."
19. Kealey, "1919," p. 37.
20. *Vancouver Province*, June 30, 1919; *Calgary Daily Herald*, July 4, 1919.
21. David J. Bercuson, *Fools and Wise Men*.
22. Nolan Reilly, "The General Strike in Amherst, Nova Scotia, 1919."
23. Nolan Reilly, "Introduction to Papers from the Winnipeg General Strike Symposium," p. 8.
24. Lyle Dick, "Politics and Discourse," p. 38.
25. H.D. Pentland, "Fifty Years After," *Canadian Dimension* 6, 1969, pp. 14-17.

❖ Bibliography

Private Papers, Correspondence, and Diaries

Bland Papers, Box I. Victoria University Archives.
Borden Diary. Privately held.
Borden Papers. Public Archives of Canada (PAC)
Dixon Papers. Public Archives of Manitoba (PAM)
Flavelle Papers, Vols. 5, 6, 38. PAC.
Ketchen Papers. Privately held.
Manning Papers, Box 3. PAM.
Meighen Papers, Vol. 5. PAC.
Norris Papers. PAM.
Rigg/Rees Papers. PAM.
Russell Papers. PAM.
Scott Papers. McCord Museum, McGill University.
White Papers, Vol. 21. PAC.
Woodsworth Papers, Vol. 14. PAC.

Unpublished Government Records and Documents

Canada, Department of Labour, Economics and Research Branch, Collective Bargaining Surveys Section, 1900-1934. Vol. 42. PAC.
Canada, Department of Labour, "Evidence Presented to the Royal Commission on Industrial Relations at Winnipeg, May 10 and 12, 1919" (typewritten). Department of Labour Library.

Canada, Department of National Defence Papers, Files 1055-2-21, HQ C1555, C2051, 2102, 2115, C3576, C3686, 5678. PAC.
Canada, Post Office Records, Vol. 124. PAC.
Canada, Post Office Subject Files, Vol. 122. PAC.
Canada, Royal Canadian Mounted Police Papers, Vols. 1, 938. PAC.
Canada, Secretary of State Papers, Vol. 156. PAC.
Manitoba, Department of Public Works, Deputy Minister Correspondence and Papers, 1915-1934, Box 7. PAM.

Published Government Material

Canada, Department of Labour. *Annual Report on Labour Organization in Canada.*
Canada, Department of Labour. *Eighth Annual Report on Wholesale Prices in Canada, 1917.*
Canada, Department of Labour. *Labour Gazette.*
Canada, Department of Labour. *Wages and Hours of Labour in Canada, 1901-1920.*
Canada, Department of Trade and Commerce. *Census of Canada.*
Canada, Parliament. *House of Commons Debates.*
Manitoba, Department of Public Works. *Annual Report of the Bureau of Labor.*
Manitoba, *Royal Commission to inquire into and report upon the causes and effects of the General Strike which recently existed in the City of Winnipeg for a period of six weeks, including the methods of calling and carrying on such strike.*
Winnipeg, City of. *Minutes of Council.*

Unpublished Proceedings and Reports

Boilermakers International Union, Lodge 126, Minute Book. PAM.
Citizens League of Winnipeg. Notebook of expenses and contributions. PAM.
Dominion Bridge Co. Ltd. Minute Book No. 1. Dominion Bridge.
Winnipeg Board of Trade. Council and Executive Minutes, Vols. 3, 4. PAM.
Winnipeg Board of Trade. Minutes of the General Meetings, 1903-1918. PAM.

BIBLIOGRAPHY 227

Published Proceedings and Reports

Dominion Bridge Co. Ltd. *Annual Report,* 1913-1920.
Trades and Labor Congress. *Reports of the Annual Convention of the Trades and Labor Congress of Canada.*
Winnipeg Board of Trade. *Annual Report.*
Winnipeg Industrial Bureau. *Annual Report.*

Pamphlets

An Address on the Subject of the Winnipeg Strike, May-June, 1919. Winnipeg: Citizens' Committee of One Thousand, n.d.
Dixon's Address to the Jury. Winnipeg: The Israelite Press Limited, n.d.
"Saving the World from Democracy": The Winnipeg General Sympathetic Strike. Winnipeg: Winnipeg Defence Committee, n.d.

Books, Articles, and Dissertations

Allen, A. R. "The Social Gospel in Canada, 1890-1928." *Canadian Historical Review,* December, 1968.
Bliss, J. M. "A Canadian Businessman and War: The Case of Joseph Flavelle." In J. L. Granatstein and R. D. Cuff, eds., *War and Society in North America.* Toronto: Thomas Nelson, 1971.
Connor, R. (C. W. Gordon). *The Foreigner.* Toronto: The Westminster Co. Ltd., 1909.
Dubofsky, Melvyn. *We Shall Be All, A History of the Industrial Workers of the World.* Chicago: Quadrangle Books, 1969.
Dulles, F. R. *Labor In America, A History.* New York: Thomas W. Crowell, 1966.
Featherstonhaugh, R. C. *The Royal Canadian Mounted Police.* New York: J. J. Carrick, 1938.
Flood, Maxwell. *Payment Systems and their Development in the Railway Running Trades.* Ottawa: The Queen's Printer, 1968.
Forsey, E. "History of the Labour Movement," *Canada Year Book.* Ottawa: The Queen's Printer, 1967.
Friedheim, R. L. *The Seattle General Strike.* Seattle: University of Washington Press, 1964.
Graham, R. *Arthur Meighen.* Vol. I: *The Door of Opportunity.* Toronto: Clarke Irwin, 1960.

Kennedy, D. R. *The Knights of Labor in Canada.* London: The University of Western Ontario, 1956.

Lipton, C. *The Trade Union Movement of Canada, 1827-1959.* Montreal: Les Presses Sociales, 1968.

Logan, H. A. *Trade Unions in Canada.* Toronto: Macmillan, 1948.

MacBeth, R. G. *Sir Augustus Nanton, A Biography.* Toronto: Macmillan, 1931.

McClung, N. L. *Clearing in the West.* Toronto: Thomas Allen, 1935.

MacEwan, Grant. *Between the Red and the Rockies.* Toronto: University of Toronto Press, 1952.

MacInnis, G. *J. S. Woodsworth, A Man to Remember.* Toronto: Macmillan, 1953.

McKenzie, J. R. P. *Weimar Germany.* London: Blandford Press, 1971.

McNaught, K. W. *A Prophet in Politics.* Toronto: University of Toronto Press, 1959.

Masters, D. C. *The Winnipeg General Strike.* Toronto: University of Toronto Press, 1950.

Moorehead, Alan. *The Russian Revolution.* New York: Harper and Brothers, 1958.

Morton, W. L. *Manitoba: A History.* Toronto: University of Toronto Press, 1957.

Murray, R. K. *Red Scare: A Study of National Hysteria, 1919-1920.* New York: McGraw-Hill, 1964.

Mutchmor, J. R. *Mutchmor: The Memoirs of James Ralph Mutchmor.* Toronto: Ryerson Press, 1965.

O'Connor, H. *Revolution in Seattle.* New York: Monthly Review Press, 1964.

Orlikow, L. "The Reform Movement in Manitoba 1910-1915." In D. Swainson, ed., *Historical Essays on the Prairie Provinces.* Toronto: McClelland and Stewart, 1970.

Phillips, P. *No Power Greater.* Vancouver: British Columbia Federation of Labour, 1967.

Reed, John. *Ten Days That Shook the World.* New York: Vintage Books, 1960.

Robin, M. *Radical Politics and Canadian Labour.* Kingston: Queen's University Industrial Relations Centre, 1968.

———— . "Registration, Conscription and Independent Labour Politics." *Canadian Historical Review*, June 1966.

Rodney, W. *Soldiers of the International. A History of the Communist Party of Canada, 1919-1929.* Toronto: University of Toronto Press, 1968.

Seton-Watson, H. *Eastern Europe Between the Wars, 1918-1941.* Hamden, Conn: Archon Books, 1962.

Shearwood, F. P. *A Dominion Which Spans the Dominion.* Dominion Bridge Company Limited, n.p., n.d.

Thwaites, J. D. "The International Association of Machinists in Canada: to 1919." Unpublished M.A. dissertation, Carleton University, 1966.

Urquhart, M. C. and K. A. M. Buckley, eds. *Historical Statistics of Canada.* Toronto: Macmillan, 1965.

Yuzyk, P. *The Ukrainians in Manitoba: A Social History.* Toronto: University of Toronto Press, 1953.

Other Unpublished Sources

Dominion Bridge Co. Ltd. Reprint of Prospectus issued September 23, 1882.

Heaps, L. "A Rebel in the House." Unpublished manuscript. London, 1961.

Johnstone, H. S. "Pension Rights of Certain Employees of the C.P.R. and Associated Express and Steamship Companies," 1945 (typewritten).

Orlikow, Lionel. Transcripts of tape interviews prepared for the Manitoba Historical Society. Interviews with R. B. Russell.

PAC. Millar Collection. Miscellaneous letters and portions of interviews.

Norell, M. "Labor in Winnipeg: The Rise of Trade Unionism." United College, Winnipeg, 1945 (typewritten).

Thompson, F. G. "OBU General Sympathetic Strike, 1919, Intervention of Returned Soldiers." Winnipeg, 1969 (typewritten).

Wilton, J. W. "Any Man." Unpublished manuscript, n.p., n.d.

Publications on the Winnipeg General Strike since 1974

Avery, Donald. "The Radical Alien and the Winnipeg General Strike of 1919," in C. Berger and G. Cook, eds., *The West and the Nation: Essays in Honour of W.L. Morton*, pp. 209–231. Toronto: McClelland & Stewart, 1979.

Bercuson, David J. *Fools and Wise Men: The Rise and Fall of the One Big Union*. Toronto: McGraw-Hill Ryerson, 1978.

Dick, Lyle. "Politics and Discourse: A Review of 1919: The Winnipeg General Strike, A Driving and Walking Tour." *Manitoba History* 13, Spring 1987, pp. 33–38.

Friesen, Gerald. "Yours in Revolt: The Socialist Party of Canada and the Western Canadian Labour Movement." *Labour/Le Travailleur*, 1976, pp. 139–157.

Horodyski, Mary. "Women and the Winnipeg General Strike of 1919." *Manitoba History* 11, Spring 1986, pp. 28–37.

Kealey, G.S. "1919: The Canadian Labour Revolt." *Labour/Le Travail* 13, Spring, 1984, pp. 11–44.

Kealey, Linda. "No Special Protection—No Sympathy: Women's Activism in the Canadian Labour Revolt of 1919." in D.R. Hopkin and G.S. Kealey, eds., *Class, Community and the Labour Movement: Wales and Canada, 1850–1930*, pp. 134–159. Wales: Llafur/CCLH, 1989.

Rea, J.E. "The Politics of Class: Winnipeg City Council, 1919–1945," in C. Berger and G. Cook, eds., *The West and the Nation: Essays in Honour of W.L. Morton*, pp. 232–249. Toronto: McClelland & Stewart, 1979.

Reilly, Nolan. "The General Strike in Amherst, Nova Scotia, 1919." *Acadiensis* no. 2, Spring 1980, pp. 56–78.

– "Introduction to papers from the Winnipeg General Strike Symposium, March 1983." *Labour/Le Travail* 13, Spring 1984, pp. 7–10.

Seager, Allen. "Nineteen Nineteen: Year of Revolt." *Journal of the West* 23, no. 4, October 1984, pp. 40–47.

Tranfield, Pam. "Girl Strikers." *NeWest Review* 14, no. 5, June/July 1989, pp. 29, 34–35.

Wichern, P.H. "Historical influences on Contemporary Local Politics: The Case of Winnipeg." *Urban History Review* 12, June 1983, pp. 39–43.

Yeo, David, "Rural Manitoba Views the 1919 Winnipeg General Strike," *Prairie Forum* 14, no. 1, Spring 1989, pp. 23–36.

❖ Index

registration, 41; and workmen's compensation, 49; and GWVA, 142
Riordon, C., 107
Riot Act, in street railway strike, 14; on Bloody Saturday, 173
Riot of June 10, 154–155
Robertson, Sen. Gideon D., 80, 81, 132, 158–159, 170, 184–185; and municipal strike, 63–64; early career, 64; and Citizens' Committee, 121; and postal workers, 134, 135; and railway mail clerks, 134; philosophy, 135–136; and mediation committee, 159, 160, 162; and arrests, 164, 165; and Bloody Saturday, 171
Robinson, Ernie, 58, 84, 113, 166; and Western Labor Conference, 80
Roblin, Premier Sir Rodmond, 24, 29; and parliament buildings scandal, 30–31
Robochy Narod (Winnipeg), 126
Royal Alexandra Hotel, 122
Royal Commission on Contract Shops, 73–74, 75; report of, 75
Royal Commission on Industrial Relations, 106–107, 201–202
Royal Commission on the Relations of Labour and Capital, 201
Royal North West Mounted Police, 88, 166, 168; and Bloody Saturday, 172–174
Rural press, 198–199
Russell, Robert Boyd, 55, 75, 83–84, 112, 203; early career, 54; and industrial unionism, 54, 97; and Metal Trades Council, 72; and 1918 contract shops' strike, 73, 74, 75, 77; and Tipping, 75, 76–77; and Walker Theatre, 85; and returned soldiers, 87; and OBU, 100; arrested, 165
Ruttan, Gen., 43

Saint John, New Brunswick, 23
Saskatoon, Saskatchewan, 155
Scott, Canon F. G., 149–150
Seattle, Washington, 146
Seattle Central Labor Council, 94
Seattle general strike, 94, 95; and Winnipeg, 96, 145, 204

Seattle Union Record, 146
Secession, 78–79, 80, 97, 99, 100; in Winnipeg, 101
Seditious conspiracy, 166
Selkirk, Manitoba, 2
Sharpe, Mayor, 12, 13
Shea, Timothy, 161
Shell Committee, 35, 192; and fair wage clause, 37; and scandal, 37
Shepherd, Alex, 115
Shops Regulation Act, 8, 9, 25
Sifton, Clifford, Minister of Interior, 2
Sinclair, Dr., 20
Single tax, 7
Social Democratic Party, 83
Social gospel, 5
Socialism, 4
Socialist Party of Canada, 26, 84, 97, 202; and Walker Theatre, 84; and Market Square riot, 86–87; and Western Labor Conference, 100
South Winnipeg Unionist Committee, 63
Southern Canada Power Co., 132
Sparling, Ald. John K., 150, 169; and Puttee committee, 60; and permits, 130
Special police, 14, 152, 153, 170; and Ketchen, 151–152; and Bloody Saturday, 173–174; mounted. *See* Mounted special police
Special Strike Edition (Winnipeg), 118, 119
Spry, Graham, 153
Street railway conductors, 34
Street railway employees, 169; and municipal strike, 62
Street railway strike, 14–15
Street railwaymen's union, 111; and street railway strike, 11–12; 14
Strike Committee, 165, 166; composition of, 120
Strikes and lockouts, 1901 CPR trackmen, 9–10; 1902 CNR shop craft, 10–11; 1906 contract shop, 15–17; 1906 street railway, 11–14; 1911 Great West Saddlery, 19–20; 1917 packinghouse, 50; 1917 Woolworth, 51; 1917 contract shops, 55–56; 1918 municipal strike, 58–65; 1918 postal workers, 68–69; 1918 contract shops, 74–76; 1919